OIA 1343743 8/9/78

J.

CONFERENCE OF THE BIRDS

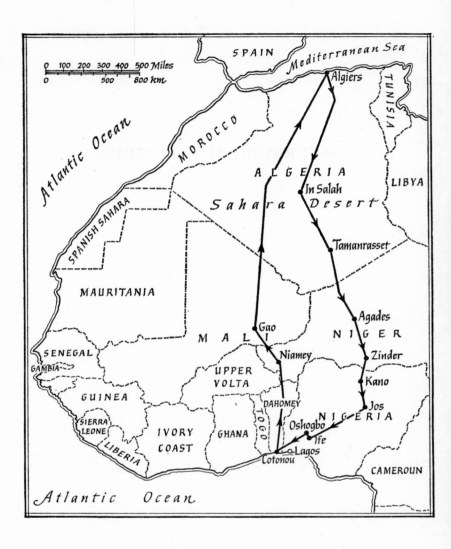

CONFERENCE OF THE BIRDS

The Story of Peter Brook in Africa

by

JOHN HEILPERN

FABER AND FABER
3 Queen Square
London

First published in *1977*
by Faber and Faber Limited
3 Queen Square London WC1
Printed in Great Britain by
Latimer Trend & Company Ltd, Plymouth
All rights reserved

c
e

British Library Cataloguing in Publication Data

Heilpern, John
    Conference of the birds.
    1. International Centre of Theatre Research
    2. Theater—Africa, West
    I. Title
    792'.092'4   PN2979
    ISBN 0-571-10372-3

FOR RACHEL,
with love

'We could start all over again perhaps.'
'That should be easy.'
'It's the start that's difficult.'
'You can start from anything.'
'Yes, but you have to decide.'
'True.'

(Waiting for Godot)

Prologue

The first stranger I saw in Africa, or thought I saw, was blind.
All week in Paris before we left on our strange journey I kept
seeing people who were blind.

The first time, I was in a taxi when I noticed a blind man
walking towards the Metro. I don't know why I kept watching
him. Just when he began to go down the staircase he brushed
into another man who was coming out. But he was blind too.
Also, he was black and the other man, the man going down,
was white. I don't know why I noticed that either. I began to
shake because I thought I was seeing a dream.

The next day, I was in another taxi en route to the research
centre where Peter Brook and his actors worked. And we passed
another Metro, different from the day before. I found myself
looking up deliberately. I knew something was going to happen.
At first I couldn't see anyone. The street was deserted. It was
raining hard and no one was around. Until there, coming out of
the Metro, was a blind man. As the taxi drove through the traffic
lights I looked back at the blind man. It seemed important to
take note of his colour, which was black.

The moment I arrived at Brook's centre I dashed to see Ted
Hughes, the poet who worked with the group. Hughes is the kind
of man who would enjoy my experience and I was convinced he
could tell me its meaning.

The famous poet was intrigued, interpreting the experience in
terms of a dream.

He was fascinated by the fact that in the first story the white
man was going down the tunnel to collide with the black man
coming up. The white man was my conscious state submerging a darker, hidden side: the black man. Both are blind, he
said, because neither the conscious nor the unconscious state

understand each other. In the first story, the two had met and crossed paths. But when the black man emerged alone in the second story, the darker side had become conscious—and taken over.

So I said the interpretation was ingenious, but there was a flaw. It wasn't a dream, for I'd seen it happening.

'That's what makes it worse,' he replied.

Then he told me of a similar incident which had recently happened to him. For the past year he had been writing a hundred poems for Brook's group that were based on an ancient Persian fable, *The Conference of the Birds*. The most important bird in the fable is called a hoopoe. One day at Ted Hughes' home in Devon a stranger called on him without warning. He wanted to sell him a stuffed hoopoe.

'It's getting scary,' I said. 'Stuffed hoopoes and blind men—what does it mean?'

'What does anything mean?' he replied, laughing. 'You're going to Africa, boy! Maybe you'll find the answer there.'

The first day, we were stranded in Algiers for eight rotten hours.

It was unfortunate. We were stranded in the airport. Mystified customs men kept going through a collection of empty cardboard boxes we'd taken with us. They kept looking for something inside.

Also, the crew hadn't turned up with the Land-Rovers. We needed the Land-Rovers to take us through Africa. 'We'll just hop off the plane and *off* we go!', Brook had told me cheerfully. It was raining outside and surprisingly green. It could have been a wet Sunday afternoon in Chipping Sodbury.

The actors were strolling round the airport, lost souls and freaks, idling away the time. They looked young and amazingly clean. Clean clothes, clean hair, clean bodies, all meticulously prepared for the desert crossing, whenever that might be. Some of them were sending home postcards with camels on the front. 'Dear Mom. It's raining in Algiers and the Land-Rovers aren't even here yet. . . .'

A bewildered African drummer called Ayansola, a crazed spirit of Africa, was dressed up in a battered raincoat like

Humphrey Bogart. A newcomer to the group, he carried a shiny new transistor radio which was tuned-in to Germany.

Helen Mirren, the English actress, was in tears: nervous of journeys.

Katsuhiro Oida, Brook's leading actor, was curled up on the floor snoring under a blanket.

A giant American-Greek actor called Katsulas tried to keep his spirits up, singing songs such as 'On Broadway' and 'I'm a Yankee Doodle Dandeeeee'. Swados, the group's prodigy of a composer, had to back him on guitar. 'You want them again?' she was saying. 'You *really* want to sing them again, huh?''

Katsulas looked as if he'd just escaped from Alcatraz. He wore baggy green trousers at half-mast and a great pair of black army boots. He never took the boots off, even in a heat-wave. But they were very important: a complete show came to be built round them. We called it *The Shoe Show*.

Katsulas was the only one who'd brought a pack of cards with him. 'Anyone want to play poker? Hey, Bruce! You wanna play a little poker? What's the matter with everyone! We may as well. I brought the *pack*.'

Brook certainly seems edgy on a journey. He has a thing about spies and plots.

'If someone talks to you in a friendly manner,' he warned us suddenly, 'just be *careful* because you might end up in prison.' At which point a vague American actor called Zeldis held up a lost pencil case. 'You didn't open that, did you?' said Brook, fearing for some reason that something might have been planted. 'Sure I did,' said Zeldis. 'And there are pencils inside.'

One time in Paris I was sitting with Brook in a crowded bar when he suddenly froze and whispered: 'Don't move a muscle— we're in a position of great *danger*.' He said it with such force you felt anything might have happened. But it just turned out to be someone he wasn't keen to say hello to. Brook has this dramatic side to him. He enjoys secret meetings, secret searches: secrets. The sub-world of spies and mysterious goings-on seem to fascinate him. He wanted to be a spy during the war. For Brook, spies pretend to be someone else, like actors.

13

'All right, everyone! We're having a conference! Can we all gather round for a conference now!' It was the laconic voice of the group's stage manager. Whenever he tried to get anything together, everyone always disappeared in the opposite direction. It was nothing personal. 'Okay—Peter says everyone's to gather round for a conference. So let's gather round for a conference everyone! Listen, where *is* everyone?'

'Hey, Bob—you wanna play a little poker? I got the *pack*.'

Miriam Goldschmidt, the young German actress, prophet of doom, was in the bar with the Frenchmen in the group. 'I feel sure someone's going to die on this trip,' she was saying. I don't think I went near her again. But quite a few felt the same way. Actors are superstitious by nature. 'I feel certain it's going to be me somehow,' added Zeldis. 'But I don't mind. I also know it's going to be all right.' I checked through my insurance policy.

'DEATH', it said in capital letters, 'means death within twelve calendar months from the date of the accident. It is understood and agreed that this policy excludes death or disablement consequent upon war, invasion, civil war, rebellion, revolution, military or usurped power, insurrection, hostilities (whether war be declared or not), acts of foreign enemies, strikes, riots and civil commotion of any kind, explosion of war and weapons, terrorist activity, murder or assault or any attempt thereat. The policy does not cover death or disablement resulting from suicide or intentional self-injury, or from deliberate exposure to exceptional danger (except in an attempt to save human life), or from the Assured's own criminal act, or sustained whilst the Assured is in a state of insanity.'

I think it meant if I was run over by Nelly the Elephant during a flood in the Sahara Desert, I was rich. But it wasn't easy getting it. Lots of insurance companies said the journey just wasn't worth the risk.

Throughout the delay Brook was bustling about, fixing this and that.

He's a fixer.

14

Something was seriously wrong with Miriam Goldschmidt's visa for Algeria. Unless Brook could fix it, she wasn't going to be allowed out of the airport.

None of us yet had a visa for the Nigerian part of the journey. Military regimes can be touchy about outsiders, particularly after a civil war. In spite of high-level appeals to embassies and cabinet ministers, cultural attachés and members of UNESCO, the Nigerian government refused to budge. We decided to leave without the visas, hoping something might happen en route. If all else failed, I think Brook was relying on a previous visit to Nigeria when a border guard had been flattered into believing he'd been made a member of the Royal Shakespeare Company.

Miss Goldschmidt's Algerian visa was fixed eventually. The priceless Nigerian visas arrived miraculously after we left. But the film crew, waiting the word in Paris, were refused entry into Algeria. Instead, they were to join us in the desert town of Tamanrasset, which is still in Algeria except no one seemed to have noticed.

The Land-Rovers limped in at last, delayed by storms.

The crew looked exhausted, which was really terrific. They'd driven through the night from Tangiers. There was also a very big drama about the weight allowance. Due to what's known as an unfortunate misunderstanding, we all had twice to three times as much baggage as the Land-Rovers were meant to carry. More baggage: less room. More weight: less speed. 'Right, that's it!' snapped one of the crew. 'That's *it*.' I thought he was jumping the gun a little. We hadn't started yet. Perhaps that was his point.

Instantly, Brook arranged the first spontaneous improvisation of the journey. There was a small puzzled audience of airline officials and assorted Arabs.

Everyone was to weigh their baggage on a huge weighing machine. If it was over a certain limit, the excess would be ditched. There was total panic. Actors were clinging to their suitcases as if there were bars of gold inside. Brook seemed unconcerned, for he travels most places with scarcely more than a tooth-brush. Katsuhiro Oida, who might have invented the word 'drip-dry', was one of the actors in the clear. With characteristic generosity and madness, an English actor called Bruce Myers offered to jettison everything except the clothes he was standing in. But the others were thrown into a flurry of devious activity. Actors were dashing in all directions—changing into their heaviest gear, hiding bulging hand baggage in secret places, stuffing socks and towels and cameras and moisturized cleansing pads under sun hats and down their pants. People could hardly move.

Malik Bagayogo, a fashion-conscious actor from Mali, turned up innocently for the weigh-in wearing three sets of clothes. He walked with difficulty, like an astronaut. That's how he was caught. Ayansola, the African Bogey, had the heaviest luggage. No man would have dared tamper with it. He had an enormous metal trunk crammed with goodies from Paris he was taking home to his family, or to sell at a quick profit maybe. But appearances were maintained: the trunk was placed on the weighing machine with a sense of ceremony. Others carried it for him. When it hit the machine, the dial zoomed round several times, and gave up. The trunk must have weighed as much as a Land-Rover. On account of language difficulties, Ayansola was under the impression he'd won a competition. He looked very proud.

I clung to my stuff, claiming a form of diplomatic immunity from the weigh-in. Shame, shame to be so conscious of worldly goods. . . .

The equipment and food supplies weighed 2½ tons. We were carrying reserves of 200 gallons of water and 700 gallons of fuel. The amount of fuel to be used on the journey was enough to run the average-sized family car for 18 years. One of the crew told me.

Apart from 8,000 tea bags—the crew were English—there were among other things, axes, crow-bars, a water filter, oven mitts, soap, vegetable strainers, a fire extinguisher, washing-up liquid, clothes pegs, frying pans, bleach, an egg beater, rubber gloves,

12 packets of kitchen towels, 4 can openers, 24 boxes of Brillo pads, 2 buckets, 8 petrol stoves, 6 ladles, 4 Volcanoes, 10 washing bowls, 40 knives, forks and spoons, 40 mugs, plates and cereal bowls, 6 kettles, 8 chopping boards, 6 fold-up tables, 20 aluminium chairs, 35 canvas beds, 35 mosquito nets, 9 tents and an extra large tent big enough for a garden party.

All this, and more, the crew loaded into the Land-Rovers and a nine-ton truck, cursing the foul weather and the overweight greenhorns called actors. At one stage, Myers the English actor went along to the warehouse to see if he could help. But he came back horrified. Apparently the crew weren't treating the group's collection of empty cardboard boxes with the right sort of deference. The actors are touchy about the boxes on account of the fact that they spend a lot of their lives living in them.

'It's obvious what they thought,' announced Myers. 'They took one look at the boxes and thought we're all mad.'

'But I thought that the first day I joined,' said Zeldis.

Why were the boxes so important to the journey? In a wonderful book by Ted Hughes called *Poetry in the Making*, there is a poem, 'The Small Box'.

> *The small box gets its first teeth*
> *And its small length*
> *And its small width and small emptiness*
> *And all that it has got*
>
> *The small box is growing bigger*
> *And now the cupboard is in it*
> *That it was in before*
>
> *And it grows bigger and bigger and bigger*
> *And now has in it the room*
> *And the house and the town and the land*
> *And all the world it was in before*
>
> *The small box remembers its childhood*
> *And by overgreat longing*

It becomes a small box again

Now in the small box
Is the whole world quite tiny
You can easily put it in your pocket
Easily steal it easily lose it

Take care of the small box.

1

There isn't another figure in theatre who fascinates and bewilders people more than Peter Brook. And few public figures are more of a mystery.

His experimental journey through Africa only heightened the mystique, particularly as it began in the Sahara desert. No one had thought of directing plays in a desert before, audiences tending to be difficult enough to come by. Also, there can be a language problem with nomads. Brook's actors, though accustomed to the unexpected from him, were stunned when the journey was announced. Others thought Brook had finally gone mad.

'He's finally gone mad,' they said.

Peter Hall, boss of the National Theatre in England, has known Brook for twenty years. And says this of him:

'His actual presence makes one think, where am I going and what am I doing in life? His talents are like an X-ray machine. If there's anything rotten, he'll find it. He's the greatest lie-detector there is in theatre. But now he's committed not to a diagnosis of what's wrong, but to a cure. He's trying to discover a form of theatre that's totally new.'

When I asked Hall what he saw as Brook's greatest asset, he replied: 'When he says without a trace of anger, "I am very, very angry."'

Glenda Jackson, who was discovered by Brook, says this:

'Ah, the Buddha! He isn't *easy*. The time and effort and suffering! Yet you will never work with a director as remarkable as him. He makes you feel anything is possible. He refuses absolutely to settle for boundaries in life. But he knows when to say no. *Very firmly*. So you begin again. And eventually he says, "No." And it goes on like this until you call for the oxygen tent. But perhaps you do discover something. And he says, "Yes, that's a bit more like it." You say, "A bit more like *what*?" To which he smiles in his benign way, and replies: "I don't know. Show me." '

Even among those who know him well, Brook has always been a subject of constant debate and conflict. This strange, restless man has a reputation for what his actors call a benevolent mystic exterior, yet he's also seen as an extraordinary showman, very much of the world. On the other hand, he can appear a cold intellectual, abrasive, like Vim. Yet another side will reveal a surprising boyishness, naïveté almost. He's a man whose nature seems to be in continual change and agitation: state of search. But at times it's as if all the contradictory and emotional views about powerful personalities have crystallized round him. He's A Topic for Conversation—

Greatest director in the world! Fake! Genius! Madman! Vampire! When he was in his twenties, considered a prodigy, he wrote of himself:

'I want to change and develop and dread the thought of standing still. I want to be a vampire of the outside world and give back the blood I have drawn out.'

That's still true.

He was born in London in 1925, the son of Russian scientists. His parents were penniless when they arrived in England, but we've a lot to thank them for. They invented Brooklax, the laxative.

Some people refuse to believe Brook's name actually is Brook. Aware of his Russian parentage, they think he's hiding something. J. Pomoroy, the renowned opera impresario, once asked him to produce an opera. 'Now tell me,' said Pomoroy at the start of the meeting. 'Let's have no secrets between us. I'm really Pomorovsky. Now you're not really Brook, are you?'

Well he is, and they didn't get to do the opera.

His wife is half-Russian. His brother is a consultant psychiatrist. Actors are fond of comparing Brook's highly analytical mind with the probing techniques of a psychiatrist. You can see where the professions of his family have rubbed off on him, for it often seems that his actors are being analysed as if on a couch—or in a test tube.

When I asked his leading actor, Katsuhiro Oida, what he thought of Brook, he replied in a thick Japanese accent: 'He is creator and *kaibutsu*.' He ran to look the word up in his tiny dictionary. It means 'monster'. He exploded with laughter, making the action of a man enveloping you.

Brook's watchful, gnomish appearance adds something to the picture. He's a stocky figure, a shade below average height, with a strong and sensual face. Usually dressed in loose-fitting denims that can look quite chic at the beginning of the week, he could be mistaken for a shambling don of the liberal kind. Or a secret agent perhaps. He tends to whisper in urgent conspiratorial tones, as if sharing innermost secrets, not to be divulged. Almost always he gestures with his hands as he talks, as if trying to pluck ideas out of the air. But there are other times when he appears in total contrast, absolutely silent and still, with eyes of ice.

For more than ten years, he has lived with his family in Paris, commuting to productions in Europe and America. He rents an apartment on the Left Bank. In London, he owns a house in the fashionable area of Kensington. Outside Paris, a small country cottage. It seems a glamorous way of life, though there's nothing flamboyant about him. He owns no other possessions, collects no art, drives a battered car, doesn't own a suit, keeps no souvenirs of the past. He drinks very little, rarely smokes. At times he might strike you as austere and withdrawn, yet he feels thoroughly at home in the showbiz atmosphere of New York, goes the rounds of parties, stays at the Chelsea Hotel. He enjoys being at the centre of events, likes to know what's going on, what the latest gossip is. When visiting the theatre, he has a reputation for falling asleep.

Apart from sport, however, almost anything interests him—particularly the unusual. He once directed a TV commercial because he was curious to investigate a theory about eggs. The playwright Christopher Fry had told him of an old country superstition about an egg not breaking when thrown over the roof of a cottage. In the commercial, which was for the Egg Marketing Board, a zoom shot followed an egg whistling through the air. It flew over the roof of a cottage and dropped without a crack on its surface in a neighbouring suburban garden. Brook says it's something to do with aerodynamic flow. Naturally the advert won a prize.

Fundamentally, he's a rootless man. A natural way of life for Brook has always been a strong sense of movement and travel. The brooding introversion often associated with Russian blood isn't part of his nature. He wants a life full of excitement and discovery. Egypt, Iran, Russia, Afghanistan, Haiti (accompanied by Graham Greene), and Cuba (where Castro took him to the movies) are some of the countries he's visited. Travel, he says, makes things happen for him. For example, several years ago he was in a Warsaw nightclub when a beautiful girl was mistakenly arrested. Immediately, Brook and another man set about getting her release. Neither man knew each other. But as they argued with the police, the stranger was referred to as 'Professor'. He turned out to be the renowned poet and Shakespearean scholar Jan Kott, at that time the most powerful influence on Brook's work.

And almost everything he does feeds his work. There are many sides to Brook: camouflages and conflicting images. At the drop of a hat he can play the hard director, the friendly father-figure, the earnest student, secretive confidant, manipulator, analyst, guide, and so on. His nicknames reveal quite a bit about him: 'The Guru', 'The Ogre', 'The Monster', 'The Buddha', 'The Gnome', 'King of the Trolls'. But his life virtually amounts to his working life. It's the one side of Brook you can be certain everyone agrees about—his voracious appetite for work. 'Never stop,' I heard him tell his group one time. 'It's a golden rule— one always stops as soon as something is about to happen.'

Although he isn't unvain, he can be reticent about himself, deliberately putting up protective barriers. There's a bashfulness about him, which surprises people. On the other hand, it's clear that he'd sooner talk about theatre, failing to see the relevance of much else. 'Could you tell me what you see as your greatest fault?' I asked him the first time we met. There was a long, agonising silence during which he stared intensely into space, groaning slightly. 'What', he replied at long last, '*is* a fault?'

In the end, he conceded that his habitual indecision might be a weakness (though he argued that in certain circumstances it might be a virtue). Brook often drives people crazy by refusing to make up his mind until the last possible second. In spite of all appearances, there's a deep and irresistible sense of chaos about him.

Then would he mind, I asked, if I took the liberty of inquiring about the small scar under his right cheek-bone? Impressed by my eye for detail, he rose to the bait. 'Not a bit!' he replied cheerfully. 'On the contrary, the scar is the source of one of my greatest fortunes.' It got him out of school for a year and a half. When Brook was twelve, he was packed off to Switzerland for what was expected to be a six-week cure to a swollen gland in his neck. In those days there was a powerful school of thought that you could cure anything by putting it in the sun. But unfortunately for the bronzed Brook, his neck got bigger and bigger, leaving him in Switzerland for a further year to recover from the eventual explosion. While he was telling me the story, he was scarcely able to stop laughing. However, ten years later he read that the great Swiss doctor who treated him had discovered that his life's work was built on a terrible mistake: it isn't that you put everything in the sun, but keep everything out of it. So it was that Brook's entire childhood culture came to be based on the detective stories from the lending libraries of Swiss Health Spas.

He hated formal education on principle. Also, he hated schoolmasters. In the end, he went to several schools—two of them among the most exclusive in England, Westminster and Gresham's School. But they made no difference. Brook's a self-educated man.

When he was seven years old he directed his first theatre production—a four-hour version of *Hamlet* for his parents in which he acted every part himself. At the end he wanted to begin all over again, which is typical. He kept a notebook of the epic production, inscribing it '*Hamlet* by P. Brook and W. Shakespeare'—which, some would say, is also typical.

At sixteen, he left school to write scripts for commercials. He claims that one for Gibbs SR Toothpaste was the best, though it was turned down, ahead of its time perhaps. An amazingly sexy actress comes off stage and starts to take everything off—her clothes, her wig, her make-up, her eyelashes, her eyebrows, her wooden leg, until revealed before the camera is a wrinkled old hag who suddenly flashes a perfect smile. 'But *these*,' she says, 'these are all my own, thanks to Gibbs SR!'

At seventeen, he went up to Oxford—one of the youngest undergraduates Magdalen College had known. There he spent most of his days dressed in a black velvet cloak directing plays and a full-length film of Laurence Sterne's *A Sentimental Journey*. Kenneth Tynan said of him: 'It was as if he had come up by public request, like a high-pressure executive arriving to take over a dying institution.' The same could be said about Brook's entry into theatre.

'He is', said Sir Barry Jackson, the producer for whom Brook first worked after the war, 'the youngest earthquake I know.' At twenty-one, he directed his first production at Stratford. At twenty-two, he was the first Director of Productions at the Royal Opera House, Covent Garden. He was the first because he invented the title himself. He became 'The Golden Boy' of theatre and now is considered the most challenging mind in it. Always with a Brook production there's a simmering atmosphere: sense of the unexpected. People want to know what he's up to. Brook has a capricious side to him, and is sometimes accused of being pretentious and over-intellectual. But no other director causes quite so much excitement or controversy, even in failure.

He's directed almost sixty productions, a terrific amount, occasionally designing sets and costumes or composing the music. He's had his disasters. Something called *The Perils of Scobie Prilt* closed after a week. But almost every kind of production has been tackled—from Genet to Truman Capote, from the hit Broadway musical about a Parisian prostitute *Irma La Douce* to the anti-Vietnam happening, *US*. At the end of that production (which was pretentious) the actors remained on the stage staring at the audience in silence. 'Are we waiting for you to go?' asked Tynan, a trifle confused. 'Or are you waiting for us?'

Three of Brook's productions which have gone down in the history of theatre: *Titus* with Olivier, *King Lear* with Scofield, and Peter Weiss's play about madness and revolution, *Marat Sade*.

24

That production gave the start to Glenda Jackson's career, winning seven major awards from British and American critics. But none of Brook's work has been so universally acclaimed as his *A Midsummer Night's Dream*. For that production, with its trapezes and juggling and magic and joy, was a masterpiece.

Yet Brook never wanted to become a theatre director. He wanted to direct films, just like all the other theatre directors.

Of his seven films, less successful than his stage work, perhaps the best known are Peter Shaffer's adaptation of *Lord of the Flies* and *Moderato Cantabile* with Jeanne Moreau and Jean-Paul Belmondo.

But he went into theatre as a substitute for films, building instead what he calls 'moving pictures'. He found that he loved the emotionally charged atmosphere, the immediacy and excitement, everything that's so intoxicating about the stage. He plunged from one end to the other with sheer enjoyment. Whatever production he did would be the opposite of the one before. Brook has spent all his working life in search of opposites, believing it's the only way he can find a reality. Somewhere among many contrasting points might be found what you're searching for. He scans, like a radar system.

However, over the years his work in theatre gradually changed and developed to the point where it totally reversed itself. The mandarin interest gave way to a clear line and purpose, as if his work had been on a narrowing spiral. It began with his famous 'Theatre of Cruelty' season after he joined Peter Hall as a director of the Royal Shakespeare Company in the early 1960s, and ended at the close of the decade with *A Midsummer Night's Dream*. He turned away from star actors towards ensemble playing, experimental work and improvisations, long rehearsal sessions, the influences of Artaud, Brecht, Jan Kott, and his friend the great Polish director, Grotowski. He confronted actors with their own self-deceptions and lies, cracking the surface of things. Eventually he opened up many questions about the accepted clichés of theatre, by implication challenging it to transform and shake itself to the foundations.

Like a child, he asked the question 'Why?' 'Why act?' 'Why go to the theatre?' 'Why theatre at all?' In many ways, the theatre's Golden Boy had become its Grand Inquisitor.

'Obviously I don't believe the *status quo* is healthy,' he told me. 'I don't believe it's even promising. Single events flicker here and there. Different schools of theatre come and go. A new playwright emerges. But I don't see much hope in any of this because I don't believe it begins to grapple with the essential problem. How to make theatre absolutely and fundamentally *necessary* to people, as necessary as eating and sex? I mean a theatre which isn't a watered-down appendage or cultural decoration to life. I mean something that's a simple organic necessity—as theatre used to be and still is in certain societies. Make-believe is *necessity*. It's this quality, lost to Western industrialized societies, I'm searching for.'

And more—something which, if Brook could discover it, would be the equivalent in theatre of splitting the atom in science.

Disenchanted with a weak and élitist *status quo*, he believes it's possible to discover the miraculous: a universal theatre. If so, the élitist barriers would fall. Theatre would at last become a truly popular art: open to everyone. For a piece of theatre would make total sense, regardless of language or class, wherever in the world it was played.

To these ends and ideals and dreams, he formed his own research centre in Paris. Directly after the opening of *A Midsummer Night's Dream*, he suddenly packed up and left the theatre he'd worked in all his life. Approaching fifty, at the peak of his career, Brook had gone in search of a completely new form of theatre.

The centre was given the forbidding name of The International Centre of Theatre Research, known to the in-set as CIRT.

He received an unprecedented subsidy from the Ford Foundation and others: a million dollars for a three-year programme.

The group of international actors was a unique experiment in the history of theatre, folly to some. Brook formed it to see if actors from different cultures and backgrounds could transcend all the standardization of contemporary life and bring a richer

26

quality into the work. 'Their disunity', he announced, 'will be their unity.'

But like so much of Brook's new work, even the conception of his international group is open to doubt. Are the cultures of his actors really different? Except for the Japanese and African in the group, everyone is European or American. Brook replies that to cast the net wider at this stage would be impossible. Even in its present state, the international principle has given the group its special identity and quality, something which couldn't be found anywhere else. Besides, it was never his intention to create a theatrical United Nations. But then, how rich is the work ever likely to be? If the group is basically Western it can only end up reflecting the less imaginative urban life of the West he's trying so desperately to avoid. He's spreading what's left of the jam even thinner. And to that Brook replies that the nature of a group, of any group in modern society, must hold the answer. Because a group is a recognition of the fact that the impoverished individuals within it rediscover a richness closed to any one of them outside. No single member is mesmerising alone but each come together to build a richer, more complete whole. But then, perhaps you might think he's still not going to make it. And to that Brook replies, 'Of course.' And carries on as if you hadn't spoken.

Ted Hughes, considered by many to be England's finest poet, joined the group. A grey and brooding presence, he was once married to Sylvia Plath.

Hughes was responsible for Brook's first major experiment— the invention of a new language of sound, which he called 'Orghast'. The group travelled to Persia to perform it in the ruins of Persepolis. The result of a whole year's research behind the locked doors of the Paris centre, the experiment was a real attempt in our time to open up this fascinating possibility of a form of universal speech more powerful than anything we have known. Brook and Hughes recognized that language as we know it has lost its real vitality and meaning. The rich local dialects and idioms of former times have weakened in expression over the centuries, watered-down like mass-produced art. Brook tried

27

to discover why spoken words from ancient languages have a flavour that directly touches the listener, reaching out to a far greater emotional response—as music does. As well as Hughes' new sound-language, the actors were put to work on the syllables, letters and sounds of Latin and ancient Greek. Also, a 2,000-year-old dead, forgotten ceremonial language called Avesta. They learnt how to speak it from diagrams.

The 'Orghast' experiment in Persepolis was described by many as 'controversial' (that is, it wasn't an unqualified success). But the work of Artaud and the 'sound-poetry' of the Dada movement are other schools before Hughes which have tried similar experiments. Professor Chomsky in America has focused attention on the theory that identical 'deep structures' of language exist in every human mind. In his massive book, *After Babel*, George Steiner traces the idea of a universal literary culture as far back as the dreams of Leibnitz. Is there, therefore, an underlying skeleton of speech common to all men?

Steiner tends to think not, believing the estimated four to five thousand languages on earth are evidence of permanent differences within man of which language is the outward symbol. The bewildering diversity of tongues is seen as a deep psychic need for separate communities, a sense of privacy, self-determination: national identity. But in the context of Brook's work it's arguable that the idea of a universal language—and certainly of a universal theatrical language—threatens neither diversity nor identity. On the contrary, it wants to maintain them. The exciting dream of a universal language of theatre is after something different, and on that score Steiner misses the point. For what can be found *behind* the identity of different nations that strikes an identical chord in everyone?

Ted Hughes talks of the search for that great precious thing far beyond words which he believes is missing from our lives and accounts for the real distress of our world. It is a spirit, he wrote, and it speaks to spirit—

'When we hear it we understand what a strange thing is living in this Universe, and somewhere at the core of us—strange, beautiful, pathetic, terrible. Some animals express this being

28

pure and without effort, and then you hear the whole desolate, final actuality in a voice, a tone. Then we really do recognize a spirit, a truth under all the truths. Far beyond words.'

After 'Orghast', Brook's group continued with new work behind the closed doors of their research centre, like scientists. Occasionally, the doors were opened and the actors would play to audiences of psychiatrists, convicts and the deaf.

They were opened again for the journey through Africa.

For the actors, this journey in search of the miraculous wasn't only an experiment in theatre. It was about themselves. In some way, they were trying to begin all over again with their own talents and their own lives. And so was Brook. He's a man driven by a passion to understand and confront and pacify everything life can offer through make-believe. Yet like his actors, he was trying to face his own barriers and deceptions, enrich himself through unknown territory: open himself to it. The Brook I saw at work could no longer be described as the all-powerful mastermind of his own experiments. Nor were any of the popular images of him appropriate. His involvement in his own research had affected him so deeply, the truth is he no longer had a role which could be clearly defined. He had become a participant in his own work, and a victim. In many ways, I saw him as a man who'd lost his identity.

'In theatre', he says, 'it's always possible to wipe the slate clean.' But theatre can only give expression to the people who create it. Though Brook's ultimate aims differ from those of his actors, in one vital sense he's exactly in tune with them. Struggling to transform theatre, he transforms himself.

The skills and knowledge of twenty-five years in traditional theatre, that touch and flair capable of scooping ideas together and staging them instantly, like an action painter, the more traditional techniques of the director, a strong sense of showmanship, inner certainty, the judgement which finally decides what has life and vitality in a production, what works or fails—these are the source and power of Brook's talent. But it was precisely this talent which was closed to him in the search for a new form

29

of theatre. By virtue of his experience, Brook led the group. But in truth, he was learning the way with it.

In his book called simply *Peter Brook*, the critic and stage historian J. C. Trewin traces Brook's career as far as *A Midsummer Night's Dream*. On the final page Paul Scofield, who has known Brook for some twenty years, writes of his friend as 'the very complex working mechanism'.

'If Brook has shifted position as an artist,' Scofield concludes, 'it is from spectatorship to participation, from remote control to a more sensual involvement. I think he would like his experience of being a director to be closer to that of the performer.'

It's a tempting conclusion, particularly as Brook has begun to flirt with acting since Scofield wrote about him. He joins in some of the group's exacting exercises, looking rather awkward. As the African journey progressed, he began to risk joining in the musical work. There was to be a historic acting début, too. But the Brook I saw struck me as a man in search of something more essential to him than performing. I think he would like to experience acting only in the sense of what he longs for from actors. I think he would like his experience to be that of the true creator.

One time, I asked Brook what his first memory of life happened to be. But a later one sprang immediately to mind. He must have been about twelve years old. He was in the country. He remembers having some sort of philosophical discussion with himself. At that moment, he was struck by a clear perspective in front of him of learning and understanding more and more by growing up. But in the same moment he was struck by the fear—what if he were closer then to understanding reality than he would ever be again? How could he be certain that any step from then onwards wasn't going to take him farther away from everything he seemed to be on the verge of knowing?

The fact that the memory remains with him means that the question is still unanswered. It's as if he's been searching for an answer all his life. But it has its dangers. 'What's Brook's greatest strength?' I asked one of his actors. 'Hunger', she replied. 'And his greatest flaw?' 'Hunger', she replied again.

It is this insatiable search for knowledge and understanding of

30

life which goes to the core of Brook's personality. It's exhilarating to witness, as if a state of emergency has been declared. He's very much a man who wants to understand life as lived, knowledge as truly experienced. Yet at times, he lusts to know. The relentless questions and probing, the analysing and thrusting, can seem out of key. It's as if within his own voracious intellect, the very part of him that makes him who he is, is too strong a force.

Before we left for Africa, Brook and the group worked with The American Theatre of the Deaf. At one point the deaf actors gave them words to translate into body movements. The first word they chose was 'inspiration'.

Brook's version was to pluck something immediately from his head. But the deaf actors gently lifted something from the area of their soul.

It was the merging of these two opposites that I saw in its development within Brook. If in some ways he had lost his identity it came from the most intense struggle to discover a fuller one: a deeper, creative impulse.

Peter Brook is a man in search of a form of theatre created from the seed.

He wants to change and transform.

I think he would like to wake up on the other side of his identity.

2

Eleven actors and Brook left for Africa and thirty actors returned. Everyone connected with the journey learned how to act, one way or another.

These are the eleven actors:

Katsuhiro Oida, about forty years old, the senior member of the group, a gentle and disciplined Japanese, watchful, very inquisitive, with the dedication of a monk. As an actor he has incredible dexterity. It would seem he can do anything. Often when a show might not be going too well, he'd be called upon to save the day. Yet when he first arrived in Paris he had never improvised in his life, could speak only Japanese and had not even heard of Brook.

The famous French actor and director, Jean-Louis Barrault, invited him to Europe in 1968 for a special experiment in theatre that Brook was involved in. But the student revolution put an end to it. Barrault fell from favour and Katsuhiro Oida rejoined Brook when he began his centre two years later. No other actor can match his commitment and staying power. It is he who puts the actors through the torture of many of the physical exercises. More than any of the others, he has a deep sense of personal search.

For twenty years, he trained in Noh Theatre technique under one of its great masters, Okura. He trained too at the Zen temples, praying and meditating. Each day he rose before dawn, cleaned the temple, worked in the fields, sitting and praying until midnight. When his father died at an early age, he ventured into commercial theatre and films to support his family. He's quite famous in Japan, though he'd never mention it.

It's strange: he was the only actor in the group who wasn't keen to go to Africa. He said that he'd miss the central heating.

He's known as Yoshi.

Andreas Katsulas, twenty-six, the giant American-Greek, born in St. Louis, the son of a one-time gambler and bootlegger who was imprisoned for a year or two in Illinois. Katsulas would be terrific playing Lenny in *Of Mice and Men*, but it wouldn't be type-casting. He's emotional, forthright, explosive—unconcerned, he likes to say, with 'the mystical shit'. He does a job. His father always said: 'Work eight hours, play eight hours, sleep eight hours. Don't do any more or less.'

So he doesn't.

His father also said never trust anyone, not even your mother. And he doesn't do that either. Also, he watches every penny he spends, which gives him a reputation for meanness. Yet when one of the actors needed quite a bit of money in a hurry, he was the only one who offered to lend it, counting out the notes in ones from a tin in a secret hiding-place. His family, many of whom live in Greece, is working class. His mother makes salads in a hotel kitchen. He paid his own way through school, ending up with a drama fellowship at Indiana University. When Brook was recommended to meet him, Katsulas had scarcely acted in the professional theatre. Incredibly, he's the second member of the group who hadn't heard of Brook. He says he joined the group because it gave him a free trip to Paris and paid well—125 dollars a week. His family are always saying to him: 'Andreas, when are you going to get a *real* job?'

His wife, Marva, came out to Africa as a cook, which led to all kinds of trouble.

Natasha Parry, who had heard of Brook if only for the reason that they're married. They met twenty years ago when he was directing opera. Apprehensive, spendthrift, private, dark, beautiful, she's acted since she was twelve. The daughter of a Russian who fled the Revolution and is said to be related to Pushkin, her first father was a gambler and newspaper man. Her stepfather's a film director. Like Brook, she doesn't seem to have had much formal education. Instead, she won quite a reputation in films and traditional theatre, playing opposite such leading men as Orson Welles, Gérard Philippe and Alec Guinness—all a world away from the current work. And she brings to it the most wonderful

B   33

qualities of pain and tenderness. She touches people. Yet she becomes fearful and tense, a stretched catapult tensed for failure. Others are like this.

She almost didn't make the trip. Just before we left for Africa she went into hospital for a minor operation. There was a danger she mightn't be fit in time. It was a tough journey. But when I visited her in hospital she was taking swigs from a bottle of vintage wine, surrounded by many maps, learned books, articles on mysterious tropical diseases, dictionaries, pamphlets, tape recordings of various African languages, and a small harp. 'Oh, miss,' said the nurse, bustling in with the steamed fish. 'You do look like Leslie Caron.'

She was fit.

Bruce Myers, thirty, who made history when he was expelled from the Royal Academy of Dramatic Art for being drunk on stage while playing Napoleon in *Man of Destiny*.

What to say about him? I've known him for so long. I married his cousin: cousin Ruth. It was quite a coincidence, amazing in its way. Of all the actors who might have been in this group, Brook ended up choosing someone I've known all my life. 'Don't laugh,' Myers said to me when we were fourteen. 'I've decided to be an actor.' He was supposed to have been a lawyer, like me. Also, his mother has a cousin, who has a daughter, who's married to a boy, whose sister is married to a man, who is the brother of Peter Brook.

I do not think this influenced Brook in any way.

Myers was to get lost in the Sahara Desert. He could have died. He can be wild and frightened, just frightened of life I suppose. And he can have moments of such calm and mastery, of wisdom almost, that your eyes would be opened. Before Africa, he took a leading role for a short while in Brook's production of *A Midsummer Night's Dream*. He was filling in for an actor who'd fallen ill, and had only a few days to prepare the part. Brook told me that his first performance was one of the finest achievements he'd ever seen on the stage. Then he lost it. The old fears returned. He *lost* it.

His favourite expression is: 'Write it off.'

The son of a lawyer, a legendary man in the north of England, someone who was so outrageous and good that people loved him and wanted to live life like him, Myers had virtually given up the theatre when he joined Brook. He left the Royal Shakespeare Company after three years because he found himself in a state of terror on stage. Also, he doesn't like cliques and hierarchies. He went to the Lake District to teach sailing and climb mountains. One day, a movie was being shot in the Lakes and Myers signed on as an extra. It was directed by Cornel Wilde, renowned for his in-depth portrayals of Chopin and D'Artagnan. 'You know,' he said to Myers, 'you could be an actor if you really tried.'

Helen Mirren, twenty-six, a star maybe, outspoken, generous, bright, luscious, lost. Violence is a part of her—part of the strange alchemy that goes into the making of a sex symbol. I'm not certain the English know quite where to place her, the national temperament tending to prefer English Roses. However, she resolutely refuses to appear in the nude except for money. 'Time was', thundered an outraged newspaper editorial, 'when actresses did it for art.'

She's famous for many fine leading roles for the Royal Shakespeare Company, two movies for Lindsay Anderson and Ken Russell, and some massive publicity usually labelling her as 'The Sex Queen of the RSC'. This can lead to tears, but you have the feeling she can't resist playing up to it. It makes life easier sometimes. 'Oh, don't let's talk about *serious acting*,' she's been known to say to earnest journalists. 'Let's talk about my big tits.' Part of her dilemma might have been that she couldn't decide whether to be a straight actress or a great big sexy movie star. You can't have both, apparently. The Brook experiment was entangled with her search for an answer. Make no mistake, she's potentially one of the most exciting actresses alive.

She was the last recruit to the group, joining the work only two months before Africa. And the group didn't accept her overnight. She was an outsider for quite a while, depressed and threatened. When she's vulnerable she can be curt and stand-offish, mannered almost. Sometimes she can't cope, like the rest of us. There's a melancholy side to her, which takes people by surprise. She's a hippy in a sense, often talking of 'freedom' and 'love' and 'togetherness'. She spends part of her time living in a vague commune outside London. When she's on form, when she's confident and happy, she's unbeatable. I've known her for a few years now. She lived with my family in London. 'For Godsake,' I used to say to her, 'you're not wearing anything.' She'd genuinely forgotten. Or didn't think it mattered.

François Marthouret, born in Paris, aged twenty-nine, the son of an engineer, charming, attractive, said to be the handsomest actor in France, mischievous, clever, he will say of someone in the group: 'He is without one shadow of a doubt the worst actor in the world—but I *love* him.' He's invariably late for everything, though no one can possibly take offence for long. Occasionally he suffers terrible pangs of remorse, going in for public soul-searching of a philosophical nature. He has a clownish quality. Also, he enjoys being part of the French tradition of romantic-poet existentialist figure. 'Wasn't it Baudelaire who said, "Everything with passion"?' he might announce unexpectedly. 'Perhaps it wasn't Baudelaire. Perhaps it was someone else. Ah, Baudelaire . . .'

He went into experimental theatre after studying literature at the Sorbonne, forming his own experimental group near Marseilles. He's well known in France mainly as a television actor in lengthy Dostoevsky serials. He's made a couple of films. Along with Mirren, he has that mysterious gift known as star quality. He's fun. Also, he refused to go with the group on their journey to Persia, objecting on political grounds. He worries, goes down with stomach complaints, cuts out of the work entirely during a crisis. He says he does so for his own sanity. You can believe him. He was one of the actors who reached breaking point in Africa.

Lou Zeldis, thirty, tall as a windmill, vague as a giraffe. You would notice him in a crowd. He's a striking bisexual, usually dressed in flowing robes as if taking part in a biblical epic. Perhaps he is. He lives very much in a world of his own, a world of fantasies and dreams, lived out with a little help from his friends. He's been busted a couple of times. The first time, Betty Grable

bailed him out. The second, he was jailed for six months down-
town Las Vegas: quite enjoyed it. Very little fazes him. He talks
rarely. When Brook has a discussion, he often falls asleep. That
is, unless he's listening with his eyes closed. If something nasty
happens, he dances.

And he began life as a dancer, touring in productions such as
Hello Dolly and *How to Succeed in Business Without Really Trying*.
He really loved it, too—roar of the crowd, smell of the grease-
paint. His finest moment came in one of the most extravagant
flops in the history of theatre. It was a show called *Wonder-
world* for the World's Fair in New York. He played Neptune.
The set changed into an underwater nightclub and he emerged
from the water at the end of a swimming routine to announce:
'I am Neptune. Welcome to my underwater nightclub.' He wore
a coral crown, a pearl beard and a fishnet gold cape embroidered
with pretty fishes. Erté designed it. 'I looked,' says Zeldis, *'superb.'*

Eventually, he drifted into the New York underground scene,
playing in the famous Café Cino and La Mama groups. He
decided to join Brook's group because it seemed like a good idea
at the time. I think he may have had his doubts since. Most of
the actors have. It's part of the nature of things.

He spent his childhood in California and Japan where his
father, a distinguished pathologist, worked for the Atomic Bomb
Casualty Commission. He lived in Hiroshima. 'Don't provoke
him,' one of the group told me. 'A part of him seems to be in
despair.' He drifts, and is all right, living in the moon.

Michèle Collison, twenty-nine, a small mountain, or a large hill,
height 6ft 1½in., weight 180 lb before breakfast. Unless you've
seen her blow her wages on a meal, you've missed one of the
great theatrical happenings. She tends to feed herself the fantasy
of Earth Mother, and others feed off it. But she likes life to be
easy, says things to please, can be tough and resilient, a medium,
changed by the people she happens to be with. She's a perceptive,
nice and easy paranoid. She's very serious and conscientious about
the work. It gives her life a sense of purpose.

Before she joined Brook she went through the same '60s drop-
out scene as Lou Zeldis, lived in communes in the Colorado

Mountains and Haight-Ashbury, made a porn movie, tripped her way round the world. She keeps bumping into Zeldis. They first met at university near Long Island, acted together in Café La Mama, and both joined Brook independently. She's the outstanding musical talent in the group: once sang in nightclubs around the Caribbean always closing her act with the lyric, 'You're not a dream, you're not an angel, you're a man. I'm not a queen, I'm a woman, take my hand. . . .'

She was brought up by a Roman Catholic grandfather, an Irish immigrant. Her father, a magician, died four months before she was born.

Sylvain Corthay, thirty, the one member of the group who might be instantly recognizable as an actor. He has the dark bearded good-looks and resonant voice of the traditional Shakespearean actor. One could imagine him striding confidently on as Fortinbras, tying up the loose ends. In fact, since studying at the Sorbonne he's spent his life in experimental theatre, once forming his own group, directing as well as performing. He's worked with Barrault and was the only actor to have visited Africa before when he toured the cities of the French-speaking countries with Jean Vilar. But that was a traditional theatre tour, culture to the underdeveloped nations in the form of Molière. Corthay's second wife, like his first, is an actress.

There's a neatness and order about him. He can be taciturn and introvert, given to brooding. The son of a Spanish mother and Swiss father, he spent his youth among the family's sheep farms and wine groves in the South of France. 'You mustn't be too hard on Brook,' he said to me unexpectedly. 'He doesn't find personal relationships easy. You see he's rich and privileged, like me.'

Some of the actors take notes on the work, but Corthay takes more than most. Perhaps he'll become a director one day, or write a learned book. He's a disciple.

Miriam Goldschmidt, German, black, wide-eyed like a child, devious as a cat. She likes to drink, goes over the top from time to time, has a wild surrealist imagination, living close to the edge of craziness maybe. At twenty-five, she's the youngest member of

38

the group. More than anyone she has a real need for the world of make-believe. Her mother died when she was two. Her father, thought to have been born in Mali, died in a car crash. Her adopted parents both died in a car crash. Her third mother died of cancer, as did her first. Her boy-friend of nine years, an archaeologist, died in a car crash.

One time during an improvisation, Brook asked her to come on last. 'I don't want to come on last,' she snapped. 'It's the story of my life. Shit to last!' People thought she was joking.

Before joining Brook she acted in traditional theatre in Germany and Switzerland, toured in a one-woman show, studied drama in Paris under the renowned Jaques Le Coq. She gravitated towards the research centre, sitting uninvited at the edge of the carpet, just watching the work. Brook asked her to take part in an improvisation. And invited her into the group.

Malick Bagayogo, twenty-eight years old, though I suspect he might be rather more, temperamental as a vain woman over such pressing matters as age, a fine actor from Mali with delicate ebony features, usually dressed to kill in silk shirts and cuban heels: a city dude. But if there's part of him that's become more of a sophisticated European since he came to live in Paris seven years ago, his background is extraordinary.

Bagayogo seems to have a perfect physical build, as powerful as an athlete. Yet he was crippled down his left side as a child. He was kept away from school—he can still scarcely write—until his father took him to a healer in the village who miraculously cured him with herbs and leaves. The treatment lasted three years. Though some of his family are now high-ups in Mali's military regime, his father was a poor country farmer. When he was eleven years old, Bagayogo met a blind beggar, a singer, who travelled from village to village. He became his guide. The beggar taught him everything he knew, songs and poems about ancient traditions, animals, sorcerers and devils, which have since been taught to the group. Sometimes, he starts to sing a melody suddenly remembered from his childhood. The actors scramble to write it down before it's gone for ever.

Brook told me there are two things you must be careful never to ask Bagayogo to do—play a slave or a drum. If he suspects he's being used or patronized, he doesn't work. He's spoilt, a gentle and disorganized man, fond of naps in the afternoon, and sometimes in the morning. When tempers are short, the others tend to resent him for this. But he's the one actor in the group capable of working totally in the abstract—turning an improvisation inside out, forcing the work closer to Brook's long sought-for world of invisible powers. He's an instinctive actor. Talk and theory fall on deaf ears with him. But he possesses a very special gift: an inner eye.

He came over to Europe with Mali's National Theatre, stayed to work in Paris with an African group and was introduced to Brook by the Polish director, Grotowski. He's the third and final member of the group who hadn't heard of Brook before he joined him. Still, three out of eleven: could be worse.

As well as the actors, several others went on the journey.

There was a doctor, the French wife of Bagayogo, who was going to be needed far more than any of us imagined.

Brook's personal assistant for several years, Mary Evans, typing out each day's progress like an official diarist.

The stage manager, Bob Applegarth, who'd been with the group since he met Brook in Persia.

Marva Katsulas, the wife of the American-Greek actor, as one of the cooks.

A young and lonely Frenchman, Daniel Charlot, sent out by the French government to observe the work.

An American photographer, Mary-Ellen Mark, on an assignment for *Life* magazine which with a terrific sense of timing was to fold while we were in Africa. She took it quite well, considering.

Others, such as Ted Hughes and the five-man film crew, were to join us en route.

The expedition was crewed by a team of specialists from an English firm called Minitrek. At one stage, Brook wanted to handle the mechanics of the journey from within the group itself. If that had happened, I wouldn't be here to tell the tale. I remember one discussion when Brook was leafing through a pamphlet called *Camping for Beginners* there was talk of everyone travelling in a specially equipped bus, like a rock group. Myers was supposed to go on a crash course in car maintenance. There were even romantic ideas about everyone sort of hunting for their own food. Sylvain Corthay, an open-air type, was said to be pretty useful with a bow and arrow.

Minitrek normally handle short trips to Africa for tourists who like to camp and play Big White Hunter. They'd never mixed with actors before: an omen. Also, they preferred to travel by the book—rules, regulations, time-schedules: another omen. There was one expedition leader, one camp master, one cook and one mechanic responsible for five Land-Rovers and a Bedford truck. Three additional drivers, specially skilled in desert crossings, had been hired to get us from Algiers through the Sahara Desert.

The cost of the expedition was 60,000 dollars.

The journey was to last almost three and a half months: 100 days.

Finally, there were two important new recruits to the group— the bewildered African called Ayansola, a man of many parts, crazed spirit of Africa, who played the talking drum and spoke no language that anyone else knew. This made it a little difficult for Brook to tell him what he wanted him to play. Sometimes he didn't feel like it anyway.

And there was the wild prodigy of a composer, the American Liz Swados, brought over from New York to transform the work. She's beautiful in a weird sort of way. She has a Modigliani face, which means that it's long. And it was to get longer and longer. Her talent is immense: rich, feverish, incredible in its range and attack. It would seem that she can do anything. She can be ruthless with herself and those who work with her. But you've never met anyone as talented. She doesn't sleep much, drove Brook practically into the ground, has been known to have her unsettled moments, kicking sweet old ladies in the street. Anyway, I love her. She's twenty-two and I'm hers for life. There's a lot of hope in Swados. Mind you, one or two of the actors thought she was a self-centred egomaniac. Don't listen to them. I like actors but sometimes they don't know their arse from their elbow.

41

All of us left with our treasured possessions. But as well as the personal baggage there was a box of musical instruments, a case of white costumes, twenty-four bamboo sticks, many empty cardboard boxes of various shapes and sizes, and a magic carpet.

3

No one, not even Peter Brook, knew what was going to happen on the journey.

It had to be so, for nothing like it had happened before. There was no precedent. We had a map, though. The route went through six countries—Algeria, Niger, Nigeria, Dahomey, Togo and Mali. And there were one or two markers on the map—special areas to head for, like Oshogbo in the heart of Nigeria, destined to be the most traumatic shock-encounter of the journey. But apart from the broad outline of the route, nobody knew what they were in for or where they were going.

So the nature of the journey went to the core of Brook's work. It would be an improvisation in the dark. Maybe there would be some light. Brook likes to begin work in empty spaces and voids: the Sahara Desert.

Also, no one in the group had any idea what would be performed. They hadn't prepared a three-act play or anything. There was no planned programme. In fact, nothing was planned. No one, including Brook, would know what might be performed until they arrived at a village and laid out the carpet in the village square. Even then you couldn't be sure.

So the actors were in another void, though they were more accustomed to this one. They had a safety net, even if it was of the flimsiest kind. A year's work on Ted Hughes' poems had given the group a shared reference, a sub-culture almost, that could be drawn on for inspiration. For instance, they'd strung together several of Hughes' poems involving boxes and something horrible. This was called *The Box Show*. Another was about an ogre that gives birth to other ogres. This was called *The Ogre Show*. But they were in a rough, scarcely begun state. If you'd asked any of the actors what was supposed to happen in these shows, they

43

couldn't have told you much. There was no mystery about it. It's just that they wouldn't have remembered. Well, they didn't when it came to it.

But I knew that Brook was hoping to develop one particular show in Africa—the Persian masterpiece, *The Conference of the Birds*. It's the story of a journey. And like many allegorical poems of the East the journey is a symbolic pilgrimage. A long search is undertaken only to find that what you're searching for can be found on your doorstep: Mecca is where you are. It's the *Catch 22* of Islam. Without the journey you never understand that you needn't have taken it in the first place.

In *The Conference of the Birds,* many birds meet for a conference to discuss how best to search for God. The Hoopoe, their leader and teacher, warns them that the journey ahead involves total discipline and sacrifice.

'If you wish to arrive at the beginning of understanding, walk carefully. To each atom there is a different door, and for each atom there is a different way which leads to the mysterious Being of whom I speak. To know oneself one must live a hundred lives. . . . We do not know nor do we understand so much as a little of our spirit. Many know the surface of the ocean, but they understand nothing of the depths; and the visible world is the talisman which protects it. . . . Walk then in the way I shall indicate, but do not ask for an explanation. . . . When you can have the ocean why will you seek a drop of the evening dew? Shall he who shares the secrets of the sun idle with a speck of dust? Is he who has all, concerned with the part? Is the soul concerned with members of the body? If you would be perfect seek the whole, choose the whole, be the whole. . . . Seek the trunk of the tree, and do not worry about whether the branches do or do not exist.'

At this the birds grow hesitant, which is very understandable. One by one they lose heart and excuse themselves from the journey. In return, the leader asks them to renounce all vanity and egotism, telling many parables and stories to reveal the timidity and self-deception of the birds. Ashamed of their weaknesses, the birds set out on the journey. But the leader warns them of many tests and trials that await them on the way. There will be seven

44

valleys to cross. The first is the Valley of the Quest, the second the Valley of Love, the third is the Valley of Understanding, the fourth is the Valley of Independence and Detachment, the fifth is the Valley of Pure Unity, and the sixth is the Valley of Astonishment, and the seventh is the Valley of Poverty and Nothingness beyond which one can go no further.

Many birds do not survive the journey. But the handful that reach the end discover the secret of truth and God.

One of the fables in the story is called *The Lost Key*.

'Man lives in a state of imagination, in a dream: no one sees things as they are. To him who says to you: "What shall I do?" say to him: "Do not do as you have always done; do not act as you have always acted."'

I have to confess that we stayed at a hotel on that first day we were stuck in Algiers airport. We didn't mean to stay in a hotel. I told you nobody knew what was going to happen.

The light had gone by the time all the equipment was loaded on to the Land-Rovers. Pitching camp can be quite a business: we couldn't have done it in the dark. We couldn't have done it in the light either, but I'll tell you about that later. It was raining and nobody wanted to camp in the rain. Not that it would have made much difference to me personally. Just over my bed in the hotel there was this hole in the roof. Things like that can drive you crazy. 'Why's it raining on *me*?'

Also: 'Why's it raining in Africa?'

The unexpected night in the hotel certainly gave me another little insight into the group. For instance, a lot of the rooms had to be shared. Apart from the fact that everyone was very busy dashing around the corridors grabbing the best rooms, none of the girls shared a room with any of the boys, except for married couples who might have all been crammed into the same room for all I knew. I was too busy dashing around looking for the best room to take note of that. But there was this division. We men were confined to our own quarters. People were rather coy about it. This group wasn't, then, the freedom-loving hippies of The

45

Living Theatre. But I mean something different from that. It's just that they're prudent with each other. There are individual friendships. But for a group as close as these actors are during a working day, they can seem almost strangers to each other outside of it. In Paris they rarely mixed closely with each other outside the work. They very much valued their own worlds and privacy. But if Brook was to forge the group into a real community in Africa, it was going to be quite a test. It was one of the major points of the journey for Brook—to see if this community was a pipe-dream or not.

Some really strange things were going on in my bedroom. First Daniel Charlot, the French observer on the trip, climbed into his bed fully dressed. Then the next thing I knew he was being dragged away by the police because something was wrong with his passport. He didn't even have to say *'Mon Dieu!* But I am not even dressed.' Then Myers, too excited to sleep, paced up and down for hours, and spent the night strolling round Algiers. I couldn't sleep either because it was raining on me and Ayansola still had his radio tuned into Germany. He was lying on top of his bed in a pair of women's tights, coloured pink, snoring the roof off. When I crept over to his bed to switch the radio off, he woke up instantly and switched it back on. Then he fell asleep again.

Sipping mint tea the next morning in the boulevard Che Guevara, the call came that we were about to leave. Mr. James Wilkins, the leader of the expedition—the other leader—had arrived with his convoy of Land-Rovers and taken charge. Our safety was entirely in his hands. At first sight, he looked like the picture of the sailor on the old Players' cigarette packs. I judged him to be in his forties: a heavy man, barrel-chested, bearded, ruddy-faced, a man who looked as if he could hold his liquor. Yet his eyes were suspicious and watchful: nervous. It turned out that he was only thirty-four, though it was almost impossible to believe. He must have been through darkness in his life.

He was secretive about his past, preferring to sketch only the outlines for me. He was born in England, a public-school man

46

who joined an aircraft carrier as a pilot. He owned a sisal plantation in Tanganyika for a while, became a coffee farmer in Kenya, owned a share in a diamond mine. 'Trouble was,' he told me, shaking his head sadly, 'there weren't any diamonds.' He's a bachelor, a drifter, who's travelled alone through almost every country in Africa. At one time he became a professional hunter. Also, he fought as a mercenary in the Congo. He clammed up about it when I asked for details. And yet there was this unmistakable atmosphere of fear about him. One sensed it immediately, that and a sadness. I don't know why he decided to work for Minitrek, ferrying tourists across bits of Africa for two or three weeks at a time.

When I joined the convoy I could see the actors clambering excitedly all over the Land-Rovers: new toys. Ayansola was busy ordering someone out of the front seat of one of them, the Land-Rover he'd chosen as his own. No one dared to go near that seat throughout the entire journey: it was his throne. A small crowd had gathered, staring. One man, an ancient man, a fisherman, was smiling at us. It was as if he was peering through a small telescope, squinting at the sight before him with his head cocked on one side. As we set off he was still smiling, long after the crowd had disappeared.

I was up front in the lead Land-Rover, squashed in the back seat between two soft bookends: Helen Mirren and Natasha Parry. Brook, more like the general of an army now, was in the front with James Wilkins, known to the crew as the Leader. Sooner or later I knew there was bound to be a little power struggle between the General and the Leader. Also, I knew who was going to win.

Maps were studied. We were heading for the Atlas Mountains along the Hoggar Route that goes straight down from Algiers into the Sahara. The Leader knew what he was doing: he'd crossed it twenty times before. He seemed to be welded to his driving wheel, as if he were part of the machinery. He was fond of his Land-Rover, too—attached to it in the way that the English are to dogs. He had a name for it. He called it Esmeralda.

Rules of the Road were quickly established. For instance, *never* overtake the Leader. Check that the Land-Rover behind is always in sight. If the convoy gets separated—*stop*! Headlights full on to stop the Land-Rover in front. If the Land-Rover isn't in front when you put your headlights on, do not pass go, and proceed to jail. 'Dear me,' said the Leader, pulling into the side of the road after about ten minutes. 'Oh dearie me, we seem to have lost the convoy.'

Someone was stuck at a traffic light. Perhaps they were taking a final look at it. We wouldn't be seeing another for a few months.

We drove for only five hours that day, scarcely 130 miles, crawling and twisting slowly up the mountain route until the Leader suddenly swung off the road, announcing that we would now pitch the first camp. Along with the others, I tried my best to appear very cool at this: magnificently tough and weather-beaten. Except for one or two, no one in the group had ever camped before.

'The desert!' someone cried, overcome at the sight of sand. 'We've *made* it!' I could see the crew wincing. The desert was some way off. As a matter of fact we were in a sand-pit at the top of a mountain, freezing to death. But the actors were too excited to notice, for the moment anyway. Several of them seemed to go berserk, charging out of the Land-Rovers towards a small sand-dune, screaming and yelling and wailing weird sounds into the distance. Brook was up on the sand-dune screaming with them. People were beginning to look as if they'd gone crazy. Brook was leaping up and down. I'd never seen him do that before.

Then one of the crew got a Land-Rover stuck in the sand, which made the rest of the crew roar with hearty laughter. 'Ho, ho, ho!' Stuff like that. 'Ho, ho, ho! Look at old Royston!' Royston was the driver's name. Then Myers, who likes to share a joke, managed to get his Land-Rover stuck in the sand. This put an immediate end to all the hearty laughter. 'He needs *taming*,' snapped one of the crew. Anyway, Myers was dropped from the list of drivers two days later. During a trial-run he drove Esmeralda accidentally into a graveyeard. 'I didn't do it on purpose,' Myers said.

The drivers were trying to get the Land-Rovers into the formation of a large square, as in the Westerns before Chief Sitting Bull attacks. With any luck, the vehicles might give us some protection from the icy wind. It depended which way it decided to blow. But the formation gave Brook a bright idea: it would make the ideal shape of a theatre. The chief could sit on the bonnet of a truck, he said, and his wives could sit on the chairs.

There were twenty chairs. When these were unloaded hysteria broke out on account of the fact that sitting in chairs on the top of a mountain when a snowstorm seems imminent was new to us. 'That's right!' said the man called Royston. 'Have a good laugh! But you'll be fighting for them before you know it.' He was right about that. There weren't enough chairs to go round. People would try to reserve them in advance. 'I'm sorry, but that's *my* seat.'

Royston Bennett, a thirty-one year old former school-teacher, was the Camp Master. As we shivered and jigged up and down to keep our freezing circulation going, we gathered round him for an important teach-in. He explained that each Land-Rover carried 14 petrol cans, 2 water cans, 1 set of sand ladders, 1 tool kit, 1 First-Aid kit, 1 shovel and 2 small fire extinguishers. He squirted a fire extinguisher to show how it worked. We were *not* to smoke near the fuel tanks or the kitchen petrol stoves. That's just the way nasty accidents happen. During the desert crossing we would be restricted to one wash a day. The amount of water to be used in the wash amounted to half a bowl. As numbers were so high, Minitrek had decided not to provide a portable lavatory. We would do our do-da's in the sand. Any questions?

No one had the courage.

Then he produced a green kit-bag. Everyone would be given their own with their own number. Commit the number to memory. It's no use moaning afterwards. Each of us would be provided with our own torch. Do not lose the torch. Inside the kit-bag was a bedsheet, a sleeping-bag and an outer sleeping-bag that zipped round you. Shake the sleeping-bag before use. Allow your body temperature to circulate by sleeping in the nude.

By sleeping in the *nude*? We were freezing to death in our overcoats. People were dying.

49

'How do you mean, in the nude?'

'It won't *kill* you,' said the Leader. That was his favourite expression. Also: 'You'll just have to use your common sense.'

'Can't we even wear our socks?'

'You'll just have to use your common sense.'

Then the Camp Master unrolled a canvas camp-bed, explaining how the legs fitted and everything slotted nicely together. 'A baby can do it,' he said.

It took me about three weeks to learn.

'COME AND GET IT!' It was the voice of Marva Katsulas, a voice to be heard, calling us for supper. Brook's face looked unusually pained. He likes things to come together silently, intuitively, as if by magic. 'COME AND GET IT, FELLAS!'

We joined the queue for hot soup and stew, doled out from great cooking pots onto orange plastic plates. 'You know,' said Lou Zeldis. 'I've got a terrible premonition of things to come.' There are just two things that Zeldis has a horror of in life: the colour orange, and plastic. It was really unfortunate about the plates.

Nobody could find any wood to make a fire. It must have been below freezing. People were huddled together shivering in Land-Rovers: blue. We were getting desperate. Malick Bagayogo was weeping with cold. He was walking around in his sleeping-bag, but it didn't help. Someone said he shouldn't have his clothes on, and that didn't help either. 'Why are we here?' he was mumbling. 'Why are we *here*?' He was really crying.

General consensus had it that the only way to keep warm was to go to bed. There would be a 5.30 a.m. call the next morning. 'I'll be by the right-hand wheel of the Bedford truck if anyone cares to visit,' said Mirren. Torches flashed, people stumbled into bodies, shrieked with laughter, ploughing off into the night. Ayansola was still wandering around in a daze with his transistor radio. He was wearing his bedsheet round his head. Andreas and Marva Katsulas had already bedded down, side by side. 'All right,' Andreas seemed to be saying, 'have it your way, you heard a seal bark.'

On my way to my little mound, my bedroom, I crashed into

Yoshi Oida. 'Velly solly,' he said, peering up at me out of his sleeping-bag. He was wearing a black mask.

It took me quite a while to get to sleep. I just lay there like the Dong with the luminous nose. The stars hung low, as they say.

Brook was the first up the next morning.

4

All normal communities are alike but a weird community is weird after its own fashion.

If Brook's actors had been a tribe about to go to war, they'd forget which day the battle was supposed to be. The chief would be there, though—along with his assistant chiefs, fuming. 'Jesus, where *is* everybody?' But the tribe itself would be lost somewhere, diverted by some strange ceremony, or just not up to the war that day.

Not that the members of the tribe would seem much different from any other tribe. It had its strongman, its warrior, its village joker, its hunter, its seer, its mystic, its wise woman, its mad woman, its trickster, its storyteller, its beggar. It had all the things the other tribes have except it's a really weird tribe. The chief is wise and continues to offer guidance but the tribe remains a retarded tribe. It's a well-meaning, nice and retarded tribe. For some unfathomable reason, it's the tribe that can't get it together.

Except when it goes to work.

But you've got to get to work first. On that score, Brook's a pragmatist. Moans over rigid washing-up rotas, plastic, tinned food, processed cheese, loss of privacy, endless hours in cramped Land-Rovers, routine, rules, regulations—all left him cold. Yet it was surprising. Though Brook has an unexpectedly commonsense side to him, everything about his nature must have secretly loathed the boring disciplines of the amateur camp. In everyday life, he's notorious for turning up hours late for crucial meetings, looking innocent. And communal activity doesn't come naturally to him. He once had a school report which said, 'Peter seems to be a fundamentally anti-social boy. . . .'

'But there's a difference!' he exclaimed when I asked him about it. 'I felt from the first day I went to school that I was *compelled* to. I didn't *want* to go! Each and every one of us volunteered for Africa.'

He made it sound ominous.

But all the new and resented disciplines of the camp couldn't have been easy for Brook either. The sons of the middle classes tend to take the chore of washing-up as a personal insult. There was little water, and many plates. But it's amazing—throughout our long journey in search of truth and light no issue managed to burn up quite so much nervous energy as the washing-up issue. Unlike most of us, however, Brook didn't seem to mind washing-up. 'I find I can do any sort of rubbing job, really,' he told me, explaining the secret of his success. 'Give me sand-papering, polishing, drying, cleaning and filing, and I'm quite content. But give me certain jobs to do with digging and I would so loathe it that I could scarcely do it. And it isn't laziness. Because I would do two hours of *rubbing* for you rather than two minutes of *digging*.'

Helen Mirren did the digging. For some reason she'd asked for the roughest job—digging a hole each day where the rubbish was burnt from the camp.

During those first unusual days as we headed towards the desert various jobs were handed out, of a symbolic nature some of them. Yoshi Oida made fire: he lit the petrol stoves each morning before breakfast. Lou Zeldis created water: he looked after the precious jerrycans of water. So he eventually made tea: one jerrycan filled six kettles. I was given the supreme symbol of putting up four fluorescent lights each night when we pitched camp. I would throw light on the entire proceedings.

They were really rotten lights. They kept falling down. People would cry out in anger.

Brook took the camp seriously, however. For him, it sym-bolized a special challenge—not just on the pragmatic level of efficiency, but something far deeper. When I mentioned to him that I really hated putting up the lights, he answered me as if everyone's life depended on it. I was teasing him, but it made no difference.

Thus it was that as the convoy headed deeper into the Sahara

53

Desert, Brook gave me a lecture about fluorescent lights, gradually developing his theme to include various thoughts on Western industrialized societies, washing-up rotas, acting groups, and the painful process of evolving living organic communities. I had begun to loathe that word, 'organic'. But as always with Brook, the words came tumbling out of him as he led up to his central message about the camp—what he called, 'the super-grand exercise'.

'Everything we do on this journey is an exercise,' he told me in his urgent way. 'It's an exercise in heightening perception on every conceivable level. You might call the performance of a show, "the grand exercise". But everything feeds the work and everything surrounding it is part of a bigger test of awareness. Call it "the super-grand exercise". But if we wish to avoid the traditional trap of living in a water-tight separation between work and life outside, all antennae must be out. If you don't notice that the car behind has stopped or someone needs help with the washing up—at that moment your general awareness has dropped fifty decibels. In so far as this is human, it can be understood. In so far as you have a choice, it's regrettable. Because if the penny could only drop, everyone in the group would be the richer for it. And if that's the case, the quality of our work will be the richer too. Everything feeds the work. Keep your antennae out when you put up your lights.'

I'm afraid my lights fell down just the same. It's no excuse, of course, but the rest of the group, the tribe who couldn't get it together, weren't so hot on their antennae either. Even in those first few days, used by Brook as little more than a training period, fixed positions were already being taken that were to change very little throughout the rest of the journey. For instance, there were camps within camps.

On one side, there was the acting camp. On the other, the crew camp. The actors rarely ate with the crew, didn't talk to them much or get to know them—and vice versa. Only the mechanic, Mr. Gerry Sturgeon, crossed the lines. He seemed a gentler, more open man than the rest of the crew: less suspicious, interested in the work, just friendlier I suppose. But one could see these two separate worlds forming—worlds of different values and habits, bound to collide at some point. So it was. Half-way through the journey, when exhaustion and sickness were high, the crew wanted to pack up and go home.

Daniel Charlot, the young French observer, a shy and awkward man, lived in his own shut-off camp too. A stranger to the group, he remained so for almost the entire journey, a lonely and miserable figure, left to create worlds in his thick diary like Gogol's madman. I do not think people find it easy to live together. Maybe it's one of the great myths that people are made for each other. But perhaps there was a special onus on the actors to draw people out: build bridges. Transforming dead situations is their business. The point of the journey was to learn new and powerful ways of communicating with people. Yet outside their work, something was missing. I think I realized what it was later on, but for the moment it was difficult to understand. I remember on the night the actors left their centre in Paris, Brook gave a small party for the workmen, furniture makers, who worked in the same building. It was a way of thanking them for being understanding about things like bird sounds driving them crazy all day long. But during the party, the actors and the workmen scarcely talked to each other. 'Why should I say good-bye to them?' said Andreas Katsulas. 'I never said hello.' Katsulas often acts as a barometer of the group's feelings, but the cruder he plays it the more certain you can be that he's reflecting a confusion and panic about something that no one can quite understand.

Ayansola had a camp to himself, of course. Well, nothing was easy with him. He wasn't exactly open house. He was the weirdest presence of all. Regal, childish, devious, indifferent, greedy, greedy with the cornflakes unless you got there first, it was as if he'd been sent by some mischievous African spirit, a trickster planted among us as a mysterious test. 'Ayansola! Go test that American-financed mostly white big-deal Western acting group with the cute ideas. And test 'em good, lover!'

If so, I think he was winning. But only Helen Mirren seemed to take time out to try and cheer him up when he was low. Otherwise, he slept with his radio, or collected sand in empty cigarette packs.

For the moment, Mirren was a tense and unhappy figure: a bruised peach, bruised by her inability to make things work. Nothing would go right for her until several weeks passed. But at least she could talk to Ayansola, using a form of sign-language. The others only made her jealous and contemptuous: strangers. Perhaps she wasn't the only one bewildered and fearful of the new community. But each night she took refuge in one of the Land-Rovers, reading books, or scribbling in a diary:

'We are supposed to live this journey as a disciplined, thoughtful, organized, organic, inspired, fun in fun time, which is not too often time, alert, helpful, hard-working, oh so together and admirable group. I dream homely banal dreams.'

Each day we travelled for eight or nine hours, heading slowly for the Sahara, still wrapped in heavy anoraks as if it were an expedition to the Antarctic. Brook was talking about everything from the origins of colonialism, to his days at Oxford, to the English spy he happened to know in the 1950s (who died in mysterious circumstances). Sometimes we'd doze off, but if I caught Brook's head nodding he'd jerk awake as if nothing had happened. Mirren was very busy reading Graham Greene's *Brighton Rock*. Natasha Parry would hand out sweets, almonds, dates, bread, cheese, Vichy water, various pills and wondrous laxatives. The only respite from the exhausting hours of travel was an occasional stop for a pee, or the hour's lunch in some wasteland off the main track. Once I saw a sign in the distance that said 'Sandwiches' in English. An arrow pointed to the sky.

The sand seemed to be blowing south in a trail down the road. It's odd: it didn't seem to be blowing anywhere else. 'The sand is migrating,' said Brook. 'On the road, some grains will fall by the wayside. But as the sand travels to warmer weather, do you know that only one tiny little grain will finally make it?'

He often said things like that, often enough to notice.

'Gosh!' said Mirren, suddenly looking up from *Brighton Rock*. 'Camels!'

56

'Camels?' said Brook, peering out of the window. 'Then this *isn't* Denmark.'

'Of course,' said the Leader, glued to his driving wheel. 'You all know the reason for the superciliousness of the camel?'

'No,' said Brook.

'You see, the Koran has ninety-nine names for God but only the camel knows the hundredth.'

'Hence his superciliousness,' said Brook.

'*Exactly*,' said the Leader.

As we passed through a small village a motorbike roared by, which gave Brook an idea for a show. A woman falls in love with a motorbike and a donkey, but she can't choose between them. 'We could do it here,' said Brook, sounding like a character in an old Hollywood movie. 'We could do the show right here!'

But the convoy ploughed on, over scrub and shingle, past small oases, bright green: unexpected worlds glimpsed through bewildered Western eyes. We stopped at a sacred Muslim village —the village of one-eyed women. The women were so heavily veiled that the only part of their body they revealed was one eye.

Swados, the young American composer, followed one of the women through the twisting narrow streets of the village. The woman was shrouded in white muslin, climbing quickly up clay steps, urgently, as if threatened by the intruder following her. Swados, a slight and distorted figure in her baggy green army coat and brown boots, followed the woman to her home. Was she young or old, beautiful or not? Did she take water from the well every day, slap children on wet behinds, wash socks, pray?

When she arrived at the door of her home the woman in white turned round and faced the intruder, staring through her veil with one eye. She was taking a risk. Contact with strangers was not encouraged in this place. Strangers were safer ignored. But the two women faced each other and stared in silence, perhaps for a minute or so. Then the woman in white signalled to the other with a thin finger pointing out of the sleeve of her garment. She was saying, 'Come closer.' Swados edged closer to her, into the shade of the stairs to her home. And the woman removed her

57

veil, only for a moment, and smiled. And both were smiling now.
She was a teenager.
She put back her veil and ran quickly into the house.

Each night after supper there were many songs and rough
Algerian wine poured from a heavy petrol can. Swados and
Michèle Collison, a team, would sing any song you named.
But everyone enjoyed the numbers from ancient musicals the best.
Actors always say they want to play Hamlet, but they don't really.
All they really want to be is Fred Astaire and Ginger Rogers.

Still, every group has its own song, its anthem. The lyric to
ours was this:

> By the waters, the waters of Babylon
> We lay down and wept, and wept
> For Thee I am.
> Be remembered, be remembered, be remembered
> Thee I am.

It looks too sentimental in print, perhaps. But we nearly always
ended a day by singing it. It could be moving when we really
tried. One thing was odd, though—Brook never joined in. He
hadn't joined in any of the songs. It was odd because you knew
he wanted to.

One night, when most of us had drifted off in search of camp-
beds lost in the darkness, Brook lingered behind listening to
Swados and the rest singing. After a while, he went up and asked:
'Will you teach me the Babylon song?'

But he was so nervous and shy that Michèle Collison held his
hand, as if he were having a tooth out. He was struggling to get
the right notes, but they wouldn't come. The others joined in, to
reassure him. Then they gradually stopped one by one. 'You're
abandoning me!' cried Brook. But he tried again, by himself this
time, fighting to hit the right notes. Sometimes he stopped and
laughed, amazed at the high breathless sound he was making. For
the man who was Director of Opera at Covent Garden when he
was twenty-two couldn't sing a note.

'It's so simple!' said one of the actors, touched and excited by what he had seen. 'Don't you see? He's a box! He's just like the rest of us! He's a *box*!'

Each day, whenever we stopped near anything vaguely resembling a sand-dune the actors, being actors, would get over-excited and serenade it with a flute. But it wasn't until the sixth day that we actually entered the desert. There wasn't any sand, though. It was ash—a great flat featureless void of ash. There was difficulty with the pee-stops. There wasn't even a tree. The girls liked to have a tree.

The crew had tensed a little, checking the Land-Rovers with extra care. Water bottles were issued. Don't lose them. It's no use moaning afterwards.

Many of us were wearing white *cheches* wrapped round our heads and faces: protection from the wind. The Leader wore a black *cheche*—traditional colour of the slave.

The first leg of the desert-crossing was to be a 250-mile drive across the featureless Plateau du Tademait as far as the oasis of In Salah. There the group would give its first performance.

We spurted into the ash-world of the Plateau, driving fast through thick clouds of dust in a diagonal formation to avoid blinding the Land-Rover behind. There wasn't a road, but a dirt track beaten into the ground by others who'd crossed it. If you lose the track, you're finished. People do sometimes, and die. But at one stage, the Leader deliberately left the tracks, cutting across them for several miles to make the route shorter. I don't know how he knew which way he was going. It seemed miraculous. We were all yelling and cheering him on with excitement. It was our first adventure.

Then, to everyone's astonishment, another Land-Rover shot dramatically into the lead. It was François Marthouret, driving for the first time. He'd decided to have a race. The Leader, black as thunder, signalled urgently with his lights. *Nobody* passed the Leader, particularly in a race. But Marthouret didn't seem to be stopping. I started yelling and screaming encouragement with the rest. I thought: he's going to write off his Land-Rover. It pleased me. It would make a change.

A stone smashed his windscreen, which was jolly bad luck. He had to retire from the race. 'You've got to respect the desert,' muttered Royston Bennett, inspecting the damage. 'It might take its revenge if you don't.'

But the Leader wasn't concerned with the Land-Rover. 'It's a machine,' he said angrily. 'I'm concerned with life and limb. *Lives* are at stake.' I never knew how much he might be over-dramatizing when he came out with things like that. Some stretches of the desert could seem just about as dangerous as a day trip from London to Brighton. But the previous year, two German tourists had died in the desert. And once, we passed an Austrian couple who were in real trouble: form of desert blindness. If they hadn't followed the convoy they would have travelled round in circles, and died.

Nobody overtook the Leader again.

That night, we descended the Plateau and camped among the rocks at its base. After supper Brook ordered two hours of musical work, taking us by surprise. Brook's stamina and enthusiasm for work are notorious. It's why Yoshi Oida calls him a monster. But when everyone was so bitterly cold in the Sahara that hands were numb, it was a little surprising that work continued in the dark as the group huddled round a dim torch. Later in the journey, plagued by mosquitoes and exhaustion in the heat and wetness of the forests, the group went on working just the same. Even in those first days Brook had set a pattern that wasn't to change throughout the entire journey. If there wasn't a performance, you kept working.

Yet the demand for work had come spontaneously from the actors themselves. By the third day, several of them began to return to the group's own exercises and folklore. During a break on the road or after camp was pitched you could see the actors gradually returning to a way of life.

Everyone in the group kneels, holding short sticks or fans. Facing them, the stern and disciplined Yoshi Oida. The actors sing an ancient Japanese song, in Japanese. Occasionally, Oida stops them abruptly, corrects the sound and begins again. Every day for two years in their Paris centre the group had struggled with this one song: a ritual. Brook sits bolt upright, watching.

Again, Yoshi leads the group, exercising in total silence with bamboo sticks six feet long: slow, rhythmic movements, shapes and patterns, bodies stretched on a rack.

Bagayogo, the African from Mali, an actor it seemed who was often like a man possessed, teaches an African song difficult enough for Africans to learn. SO KO NI OULADALEE M OULADALEE OULA. It's the traditional song of tribesmen the night before a circumcision is done by the local blacksmith.

After the song he teaches a flicking movement with his neck, fast as a snake's tongue.

In silence, silence made more mysterious by the desert, the group returns to T'ai Chi. A 1,200-year-old exercise developed by Taoist monks, still widely used in the streets of China and now quite fashionable in America and Europe, the actors look forward to it like a fix. The slow, ethereal movements are very relaxing. Brook asked me to join in. I was shy at first, though, and asked him where I could stand so as not to be seen. He gave me his place.

The carpet is laid out and an empty cardboard box appears. An actor climbs in, as a bird. And makes bird sounds. Intrigued, another actor approaches the box as a bird. And opens the box. Bird inside leaps, and kills.

A little ancient Greek is tried, perhaps Aristophanes. Exercise in sound and rhythm, as with all the work in language. TOTOTO-TOTOTOTOTOTOTIGKS! If you don't get the right number of TOS, it isn't any good. Stranger things have happened in Transylvania.

Other sounds, screamed into the void:

ELELEU! ELELEU! AUSFAKELOSKAI! XOODEDOM! EPOPOPOI! POPOPOPOI! POPOI! SCLEEOOOAAAAAH! OOOOM! HAAAAAR! OKKAKAKKO! POPOPOPOPOPOPOI!

One time, when I was more confused about the work than usual, Natasha Parry held out a key. The key was a Lorca essay, 'Theory and Function of the *Duende*'—which Goethe defined when he attributed to Paganini 'a mysterious power that everyone feels but no philosopher has explained'.

61

'All that has dark sounds', wrote Lorca, 'has *duende*. It is not a matter of ability, but of real live form; of blood; of ancient culture; of creative action. To help us seek the *duende* there is neither map nor discipline. All one knows is that it turns the blood like powdered glass, that it exhausts, that it rejects all the sweet geometry one has learned, that it breaks with all styles, that it compels Goya, master of greys, silvers and of those pinks in the best English paintings, to paint with his knees and with his fists horrible bitumen blacks.'

Now the box of musical instruments was unloaded for the first time. Here are some of Swados' collection of instruments:

A Japanese dinner gong, a wooden Tibetan drum, eight pieces from a Balinese gamelan, tambourines, a hand-made replica of a medieval court harp, a dinky xylophone, slide whistles, Indian bagpipe flutes, Latin-American bongo drums, a saw, a bugle, rattles made from bean pods, a toy piano, one raunchy harmonica, recorders, two conches, Iranian flutes, kazoos, sandblocks, maracas, Jews' harps, claviers, Indian stomach tasangers, a Chinese circus drum, wood-block cymbals and ratchets, crystal glasses, various pieces of scrap metal, and specially designed tuned cowbells from wonderful Copenhagen.

Ayansola would join the musical workshops with his talking drum. It really did talk. He used to bang it with a stick, like a claw, rocking gently as he built the sound to a terrific pitch and rhythm, and came to life. He was a master. But he didn't get on with Swados, and Swados didn't get on with him. For generations the male line of Ayansola's family in Oshogbo had been drummers. But he was a Yoruba. Yorubas don't take orders from women. So there could be awkward moments. 'Ayansola, you please play drum now? Drum now, yes? Jesus Christ, doesn't anyone speak Yoruba round here!' Ayansola would stare innocently into space, puffing on someone else's cigarette.

He certainly wasn't feeling up to much that night in the desert. The day before, he'd sold his transistor radio to an Arab on a donkey. The batteries had run out. 'I don't know what you find so hysterical,' Mirren said to me. 'Poor Ayansola. *Poor* Ayansola.'

Part of the trouble was that Swados thought the talking drum wasn't too bright an idea in the first place. It's a very specialized instrument, not easily blended into acting. Brook had been excited by Ayansola's drumming at a party he went to during a short trip to Nigeria. That's how the talking drum came to Paris. Brook often acts on impulse.

Swados drives herself hard—harder even than Brook, which would seem to be impossible. Also, her patience has been known to hit all-time lows. Patience is one of Brook's greatest assets: he understands the strange psychology of actors, when to step in or hold back, encourage or smash. But at twenty-two, Swados waits for no man. Brook had to calm her down from time to time. But she has this demonic energy in her. Peter Seeger, who's a friend, taught her many things about music but most of all how to work best without ever stopping. She composed her first song when she was four—a song for the ritual sacrifice before stuffed dolls of her nursery-school teacher. At High School she wanted to be a great writer—wrote three novels, receiving 253 rejection slips. She was a college radical, lived on various communes, some of them political, writing thousands of protest songs and so on. She worked for the Café La Mama for two years, working a lot with American-Indian groups, Chinese and Black. When she joined Brook she'd just won an Off-Broadway award for work that was recognized as being years ahead of its time. Her father's a lawyer in Buffalo, New York. Her grandparents were Russian: one a pianist, the other a concert violinist. Anyway, she's the one member of the group who can't help screaming with laughter at some of the things that go on. Swados takes herself seriously all right, but she has that quality. I relied on it.

Also, she was going out of her mind. It wasn't easy working at this level with a bunch of actors whose musical ability used to be no more developed than yours or mine. Only Michèle Collison and Malick Bagayogo possess that very special gift—the irresistible need to make music, for the joy of it really. One couldn't imagine their lives without song. But with the others, so highly trained and confident in other fields, music is something to be

63

feared. It would drive Swados to distraction. There are one or two members of the group who seem to be tone deaf, excluding Brook. She would resign most days. You could watch her sitting on the edge of the carpet contemplating mass murder.

Yet in just three months' work before Africa, the musical range of the actors had been transformed. At first, Swados concentrated on a crash course in basic music—constant and demanding work on different kinds of rhythm, choruses, pitch, sounds and harmonies that took them a little further than the customary wailing and clanging of so many underground theatre groups. Slowly they build up a repertoire of songs, some of them taught by Bagayogo or composed by Swados. But they were no more than a safety net, as the little shows were in the group's acting work. No, the real musical work was about learning how to improvise, compose, create music and sound on the spot, like a jazz musician. I knew they had a very, very long way to go before they got there. But why this stress on music? For it was absolutely vital to the work.

Tolstoy wrote: 'People are like rivers: they all contain the same water everywhere, yet each river at times can be narrow, swift, broad, smooth-flowing, clear, cold, muddy, warm. So it is with people. Each man carries within himself the germs of all human qualities.' So Brook's actor must be the composer, the singer, the poet, the dancer, the writer—each is a part of him, to be rediscovered, in time.

But it cuts even deeper than this. In line with Brook's theories, Swados was trying to discover whether music can be taken beyond the traditional format of performance— the masterpiece performed on the stage, the big number of the stage musicals, the singer crooning into the microphone. Sometimes the very best jazz musicians or folk singers have this special quality Swados is searching for. And Africans too, as she was to discover. It's difficult to describe. But she had a shot at it for me:

'Supposing you want an actor to capture in music the feeling of loneliness. Well, an opera singer would be limited because singers aren't really actors. Technically they'd be perfect but there's no emphasis on real acting. On the other hand, you can't give an actor the melody of a song. The melody limits whoever's using it. It's something imposed, *given* to the actor, unless you want him to sing "I Left My Heart In San Francisco". I mean that would be fine, but the actor wouldn't be able to take it too far. He would "act" the song. But Shakespeare used words that had such rhythms they could really be *manipulated* by an actor to suit the scene—the musicality of the words, the consonants, the vowels, the miraculous way they flowed—mostly the movement, the pauses, the stops, the breaths. I once set *Romeo and Juliet* to music and it was just incredible how you could set each scene a hundred different ways—the ballad, the blues, rock and roll, anything. So the actor can come along and take these words and really *develop* them. The words are his base, right? So what I'm trying to find is rhythms, flows and directions of sound—I'm really trying not to get abstract—but movement and intonations of voice that can reflect a character. I've got to find an *indication* of a melody. Something that doesn't restrict or illustrate—just a couple of notes perhaps, something within the actor's range that really reflects emotion, really reflects a state of being. It isn't something that's incidental or background music. It isn't virtuoso technique. I guess I'm trying to find the simplest elements that give a *source* to emotion. But the elements are a base. The actor can manipulate them for his own use. It's like having a really great text. Except that what comes out isn't necessarily a song. It might just be a sound. The sound somehow encompasses an entire feeling, and conveys it.'

You can understand how Swados could be driven to distraction. She was searching for Ted Hughes' 'great precious thing far beyond words'—the being pure and without effort that some birds express, and animals.

Even during that first musical workshop in the desert there wasn't a second to waste. There's such urgency about Swados. Sometimes, when things aren't going too well she remains sublimely calm whilst secretly plotting revenge against the world in general and vain actors in particular. Other times: no mercy.

'*Listen!* You forgot the tune. You weren't listening. You had no base. You left no room for anyone else to come in. You were going like a train at a thousand miles an hour. Congratulations, you really fucked it up.'

This would be followed by:

'What I *mean* to say is, it's coming along very nicely but we're not quite there yet.'

There was a performance the next day, the seventh day.

5

Nobody was expecting anything to happen when the convoy drove into the oasis of In Salah, an ancient fortress town in open desert, a town sometimes buried completely by sandstorms. The oasis is 500 miles from Algiers. It was nine o'clock in the morning. We'd stopped to buy petrol and water.

Also, it was really hot for the first time and this only added to our lethargy as we strolled around the small market-place in the heat and dust. Caution was needed, warned Brook. If there was trouble we might be mistaken for thieves or a terrorist gang. The Leader was on his guard, too. 'This is Algeria, George,' he said to me. He'd taken to calling me George. But the people of In Salah didn't seem to be suspicious. They were a mixture of Algerians, Negro descendants of slaves and the famous 'veiled men': Tuaregs veiled in indigo, quiet and unhurried people who smiled at the unexpected strangers among them and went casually about their business. The market-place was almost deserted, yet it was a large town. When I asked a man who spoke French where everyone was, he replied: 'Cultivating their gardens,' and gave me a huge smile.

Turnips, carrots and mint were laid out for sale in neat piles on the ground. Bracelets and necklaces were offered. Two ancient men in rags squatted over a battered kettle, untroubled by the flies, gossiping quietly to each other. I think they met every day. A cobbler was working indoors, a dark place, more a hovel. He looked up and said hello: no teeth. A white camel sat sadly in one corner of the market, resigned to its fate. It would be slaughtered and eaten. Camels are more useful than Land-Rovers in the end. You can't eat a Land-Rover. There were very few women. This was a Muslim town. The women stayed indoors, peeping through veils at us from behind open windows.

Brook was looking around on his own when I joined him. 'Now this is the sort of place we should perform,' he said. 'It has something. I wish I'd known.' He had planned the first show for Tamanrasset, a bustling desert town 400 miles further south. It seemed as good a place as any. But half an hour later I saw Brook walking purposefully ahead of three important-looking men, local officials in Western clothes. 'We play,' he said to a group of actors munching hot bread. 'We're going to play!'

Play what, I thought. For nothing was prepared. The actors took the news calmly, though one or two were holding their breath. Instructions were sent out for the carpet and the great metal music box. The rest of the group were rounded up. 'Did someone say we are to *play*?' said François Marthouret, running excitedly to help out with the carpet. It was laid out in a corner of the market where a small donkey was chewing a carrot. As was appropriate, Brook was the first to sit on the carpet in his customary crossed-legged Japanese sitting position. People stared and giggled at this strange sight, ambling over to see what was going on. There had been no announcement. There had never been a strolling player or anything resembling what was going to happen in this place before. I don't think we could have been mistaken for thieves or terrorists. But we might have been strange missionaries or salesmen of an exotic kind. Brook was very busy nodding and twinkling and beaming good will at the small crowd as the actors strolled over to join him on the carpet. As always in Africa, a crowd can appear from nowhere. For the moment, fifty or so people were standing round the edge of the carpet waiting for something to happen. Many of them were children, giggling behind their hands.

The music box was opened, everyone choosing an instrument. There were flutes and drums mostly. Brook had two sticks to bang. As I'd been included in some of the simplest musical work, Swados gave me a cowbell. It wasn't exactly a major instrument. Still, Brook asked me to join the actors on the carpet—part of the show. I promise you, it was quite a compliment. Not even George Plimpton would have got on that carpet. But as I sat

68

there, shaking with nerves, the thought occurred that none of us need actually do anything. The crowd seemed mesmerised by the freaks sitting round a carpet in the corner of their market. They were particularly fascinated by the sight of Yoshi Oida: yellow man in kimono. I think it's just about possible that the group's presence alone could have passed for the performance.

It did for a while. It was about half an hour before anything actually happened. Brook and the group were holding a discussion with Swados about what to open the show with. Nobody seemed to mind. The pace of the oasis was slow and people were used to life taking its time. So there was an instant sense of a completely different atmosphere to Western theatre. Whatever else happened there would be no wall between actor and audience here. Everyone was very relaxed. I may have been alone in thinking the group should get on with it, which is what Brook likes to call 'Western conditioning'. This is the conditioning that whispers to you: 'Give me a result! Make it quick and make it good!' The actor hears the same voices too. God help him if he's deaf. But if these pressures are absent, something fresh might be discovered. A frightened actor does not take risks.

After the long discussion, the actors returned to the fringes of the carpet. The start of the show had been decided. We would play an overture.

This improvisation was greeted politely. I would not say it bowled the audience over. The group had worked on the overture a little in Paris. Michèle Collison guided the group on the Balinese gamelans. One-two-three and bang the cowbell! I kept missing the beat. So I followed Myers, but he kept missing his too. Hence the African proverb, 'Copying everybody else all the time the monkey one day cut his throat.' After the overture, two songs. Swados yelled out what they should be. The first, the group forgot entirely, got lost, felt embarrassed, was glad to hear the bell. The other was sung by Malik Bagayogo, but his voice cracked in the heat, which brought laughter of the gentlest kind. Myers whispered to me: 'Don't worry about a thing. They're just going to crucify us.' I was really nervous. I had a look on my face that was trying to say: 'I'm not really one of them, you know.' But the third song was a terrific success and brought applause. Brook cheered with delight. The actors were laughing happily and so was the audience, who knew a sense of relief when they saw it. The Arabs among them couldn't have known they were applauding an Israeli song. Maybe they didn't care.

The crowd was growing now—300 or so spilling onto the carpet. A fat and furious schoolmaster was pointing angrily at his watch, lashing out at his truant children. They just dodged away and dodged back again. The village mad woman, an old hag holding a mirror and comb, stopped the show when she decided to jig around on the carpet for a while. Who would have her? She was singing and admiring herself in the little hand mirror. Who would have her? A violent row blew up amid laughter from the crowd, for there were no takers. Then Sylvain Corthay took off on a risky solo, making wild and strange sounds to a basic beat from the group. The audience collapsed with laughter. They were like lightning. The second he made it, striving and straining after a specially meaningful sound, they just roared with laughter. They weren't cruel or anything. They just couldn't help it. 'You see,' Brook whispered to me, 'they've good taste.' Corthay gritted his teeth, ploughing on with the solo in a daze.

Then the group began many improvisations based on some of the archetypes they'd worked on in Paris—a trickster, a king, a giant, a corpse—the first tentative improvisations performed in ones and twos as the white camel was slaughtered in another corner of the market-place, groaning and spitting blood.

Perhaps what followed might strike you as very naïve. Brook met Bertolt Brecht shortly before he died. Brecht said: 'You know what my real term for the theatre is? My term is the Theatre of Naïvety.'

'Quick!' said François Marthouret. 'Give me an idea!' 'Search me.' Then he was on the carpet, struggling with a cardboard box. The crowd fixed on the box with total attentiveness. There was a stillness about the people, an expectancy. What's in the box? Another box is in the box. What's in the second box? Marthouret struggled with the box again, a Kaspar character, someone who could not speak, struggling with sounds and objects as if they

70

had just been discovered. He buried himself in the box, head first. The crowd laughed. He emerged with a conch. No sound would come. Blow harder: no sound. *Harder!* He got a sound. Mathouret grinned from ear to ear, as did the audience.

Helen Mirren went on the carpet, blowing on a slide whistle. She talks with the whistle to Miriam Goldschmidt who replies with a flute. Michèle Collison joins them, is lured by them, on to the carpet. She has a flute. The three women talk to each other. Enter a corpse: Lou Zeldis, the tallest corpse in the world, taking a great theatrical bow. The actors laugh but no one else understands the bow. What's a bow? But the corpse is dead on its feet. Bagayogo takes its hand: the hand sticks to him. Myers goes to the rescue: corpse envelops the rescuer. No one escapes a corpse. The crowd enjoys this slapstick and cheers the corpse. Zeldis, now an actor, takes another bow. Ah, so *that*'s what a bow's for!

What next? Nobody knew. Brook wasn't saying anything either. Enter a void! No actor was moving. Until Katsulas suddenly took off his huge army boots and placed them in the centre of the carpet. Then he abandoned them there.

The crowd stare at the boots. The actors stare at the boots. Everyone in the place is staring at a pair of army boots. It was as if we were all seeing them for the first time. Then Katsulas, who must have been having a little think, approached the boots. What luck! To find a pair of boots in the middle of nowhere. So he put them on, for he hadn't a pair of his own. Then he's in those great boots, and he's feeling really good, and he's strutting around that carpet a new man, a powerful man, a *giant* of a man! Sometimes the boots won't walk where he wants them to. They kick and fight him. But Yoshi Oida decides he wants the boots, confronts the giant, grows frightened, hides in the crowd. Uproar! The giant goes after him, but grabs a child instead. Everyone's laughing now, except the child who's really scared. So the giant, who's a gentle giant, takes off one of the boots and gives it to him. The child doesn't know what to do. 'Blow,' mimes the giant. Marthouret is on the carpet now, blowing into the boot for the child. No sound. Blow harder: no sound. *Harder!* The boot makes the sound of a conch. Swados is blowing her brains out on the conch at the edge of the carpet, and everyone knows this but it doesn't matter. The child's eyes are wide. The giant asks him to try. He blows and blows, and the sound comes. The child just looked at the boot and he looked at the sky, and he couldn't say a word.

Enter Ayansola on one leg. Goggles over the bedsheet round his head, tartan socks tucked into his natty Italian shoes, a terrific sight. Ayansola gets that claw working hard on his talking drum as he hops about on one leg for extra effect. The crowd loves this showmanship and cheers him. SCLEEAAAAH! Katsulas is in there now, screaming, seizing the moment, cartwheeling across the carpet to the surprise and delight of the crowd. Others join him, running, diving, tumbling—acrobatics of a sort, which create their own energy and excitement. A dance begins to drums. Those actors were really enjoying themselves. With all its limitations the show had gradually become an ideal theatre performance. It was an *event*.

Work with sticks followed, exercises in rhythm and timing, audacious patterns and images, at which the crowd often fell still and watchful. They didn't mind when things went wrong. But they really loved it when they went right. When the sticks bent into an invisible circle, something that really needs incredible discipline to make, a perfect circle, slowly building from the ground to the sky, each arching his stick in precise timing with the next until the sticks seem to take life, a life of their own— that can be miraculous when it works and the crowd sensed it, watching in total silence until the invisible circle was made, and applause. A song followed. And that was all that was attempted in the market-place of In Salah.

I don't think I've ever seen the actors or Brook look so happy. That was a very special day. It had been a meeting of innocents: a celebration. But once gained the innocence was to be lost as quickly as the next performance, and never found again.

That audience had seemed reserved and gentle: open. They were totally free of any conventional theatre associations. They hadn't seen an acting group before. The name Brook meant nothing to them. They just received the work in the most open way. They were Brook's 'searchlight'—he often used the term—new eyes that really challenged the actor's sense of clarity and simplicity. This was one of the best reasons for going to Africa: whenever the group performed something obviously dramatic or arty, the audience found them out every time.

Why had the people of In Salah laughed so much when Sylvain Corthay made his strange sounds? I've heard actors make similar sounds in experimental work in Europe and America—and they've passed muster, even been acclaimed. After all, Brook spent a whole year inventing a new language of sounds, Ted Hughes' *Orghast*. But In Salah rejected them, Brook explained, for one very simple reason: they weren't good enough. What the actors and Brook did on such occasions—throughout the entire journey—was in its way equally simple. They began all over again. In this way, the second-to-second vibrant response of the audience was the best teacher the group could have. When the people of In Salah collapsed with laughter at Corthay's sounds, Brook compared it to the moment in Zen teaching when the pupil earnestly asks a vital question only for his revered master to reply by swiping him over the head. For the Zen pupil such a shattering moment might lead to illumination, and set him on the right path.

It's strange: when I asked Corthay what the laughter felt like, he said it was just like being hit over the head.

But the lightning responses of the African audiences were only one side of the coin. Brook may have been searching for a vital quality of naïvety in his work, but the people of In Salah weren't naïve—far from it. Primitivism doesn't apply to any part of Africa we went to. Away from the modern cities, the African had something else to offer and it was just as precious as his openness. The traditional culture of African civilizations is not only extremely rich and complete, but in relation to theatre it prepares the audience in a unique way.

If you take a cardboard box, it's just an object. But if you put an actor inside a box, it becomes a metaphor. For the Western audience, reality and fantasy are different things. But for the

73

African brought up in a traditional way of life they are two aspects of the same reality. There's no division. The African understands the double nature of reality. For him there's free passage between the concrete and the abstract, the visible and the invisible. When we were in Nigeria there was such a powerful sense of deities and poetry and myth as a living reality that the group was practically broken by it. Death for us is separate from life: perhaps it's an after-life. I think that death for the African is a different form of life.

Fifty years ago Jung visited North Africa to see what it could tell him about the nature of dreams. But he returned from his journey with a greater insight into himself. In Africa, Jung discovered that part of his personality which had become submerged under the pressure and influence of being a white European. And the discovery shattered him. For the first time he realized how inadequate life is when experienced only through the intellect. Western Man is split and divided within himself, for he exists in an age when myth and nature as living realities have been lost to the modern, scientific world. For Jung, it accounted for the neurosis of the white European.

In the same way, Brook warned me from the outset to watch out for this division within us, for Africa would reveal it. He pointed to the imbalance within us where the golden calf of the intellect is worshipped at the cost of true feelings and experience. Like Jung, he believes that the intellectual—the intellect alone— protects us from true feeling, stifles and camouflages the spirit in a blind collection of facts and concepts. Yet as Brook talked to me of this I was struck forcibly by the fact that he, a supreme intellectual figure, should express himself this way.

'Well,' he said after the show, 'the imaginary work is over.'

We had mint tea with the schoolmaster before leaving, sitting shoeless around the white-washed walls of his home. It was just an empty room. We drank three cups, as is the custom. The schoolmaster had recorded the show on an ancient tape recorder. Brook teased us that he might have been a secret agent in disguise. The tapes would be sent urgently to headquarters in Algiers where a team of experts would crack the code: snatches of ancient Greek, Latin, Avesta and gobbledygook.

Many children stared at us through the window of the empty room, asking for souvenirs. François Marthouret gave a youngster his pencil, feeling guilty for it wasn't much to give.

'We will share it!' announced the child proudly to his friends. 'Each will take his turn.'

Now the market was as before, a tranquil and silent place.

Within minutes we were back in the desert.

6

There had been a little incident, an accident, during the show: unlucky omen.

One of the sticks flew out of someone's hand, cutting Helen Mirren just above an eye. The blood spurted, and tears. Even the fun and joy of In Salah would be denied her. 'I don't like it,' said Miriam Goldschmidt, the prophet of doom. 'Such a thing has never happened before.'

The next morning, the English actor Bruce Myers was missing. He had disappeared in the desert.

In its way, the wild and desperate search for him was among the most dramatic improvisations of the entire journey. Brook didn't direct it, though I think he wanted to.

The Leader directed it.

It was six in the morning, breakfast time, when we realized he was missing. He wasn't in the queue for the Rice Crispies. If he wasn't careful someone else would grab his share, which was always the case if you were late, and sometimes if you weren't. Yet Myers was usually one of the first to be seen around camp, packing up his kit expertly or taking a strip wash in half a bowl of icy water. Some of us would still be waking in a confused sort of way, wondering where the roof and the bookshelves and the family and the cat had gone to. My eyes would focus on the sky in disbelief. Then I'd hear people pissing patterns in the sand.

At first we thought Myers might be sleeping further away from camp than usual. Most of us slept well away from base, spreading out in different directions, trying hard to cling onto what privacy was left. Swados would sleep as far from the camp as possible, dragging her guitar case behind her as she disappeared into the distance. You could hear her singing most of the night. Apart from the crew only Yoshi Oida, who lit the petrol stoves first thing each morning, and Katsulas, who'd decided to act out the role of camp commandant, slept in the camp.

The crew always slept in the camp, for it was thought to be safer and the Land-Rovers protected them from the wind. The Leader was bewildered and angry at the rest of us for spreading out in the desert. He thought someone would be silly enough to get lost.

Brook had got lost the night before. Out for an evening stroll with Natasha Parry, he lost track of the camp. We were camping in open desert for the first time—open and fantastic desert surrounded only by sand and sky, ravines and valleys. Sometimes you would come unexpectedly across a car wreck, pop art, left as a warning. The Brooks were no more than fifty yards from base yet they lost the camp, walking in circles for over an hour.

'Take every care,' warned Brook, who looked relieved to see everyone again.

As we ate breakfast, Michèle Collison mentioned that Myers must be on the way back from one of the mountains in the distance. Before going to bed, he said he might climb a mountain at dawn.

We were just beginning to glimpse the spectacular range of Hoggar mountains where the feared and despised Tuaregs, former lords of the desert, used to plunder and murder strangers passing through.

The previous afternoon, we drove seven times round the shrine of a holy man. The tradition brings you luck.

Two miles away from the camp were two high mountains to the right of three valleys. It was the only place Myers could be. Ever since I've known him, he's climbed mountains. It's his hobby. Nobody was worried or anything. We just assumed he would be strolling back from his climb. Brook went ahead with the usual post-breakfast meeting. It was a way of collecting thoughts, of bringing the group together for the long day ahead. There would usually be exercises or a discussion of ideas to be thought over on the road. Songs were often composed and practised in the Land-Rovers. But as the time to strike camp grew closer, the Leader decided to drive out and pick Myers up. I went with him. The Leader wasn't saying a word. He had about him that unexpected atmosphere of fear I'd sensed in our first meeting.

As we left, Marthouret mentioned he heard the sound of cries in the night. Also, dogs barking.

'Dogs?' said Brook. '*Barking?*'

We drove out of the camp at top speed, churning up the sand. But Myers was nowhere in sight. The Leader accelerated towards the valleys, stopping a hundred yards or so in front of them. No life was there, nor could anything live there for long. Several times the Leader scanned the landscape with his binoculars, climbing up on the roof of the car, watching and listening in silence. 'Listen,' he said. 'Listen hard.' Oh Christ, I've never heard a silence like that in my life. For there in that incredible void the silence hit back at us. This was no passive response, silence of indifference and emptiness. It was more a statement. Astonishment and fear are part of this terrible silence. It is inhuman silence. The Leader shattered it, suddenly ramming his hand onto the car horn so that the blast shot through the valleys. But the sound only echoed and stretched round the ravines and valleys, and returned. We shouted his name, screamed it now, human voices demanding human response. But our own voices returned.

'It might take us three days to find him in there,' snapped the Leader. 'Without water he will die in a day.'

He looked white, taking drags on a cigarette. It's terrible but I could feel myself starting to laugh.

'What's he like this friend of yours?' he asked as we drove urgently back to camp.

That jarred a bit, this friend of *yours*. I didn't know what to tell him. Myers has a reckless streak, all right. He's been known to make the odd mistake. When he worked in Stratford for the Royal Shakespeare Company he built an incredible sailing boat. He built it in the spare room of his cottage, working on it

78

lovingly for several months. People used to watch him. But when the boat was finally finished, he couldn't get it out through the door. So he sort of jumped up and down on it. Then he built it again and it was really beautiful. Except when he launched it in the River Avon, it sprang a leak and sank. He went down with it, laughing hysterically.

'What's he like this friend of yours?'

'I'm not sure. I think he sees the funny side of things.'

When we got back to camp, the Leader leapt out of his Land-Rover and started sniffing round the sand.

He was searching for *tracks*.

He found fresh footprints leading out of the camp. The tracks went to the right of the valleys towards the two mountains. They made a distinct corrugated pattern, medium-size.

Then we hurried to find the group who were sitting quietly on a sand-dune, listening to Brook. The Leader took charge.

'I would like to see everyone's feet,' he announced in a grave voice.

People looked puzzled.

'I mean I wouldn't like to see everyone's feet. I would like to see everyone's *shoes*.'

So everyone turned up the soles of their shoes. But only Yoshi Oida's were similar to the tracks.

'Did you leave the camp last night?' demanded the Leader.

And Yoshi said, yes. He'd gone to make pee-pee.

'*Where* pee-pee?' asked the Leader.

'Where?' thought Yoshi, who seemed bewildered.

'You pee-pee in direction of mountains?' asked the Leader.

And Yoshi said, no. In the direction of the Bedford truck.

Even so the Leader, who seemed to mistrust the mysterious ways of the Orient, was taking no chances. Yoshi's tracks would have to be compared with the tracks leading towards the mountains. Best to make certain, right Peter? Everyone ambled down to the edge of the camp for the track-making ceremony. 'Did someone say Bruce is missing?' asked Bagayogo, squinting at Brook through his glasses.

79

Yoshi Oida looked hurt, as if he were being accused of something. But he made his tracks next to the others and they turned out to be about ten times smaller. Still, they were peered at, walked round, studied and scrutinized from every possible angle until the whole matter was beyond any conceivable doubt. 'These tracks do *not* belong to Yoshi,' the Leader announced at last. 'We can conclude that Bruce *definitely* went to the mountains.' At which point one of the crew returned from a search party to say that he'd found fresh tracks going away from the mountains towards the valleys. The Leader looked as if he'd been hit over the head with a meat axe. 'Well he's out there *somewhere*,' he said.

I couldn't believe Myers had gone to the valleys. He would have gone for the highest of the two mountain peaks just behind them. He wouldn't have gone for the valleys or the other mountain. He would have gone for the climb that might have beaten him.

'Leave this to me!' shouted the Leader as I began to tell him my theory. 'It could take three days to find him in there. Everyone follow me! *Lives* are at stake!'

As in the army, never question the judgement of the commanding officer. We followed the Leader. There was a frenetic scramble for the Land-Rovers. Marthouret got over-excited and thought he'd lost the keys to his in the sand. Bagayogo lost his Gucci-style bags. He never went anywhere without them, even on a search. Mirren was in tears. Goldschmidt seemed to be mumbling strange incantations to herself. Ayansola was busy kicking someone out of his front seat. Then we pulled out of camp. As the Leader's car began to leave, I could see this stocky figure pounding after us. It was Brook, anxious to be at the hub of the action. 'Step on it, James,' I said to the Leader, 'lives are at stake.' But Brook caught us, jumping breathlessly into the back. He sat in silence for a while, thinking things over. 'It's frightening and it may end up a tragedy,' he whispered to me eventually. 'And yet one can't help laughing. It's black comedy.' And we both started to laugh in a nervous sort of way. 'What's the *plan*, James?' asked Brook, leaning over the Leader's shoulder.

The plan was that everyone, the entire expedition, would march on the valleys.

This was how I came to have a clearer understanding of what went wrong in The Charge of the Light Brigade. Someone was definitely pointing in the wrong direction. 'Don't ask *me*,' shouted one of the crew as we began to form a line facing the valleys. 'Just do what the Leader says. Do what he *says*.'

We were told to advance fifteen yards apart, as search parties do searching for bodies in marshes and woods.

'Now then,' announced the Leader. 'We will make two signs— arms straight up if we find him. Arms in the shape of a cross if he's injured or . . .' His voice trailed away. Or dead, I thought with a smile. 'I say, James!' shouted Brook from the line. 'Shouldn't we advance with Ayansola playing his talking drum?'

I think we were all enjoying it really. We were scared all right, but excitement and danger had come our way at last and there's perverse pleasure in that. Also, comfort of a special kind. *Schadenfreude:* enjoyment at other people's misfortune. In my experience there's nothing to beat a friend in trouble. But in the midst of my own panic and fear, old Myers had given me a terrific role to play. I was playing the lead. I saw myself as The Saviour. I would find him and save him. Thus becoming The Hero. 'I'll get you out of here, old fruit. Just hang round my neck while I slide 3,000 feet down this crevice. Don't worry about my vertigo. It's going to be all right, everything's going to be *all right* . . .' I knew that I'd be the one to find Myers and I knew that Mirren thought she'd be the one to find him. So there was a bit of a rush on.

'SLOW DOWN!' screamed the Leader as we began the advance. We were practically running. 'This is *useless*,' moaned Brook at the chaos. 'This is no good at all! What we need is a secret calling code.' The Leader rose above that. 'I don't think a secret calling code will be necessary, thank you very much Peter.' But something really disastrous was happening as the line advanced. We were spread so far apart, the end of the line was completely missing the valleys. Several people were strolling happily off into open desert. 'Are you *there*, Bruce?'

I could hear one of the crew, a sweeper-up behind the line, cursing actors with more venom than a playwright. He thought the search party was going to get lost. Some of us should have stayed behind as a reserve search party. The reserve search party could have searched for the search party. All this time I had a growing suspicion that Myers was maybe back at camp wondering where everyone had got to. Sooner or later he would decide to march on the valleys because he thought everyone was lost up a mountain.

The sun was up now, and burning. I tried to keep up with the urgent steps of the mechanic, scrambling up the side of a deep valley. He was the only one who'd remembered to bring his water bottle. People were draped round rocks gasping for air, water, shelter—*release*. After half an hour, I thought I couldn't go on. The sun was killing us. I slumped exhausted by a hillside. Two great circles had been carved on its rock surface. I stared at them in horror. They're the traditional sign of a nomad grave.

I climbed higher, struggling with the rest. And could see the Camp Master cutting a dash on the bonnet of his Land-Rover as it patrolled and circled the desert below. He was making desperate signals that Myers was still nowhere to be found. He wasn't even at the mountain.

Actually, he was up the mountain.

He was climbing it.

We couldn't see him because he was hidden in the shadow of its crevices. And he couldn't see us because he was too busy climbing the mountain. It was the one with the highest peak.

Four hours after the search party left, Myers descended the mountain. And that's when he was picked up.

He told me ages later that he almost made the summit.

The inquest on the search marked the first open split between the crew and the actors. It was inevitable.

Brook ordered a full-scale conference that night. Everyone was to attend, even the crew. Myers was looking bashful. Swados strolled along singing 'Climb Every Mountain', which didn't help. We sat in the semi-darkness warming hands on hot mugs of tea. There was always a conference after every performance and the mountain rescue operation was to be no different. Brook likes to analyse events—what went wrong or right, what could have been done better, areas to work on in the future, and so on. He likes to swop ideas. So each step of the disappearance and search was examined in detail as the crew looked on in a bewildered group outside the circle of actors. They were tight-lipped. They didn't want to have their expertise in desert crossings analysed by a bunch of *avant-garde* theatre intellectuals. You could tell. Also, if Myers hadn't disappeared there wouldn't have been a search.

It was when Brook brought up the question of a secret calling code again that one of the crew finally cracked. Someone suggested making bird sounds. If you're lost, make the sound of a crow. Then someone else said maybe it should be a sort of duck sound. And everyone started trying out different bird sounds, crows and ducks and owls and partridges echoing out through the desert. 'What about a *hoopoe*?'

The member of the crew who cracked was one of the young relief drivers due to leave the expedition at the next stop in Tamanrasset. 'What a load of cobblers!' he shouted without warning as people continued with the secret bird-sound calling code. 'What a load of old *cobblers*!' Brook wasn't fazed, however. 'Well, that's just what we've been waiting to hear,' he replied, waving the rebel into the centre of the circle to say his piece. Surrounded by quizzical forces the youngster got stage-fright, losing all confidence. He managed to say the group should go and play games elsewhere, preferably in a monastery. Also: 'Do what the Leader *says*. Just do what the Leader *says*!' At which the Leader and the rest of the crew nodded vigorous agreement.

Brook continued the conference with the suggestion that the secret calling code needn't be built round bird sounds. Not necessarily. It could be built round car horns. Two toots for 'Where are you?' One terribly long toot for 'Come back wherever you are.' Brook tried them out for himself, making the tooting sounds. 'Is it going to be TOOOOT TOOOOT?' he asked. 'And what do we think about TOOOOOOOOOOOOOOOOOOOOT?'

And the actors analysed this latest development of the secret calling code. And the jaws of the crew sagged open. And Brook never did decide about the toots.

7

All the joy and innocence of In Salah, the innocence more than anything, was smashed at the next performance.

Two days after the search we reached the bustling desert town of Tamanrasset, famous capital of the old Tuareg empire, and pitched camp among the rocks and boulders of the surrounding desert. We seemed to be living on the moon. As usual we rose at six in the morning. But to my surprise Brook ordered work on one of the little shows the group had worked on in Paris—*The Box Show*. The order came over breakfast. Then he took a Land-Rover into town to find a place to perform and make contact with the local officials. They were expecting him: Algiers had warned them we were coming.

About twenty cardboard boxes were unloaded from the truck. A clearing was found and the carpet laid out. After exercises and musical work, the actors spent the rest of the morning playing with the boxes. Boxes, like sticks, are part of the group's own folklore. Everyone seemed thrilled to see them again: identities. And homes too. Yoshi Oida grabbed two for himself and slept in them at night.

The Box Show involved a lot of boxes. Based on improvisations of several of Ted Hughes' unusual poems, there were breathing boxes, singing boxes, ballet boxes, sound boxes, mask boxes, coffin boxes, tunnel boxes, tower boxes, lots and lots of boxes. There might be one box, a Pandora's Box, with three sorceresses inside, who emerge playing violins. A walking box walks and is knifed, walking. A tree box laughs and speaks and spews out gifts. An ogre leaps from an ogre box, and kills.

A lost man is born without the power of language into a world he cannot understand. The man is born into a world of boxes.

They'd never done the show in public before.

When Brook returned, the group went through a rough order of events for the show and broke for lunch. There was usually tinned tuna fish. The flies came with the blazing heat. The flies would break the best of us in the end. Swados, who always scribbled down notes and songs and half-poems, took it out on her notebook: 'Don't fuck on me flies, you can do what you want, twenty or thirty flies on my shoe, I couldn't care less, make nests in my hair, inhabit my ears, make me dizzy with your stupid whamming and buzzing, hold great meetings, elect presidents, make gorgeous fly music, fly shit on my clothes, fly constellations on my legs, make me your countryside, swimming pool, but don't fuck on me, don't fuck on me. That's too much.'

Apart from the flies, Andreas Katsulas was busy going yummy-yummy at the tuna fish too. Also at the pilchards. Actors are big eaters by nature. Maybe it's an outlet for nervous tension. But only Katsulas actually enjoyed the food. His wife, Marva, was one of the cooks and I think he liked to wave the flag. 'Real good, Marva. Any seconds going? Let me know if there's any *more* going, Marva.' 'You'll just have to wait your turn with the rest, Andy.' She didn't want to give him preferential treatment.

Marva and Deirdre were the two cooks, or tin openers, and they had the artistic temperament of cooks. It wouldn't do to get on the wrong side of them. Sometimes the two French actors, with fond memories of Paris and chilled Beaujolais in their blood, would give Marva and Deirdre the look of a dead albatross. One day there was going to be trouble. But minds were on other things for the moment. The camp, normally relaxed, had become still and quiet. Something was wrong. The group was tensing up. They were fidgeting with the boxes or rearranging their kit-bags. They were nervous.

The white costumes were worn for the first time. But they created their own strange atmosphere. Somehow it seemed as if the actors had slipped back into the strained and artificial atmosphere of the traditional first night. The only point of the first night in a theatre is to get the actors through to the second. To hell with critics. But there, in the desert, as the actors paced nervously around in their new costumes it was as if they were waiting for the five-minute bell. Brook looked relaxed, though. Performances never worry him. He gets nervous on only two occasions—right at the beginning of a production when there's nothing but a stage, the empty space. And on the first day of rehearsal when all the actors and designers and technicians have been brought together for the first time. For Brook, it's the day when everything is literally made or marred. By the time you get to the first night there's no need for nerves: the die is cast.

We crammed into two Land-Rovers, ovens, for the five-mile ride into town. It was the stage manager's job to round everyone up, counting faces to make certain no one was left behind. 'Jesus, where is everybody?' François Marthouret was always late, always the last to arrive. Then the counting would begin all over again as nerves jarred and people sweated and stewed in the blazing heat. 'So that's one, two, three, four . . . Hey, that makes only four! Jesus, where *is* everybody?' We left camp just before three o'clock—the hottest time of the day. The back door to one of the Land-Rovers flew open on the way. A bad sign, if you're superstitious.

We didn't find the peace and tranquillity of In Salah. For Tamanrasset seemed a place with far more worldliness about it, a busy desert crossroad for military men, camel trains, tradesmen and a few tourists masquerading as the toughest adventurers in the world. One sensed bustle and pace. There were a few dingy cafés and shops, a small post office, a sense of modern life among the mud hovels and Tuaregs veiled in astonishing blues and yellows. A Land-Rover full of South Africans went roaring and hooting through the centre with all the counterfeit swagger of an English rugby club. It would not be easy to play in this place.

Brook pointed at a tree in the dust of a narrow track leading into the market square—the carpet would go there. A small crowd, kids mostly, followed the Land-Rovers, running alongside them banging on the windows. We waved and smiled back, anxious to please. As the carpet was laid out an official made himself very busy and asked Brook if he had permission to do whatever it was he was supposed to be doing. He demanded to see

86

written permission. 'But I have *verbal* permission,' said Brook, feigning outrage. 'Well if you have verbal permission,' replied the official. 'That's all right.'

Who said a verbal promise isn't worth the paper it's written on?

As soon as the actors sat round the carpet, they were ambushed. Brook had made a tactical error—the street was too narrow to hold a huge chaotic crowd that appeared unexpectedly from nowhere. The group tried to keep calm. People were spilling onto the carpet, forcing the actors back against a wall. 'Just keep calm and everything will be *all right*.' As soon as you sat down, ten kids sat in your lap. When you moved them off, twenty more took their place. The crowds were climbing walls, clinging to trees, submerging Land-Rovers, shouting, calling, laughing, fighting to see what was going on. Instant Stravinsky was going on. The actors had launched into a little esoteric musical work. But the songs were too hesitant and gentle. Nobody could hear them. 'Keep calm. Just keep *calm*.' Ayansola was sent in with a pat on his back, like a substitute footballer to save the ball game.

He knew he couldn't go wrong. He really had an evil grin on his face as he took his drum and whacked it so hard they could have heard it back in Algiers. Cheers from the crowd! But some of them were ironic. Brook laughed when he heard them, taking the point. 'Now that man can play! That man knows what he's doing!' Swados screamed for a faster number from the group. 'They want action!' But a battered old truck was forcing its way through the audience at the time. We had to roll up the carpet to let it through. It was a sort of interval.

'*Box Show!*' ordered Brook, who seemed intrigued and excited by the chaos. He likes the unexpected to happen. The crowd was growing, buzzing with the flies around the freaks who'd come to town. The village elders gossiped and giggled together at the back. The kids were having a wild time. But the veiled Tuaregs created a sense of distance: bewildered eyes. A tough group of young men in Western clothes stood at the front with their arms folded: critics.

François Marthouret, white in the face, entered the carpet to save the show. Have you ever seen the glazed eyes of a boxer just before he's sent sleepy-time Joe?

Marthouret played The Lost Man born into a world he can't understand. For a split second he glanced at Brook. Brook stared back with eyes of ice. Marthouret was lost, all right. Panicked and confused by the chaos and the noise and heat and flies, he looked desperately at the actors around him. But he must have seen his own face. The others were pole-axed too. They couldn't get to the boxes through the crowd. They couldn't get in them. The precious boxes were piled up behind a tree. The children were sitting on them. 'Guess what?' Myers whispered to me, fighting his way towards the boxes. 'We're all going home tomorrow.' He was whispering it in that sing-song way people do when they're about to get hysterical.

'Oh Christ,' murmured Mirren, staring in disbelief at the carpet. She could see several actors in boxes had made it at last, crashing into each other in the confusion. There was a pile-up in the centre of the carpet. Marthouret was playing the Lost Man as never before. Katsulas looked wild. 'We will *not* be going down in the history of Tam,' he announced, slipping into the vernacular. The in-set called the place Tam. Zeldis had the giggles, appeasing the gods with a little dance to himself. Then Bagayogo, who's a bit short-sighted, strolled on to the carpet at the wrong time. Brook's face lit up. He was waiting for someone to abandon the boxes and throw the show in a different direction. But Bagayogo decided to stick to the text, squinted at the helpless Marthouret and strolled off again. The story was lost. Jokes fell flat. Scenes were cut, confused, thrown away. The actors didn't know where they were. Brook looked resigned and embarrassed, pouting.

Unable to move freely around the carpet, the actors were forced to wait in a space behind a tree to make their entrance. The tree had become the wings of a theatre. The carpet had become a stage. By accident the group was travelling back in time towards the format of the traditional theatre. The audience was 'out there', and feared. Even the group's fear belonged to the past. Those marvellously relaxed moments of real improvisation were missing. 'Get through it,' they seemed to be saying. 'Get *through* it.' You had only to look at two faces in the group for an expert reaction. Swados—scowl, squirm, cringe, kill. Brook—pout, and in this nightmare, more pout. Brook watches every performance with all the intensity of a laser beam but when he pouts—that's it.

The audience didn't seem to mind too much, though. At least they weren't throwing things. A couple of scenes worked, and they were fun. The crowd was more baffled than anything, like the actors. They weren't what Brook calls 'a natural audience'. A natural audience is one in which both sides—actors and audience—relax to the point where judgement and defence melt into shared experience. For Brook it's what theatre is all about. It becomes a spontaneous event. The last line Bottom speaks in *A Midsummer Night's Dream* is 'The wall is down.' It's the key to Brook's entire approach to theatre. But no walls were down in Tamanrasset, for nothing was shared. That first celebration of innocence at In Salah seemed like a miracle now.

Marthouret looked punch-drunk, exhausted and drained by the heat and tension. 'It's a marathon,' he gasped, as the others did their best to help and turn the tide. A tower of boxes was built. Mercifully, the box tower signalled the end of the show. The actors sang as they built it, a hymn of praise prepared when hopes were high. But the box tower tottered and collapsed, tumbling into the crowd.

People drifted away. No applause.

Perhaps the best thing about Brook's actors is that they never blame anyone except themselves for a failure. The conditions were to get far, far worse than Tamanrasset but I never heard them take it out on the impossible conditions, not really. Yet it was incredibly difficult for them, more difficult than it was for Brook. Brook is in the business of research—opening up questions. If he'd wanted to put on a successful show in Africa he could have prepared and perfected one, and hoped for the best. But this wouldn't have helped him find an answer to what he's searching for. Part of the crippling nature of the work is that the moment anything is a success it must be abandoned. If not, it becomes set and closed—unable to teach anything fresh.

It didn't particularly help the guilt and depression of the actors after the disaster of Tamanrasset, but Brook never went to Africa to 'please' an audience. It's just that he put the emphasis on risking failure, failure in every direction, in the hope of learning something new. But it can be a terrific strain on actors. They understand what's expected of them, yet their natural instincts are to please and entertain. They volunteered for the Brook Experiment but they panic, lose all confidence, go through crisis after crisis, looking back to the good old days when there was such a thing as a well-made play, and a script, with dialogue. It's why Brook's critics often see him as the all-powerful master-mind using his actors as helpless guinea-pigs. But I think they might be wrong about that. Everyone on this journey—Brook, the actors, Swados, the audiences, even myself—everyone was the guinea-pig.

Brook led the conference after the show, more a post-mortem, over warm beer in the fly-blown bar of the local rest house. Nobody blamed anyone or anything. Acting groups, like the rest of us, aren't usually allowed the right to fail. In a very different context George Devine, the legendary director of the Royal Court Theatre during its great period in the 1950s, insisted on this right and the future of theatre was changed. Brook has the same credo. He discussed the show quietly, talking in terms of greater urgency and pace. Change direction, switch with the different moods of the audience. It was no use hoping for the ideal audience we'd found at In Salah. There was nervous tension here—noise and movement, demanding speed and action. A far greater involvement was needed, more urgency, more danger. The playing area was too cramped for the boxes. It had been a mistake—but why not abandon them, take more risks, begin again?

'It is our whole reason for coming to Africa,' warned Brook. 'Change and develop with each audience—or we're lost.'

Still, I think Brook might have been privately pleased with the disaster of Tamanrasset. Failure can be more valuable than success, if you look at it the right way. If there was any complacency left in the group, the shock-encounter had finally smashed it. No one could now take anything about this journey for granted, including Brook. For in Paris he thought *The Box Show* a direct and simple piece of theatre. Perhaps an audience schooled in Beckett or the Theatre of the Absurd might have found the boxes a powerful image. Yet in spite of all the chaos and panic, the boxes seemed highly complex in Africa. They seemed presumptuous. They were shown to be no more than what they were—a theatre convention that could have no meaning to people who couldn't recognize the convention. A way must be found to create a direct response. The event had to justify itself totally, living or dying on human terms alone. And so one is forced to create a new language, more powerful ways of communicating than anything these actors had known. But *how*? What is simplicity? Perhaps Africa would tell us.

The conference went on until after dark—discussions about such apparently straightforward topics as how to keep breathing with flies up your nose. How do you stop an audience spilling on to the carpet? What's the best time to start a show? Do you have to keep going? How long can you risk stopping for? There was no precedent. We were learning to play a new musical instrument, said Brook. And that was true, except there might have been another reason for the failure of the show.

We forgot to laugh with the Tuaregs.

It's only a thought. But Father de Foucauld, the saintly monk and evangelist who made Tamanrasset famous, wrote about the people he came to live with: 'You must be simple, affable, and good to the Tuaregs. You must always laugh even in saying the simplest things. As you see, I am always laughing—showing very ugly teeth. When you are among the Tuaregs, you must always laugh.'

He must have forgotten one night, because it was a Tuareg who killed him. We should have laughed with the Tuaregs.

After dark we found a huge rubber tyre near to camp, and lit it. It was quite an event: our first camp-fire. There were many songs and talk and wine, and spirits lifted a little. Eventually Brook drifted along singing 'The Desert Song'. He was trying to get the words to the great song from Sigmund Romberg's light opera about the intrepid and elusive 'Red Shadow' who made hearts beat faster beneath his magic spell. Brook was gazing up at the stars, mouthing the words in his amazing breathless voice—

> *Blue heaven, and you and I*
> *And sand kissing on moonlit sky*
> *A desert breeze whispering*
> *A lullaby*
> *Only stars above you,*
> *To see I love you.*
> *Oh, give me that night divine*
> *And let my arms in yours entwine*
> *The desert song calling*
> *Its voice enthralling*
> *Will make you [big note] mine.*

It was practically a duet. But his secret was out! For all its symbolism of voids and empty spaces the journey through the desert was the fulfilment of a childhood dream for Brook. One of his first experiences of the theatre had been several visits to *The Desert Song* at the local Chiswick Empire. His parents couldn't keep him away. He used to march up and down the garden of his home in his dressing-gown with his father's walking stick stuck through the cord, like a sword. He was transformed by it. He was 'The Red Shadow'.

'How does it go *again*?'

Yoshi Oida sat in silence by himself, as he often did. Sometimes he seemed to disappear completely and you might not spot him for days.

'I have paradox,' he told me unexpectedly. 'Actor needs people. But I don't like people. I hate people. I don't like people yet I need them. So have paradox. No people in desert. Velly happy in desert.'

And he laughed and opened up a little. Before he became an actor he worked on the Stock Exchange. His father was a bicycle manufacturer.

'Hate merchants,' he said. 'In world of commerce everyone cheats, everyone is charlatan. So I thought maybe artistic life for me. Find only truth. Find sincere people with no desire for money. Find no trickster. But acting life worse! Find out too late.'

So I asked him about the work with Brook.

'It is good. Never meet people. Sometimes, yes. Then have paradox. But improvisation is good. Improvisation saves you from going mad—makes worlds.'

Always he watches Brook like a hawk, and is fascinated. Brook helps him make the worlds. Yet I don't think Yoshi looks on him as a director. This strong and gentle man needs masters, or teachers. For him, Brook is more of a guide—as two famous men were in Japan. One of them was Okura, a great Noh Theatre actor. The other was Mishima, an incredible public figure in modern times, a national celebrity and novelist, who became a samurai, ran a private army and ended his life in ritual *seppuku* —suicide by means of disembowelment after which he was decapitated by a friend.

I asked what these men had taught him, though tentatively. Yoshi's a very private man. You have the feeling that questions intrude on a secret world.

'It is difficult. I think Okura taught me how to exist. Mishima may have taught me how to destroy myself. Brook teaches me how to create.'

He laughed again. Exist, destroy, create. It's a classic combination.

Then I asked why he became an actor. Perhaps he's the only member of the group who could have attempted a real answer.

'I look for something. I'm not certain. What is it? When I work with Noh Theatre I train hard for many years. But it has limitation. I discover that theatre mystery is beyond technique. There must be something extra. So I went to the Zen Temple to find it. The great Noh Theatre actor, when he stands or sits, he can tell many things to audience. When he appears on the stage he can tell all his feelings, just by movement and looks. One day I asked the great Noh Theatre actor: "When you enter the stage,

93

what do you think and feel?" But all he replied was: "I think only that I must move three-quarters of the way across stage, stop for thirty seconds, turn round, and sing song." And that was all he said. But when I tried to do it, audience did not understand. You see, that's the theatre mystery. So I went to Zen Temple to find secret. For me Temple was a way to become good actor. But somehow this changes through my life. Acting has become a way to find God. It's normal.'

Then, thinking perhaps of the afternoon disaster, he laughed again.

8

There was another crisis the next day. No petrol was left in town. We couldn't make the final stretch of desert across the border into Niger. We were stuck. 'It looks as if we're stuck,' said Brook. He was laughing at the news. Everyone was, except the crew. They were far too busy praying towards Mecca.

'This looks like a dangerous situation, Peter.'

'Quite, James.'

Brook gave us the day off and bustled into the centre to pull a few strings. The Préfet of Tamanrasset was about to become a close personal friend.

A day off! Yoshi Oida had his drip-dries out on a line before you could say 'Made in Japan'. Most of us seized the chance to do a little washing, though the water was now strictly rationed. It hadn't rained in the area for five years. Others sunbathed, slapping on face creams and Ambre Solaire. Sylvain Corthay emerged in a fetching denim outfit, equipped for the beach in St. Tropez. Natasha Parry sat under an orange golfing umbrella nibbling butter cake from Paris. Lou Zeldis struggled with the chore of letters home. 'Dear Mom,' he announced, trying things out. 'Well, here I am stuck in the middle of the Sahara Desert. We have Ayansola along and he wears a bedsheet round his head.'

The crew serviced the vehicles, checked food and water supplies, and relaxed together in the garden chairs, sipping tea. Somehow the mechanic managed to tune his radio into the BBC. He got 'Family Favourites'. Bing Crosby was singing 'I'm Dreaming of a White Christmas'.

The French film crew, miraculously clean, turned up by plane with five million tons of equipment. Crates of film were piled round Esmeralda. Where would they all go? The Leader was holding his head in his hands murmuring: 'All I want to avoid is a disaster.'

The film crew pitched tents immediately. The French are renowned camping enthusiasts. They win prizes. They built a cosy cluster of five tents—another camp within the camp. Intrigued by the first sight of tents, Ayansola demanded one for himself. He was exceptionally keen on it. He used to pitch it when we weren't stopping anywhere. The Frenchmen helped him out, a separate group, hesitant of the strange new community. Except for the cameraman, loud and fat, sweating and joking in the heat, a parody of the American tourist dressed in expensive cameras and a snappy little trilby. He handed out Kodak Instamatic pictures to the natives, like food parcels. Brook shut his eyes. The fat cameraman was a 'character'. His name was Monsieur Ozoom.

I dozed in the shade of the wheel of the Bedford truck, blowing on flies. Before I left on the journey I asked my daughter how you wrote a really important book. She said eat chocolate bunnies. She was four then. I thought of her.

After a while I fell asleep and woke to see Ayansola sitting proudly outside his tent still in his pink pair of ladies' tights from Paris. At the start of the journey his talking drum never left his side. He used to wrap it in a blanket each night. Then it was joined by his transistor radio, and replaced by it. The talking drum was getting damaged now. I watched Ayansola puffing vacantly on a cigarette, sad and alone outside his new home. Who was he?

Someone said he was beginning to smell.

White people never smell, right?

Suddenly he got up, squinted through the sun, and came towards the back of the truck, glancing furtively over his shoulder. Nobody could see him except me. I was following him. He went inside the truck and opened his great metal trunk that no one dared touch. I could see rolls of cloth and bottles of whiskey and new shoes and jars of jam inside. He rearranged everything neatly, took out a parcel and locked the trunk again. When he returned to his tent he opened the parcel very slowly and carefully. He smiled when it was open. It was a portable record-player run off batteries.

'At least they'll run out sometime,' I said to Mirren.

'That's *not* funny.'

He played it at full blast, the same record over and over again. He only had one record, the same song on both sides. It was a rock and roll number. He played it the entire morning and was very happy. He played it whenever he could. People used to hide behind sand-dunes.

Brook returned after a couple of hours in town—perhaps there would be petrol tomorrow, or perhaps the next day. In any event there would be another performance the following afternoon. A come-back! Then he huddled into a lengthy conference with the crew, persuading them to spare petrol for a visit to Father de Foucauld's hermitage, thousands of feet up the mountains. The crew tensed again. I think they felt the petrol crisis wasn't the time for day-trips. I didn't go with them, though. I stayed behind to write a show about a pair of shoes.

We called it *The Shoe Show*.

It's quite famous in Africa. It may not prove much but if yuo went to some villages we visited and put your shoes down in the village square, lots of people might make you very welcome. You needn't speak the same language.

Why a show about shoes? The idea came from the first fragmentary improvisation at In Salah. Brook was fascinated when all eyes fastened on Katsulas' enormous pair of army boots in the centre of the carpet. They fascinated him because the unexpected event was a genuine beginning from zero. First there was an empty space. Then a concrete object: the boots. You didn't need a conception of theatre. You didn't need to know what acting was. There was nothing the actors could prepare. Here was the first step: a pair of boots. We must discover more, said Brook afterwards. We must build a show round them! Brook wanted to involve me in the work and commissioned the script. Besides, there wasn't anyone else. Ted Hughes wasn't due to arrive for another month.

Also, even a pair of shoes can have a serious side. As far as Brook's concerned, everything the group performs amounts to

D   97

the same show. For at many different levels each show opens up vital questions—questions taken for granted or rarely asked.

What is simplicity? What is a sound, a song, a movement? What is fantasy? Can one discover a universal language? Is it possible to transcend cultural and racial conditioning? What does open-air theatre actually involve? Does the audience have a role to play? What can be learnt from children? Can actors create? Does creation happen by itself? What is the relationship between the abstract and the real? How freely can one move between the two? How can one fuse the popular and the élite forms of theatre? Is it possible for them to exist in the same moment? So many questions that Brook would like to glimpse an answer to. If you take absolutely nothing for granted—no precedent, no rule, no convention, no dogma—you might discover something new. But it isn't easy. How many angels can dance on the head of a pin?

What *is* a play? Brook put the question to me when he asked for *The Shoe Show*. But I wasn't sure what a play was any more, and asked Lou Zeldis. 'A play,' he replied in the tones of an oracle, 'is anything with me in it.'

I made sure he had a star part. But *The Shoe Show* didn't exactly tumble out. Although I'd written plays before, a theme about a pair of shoes had never sprung immediately to mind. Also, I wasn't allowed to use any dialogue because of the search for a universal language. Brook's group doesn't use everyday language, so there wasn't any dialogue to be written. Anyway, none of us spoke Arabic. I ploughed ahead with the script, more a scenario, as the group left for the hermitage and Ayansola grooved around to his record. Brook wanted me to write an episodic play in which the different episodes somehow made a whole. He wanted to discover to what extent strong narrative is essential to theatre. He said the last playwright to master the episodic form was called Shakespeare.

I placed my shoes in front of me, leaping into them from time to time in search of inspiration. I analysed them. What *is* a shoe? A shoe is something you wear on your feet yet it isn't a sock. But what if there aren't any feet in the shoe? Is a shoe a

98

shoe if it's empty? I decided if a shoe is empty, it's a *magic* shoe.
It may as well be. It's doing nothing else. So I tried to use the
shoes as transforming elements—hags transformed into princesses
by the magic shoes, slaves into masters, one-legged men into
two-legged men. They were little more than ideas, images perhaps
—a springboard for the actors' imaginations to work from. The
show was eventually changed and developed by the actors, rewritten many times, until it was thrown away.

Here's the *Shoe Show*—

A shoe collector abandons a pair of shoes.

An old hag finds them, wears them, and is given youth. She
dances and sings.

A greedy King falls in love with her. She lets him remove the
shoes, playfully. Then she becomes an old hag. She curses the
shoes.

The greedy King is rather confused. Curious, he wears the
shoes. Greedy King becomes Super King, and is pleased. Preen,
preen, preen. Super King sleeps, guarding the shoes.

Two ridiculous thieves try to steal the shoes, bungling the job.
They're the most ridiculous thieves you ever saw. But they get
the shoes. Super King, now Silly King, weeps buckets. Ridiculous thieves share one shoe each. The shoes do ridiculous things.

Enter a one-legged shoe polisher. Ridiculous thieves offer
shoes, hoping for reward. Only one is required, however.
Arguments follow. The one-legged shoe polisher tries one shoe.
Other leg appears. Horrified, he removes the shoe. Leg goes
away again. He is a happier man, distrustful of change.

Disillusioned, ridiculous thieves throw shoes away. The shoes
return, again and again. The ridiculous thieves run for their
lives.

Enter a slave carrying a corpse. He finds shoes and puts them
on the corpse for safe-keeping. Corpse comes alive and strangles
slave. He carries the slave's corpse. It's the least he can do, after
all these years. They travel and rest.

A devious merchant offers rags in exchange for the shoes. A
deal is made. The merchant tries the shoes, goes wild, rages,

rolls, runs and runs. Cries for help. Others laugh. The shoes run him into the ground.

A beautiful woman takes the shoes from the merchant and becomes a beautiful camel. The merchant beats the camel. The camel shrieks. And eats the merchant. The merchant does not like this.

An incredibly proud hunter captures the camel in a box. The incredibly proud hunter is dragged into the box. Only the shoes remain.

A practical joker buries the shoes.

The old hag returns. Discovers the shoes. She often likes to dig. Trumpets! Song of celebration! The old hag is beautiful. Treasuring the shoes.

First thing the next morning, Brook put the actors back to work —six hours of exercises immediately after breakfast. They were going to need a little inspiration for *The Shoe Show*. In many ways Brook is a disciple of the great Russian director and theorist, Stanislavsky. And perhaps in one way, in particular. 'Inspiration is born of hard work', wrote Stanislavsky. 'It is not the other way round.'

Musical work, sound, movement, ancient Greek and Japanese, new African songs, T'ai Chi, acrobatics, bodies, jaws, throats, tongues, exercises in rhythm and timing, balance, awareness, concentration—everything was worked on for many hours as Brook sat cross-legged on the edge of the carpet, watching. Only the stick work was missing. The sticks were lost in the desert. They'd fallen out of the truck. 'It's for the best', said Brook. He often said that when something vital went wrong.

One of the exercises for the body involved lying on your back as you worked through a series of horny hip movements. Brook usually joined in, and I followed him. As a general rule he told me to try everything he did. It was safer that way. I found that I tended to lose concentration during the hip exercise. It could get embarrassing. I had to think of stainless steel pocket calculators. I don't think Brook would have approved. Also, Moshe Feldenkrais.

Moshe Feldenkrais invented the movements and teaches the group in Paris. A silver-haired Israeli with a spectacularly rich career, he was a leading physicist in England during the war, a former judo champion of France, who evolved a world-famous science of body movements. For a while he was influenced by the famous cult figure, F. Matthias Alexander, founder of the Alexander Technique of body awareness and better health that influenced Bernard Shaw and Aldous Huxley. Feldenkrais now uses his own system as therapy—General Dayan is among his pupils and orchestral conductors have studied under him, as well as many deprived people in America. Basically, he works to increase awareness of the natural function of every part of the body. A transformed understanding will liberate the muscles to the point where the body can move with minimum effort and maximum efficiency. The ultimate aim is the transformed state of what Feldenkrais calls a 'potent state of mind and body'.

It's arduous work and it comes through practice—just as the ethereal T'ai Chi movements raise both mental and bodily powers through constant and demanding repetition. But Feldenkrais doesn't work to a system, which is why Brook finds him so valuable. Brook doesn't believe in any system or school. He wants to liberate the actor from methods. For any one method would clash with the other. Or create an imbalance, overdeveloping one skill at the expense of the rest. In the same way the voice isn't trained through traditional techniques, but song. Stamina isn't developed through physical exercise, but the more creative T'ai Chi movements. Everything Brook does links eventually. Everything searches for unity. Everything is used to create.

But there's danger involved. The organic actor takes years and years to develop. The fully creative actor—creating from nothing as a painter fills a blank canvas—I don't think the fully creative actor actually exists. It's why Brook believes it's a crucial area to work on. Why not try? But you need the patience of Job. Brook kept telling me to be patient.

I didn't find it easy. Actors stumbling in the dark. I suppose they had to be patient too. I used to watch Swados BEING PATIENT. For instance, that morning she took the group for a three-hour musical workshop and this scrawny, emotional, funny, incredible composer was going from ecstasy to hysteria every two minutes, but VERY PATIENTLY. It was a struggle for her, and I don't expect it was any picnic for the actors. But Swados was being drained. In three months with the group she'd never heard one piece of music performed as she imagined it. Part of the impossible battle was to get the actors to create with her. Professional musicians could have shared the music, and more. But the actors weren't equipped for that or didn't have the talent—not yet anyway. It's why for all her vitality and energy and faith, sort of faith, Swados sometimes got desperate. You know, the strait-jacket.

Still, she kept plugging away—at the harmonies, the choruses, patterns, sounds, chorales, staggered times, beats, rhythms, rounds, rock, folk, jazz, African songs, circus music, every kind of music, trying hard to encourage, give out, keep going, keep PATIENT. But there wasn't the same level of imagination in the music as there was in the acting. Perhaps Brook went through the same kind of despair as Swados. Except he'd never let you know about it. He wouldn't tell you. One time he asked me if I thought the actors really understood the nature of the journey. And the fact that he asked the question must have meant he had a few doubts. But he isn't like Swados.

So I asked her what was really going wrong. Apart from everything else.

'See—the biggest, *hugest* tragedy. Why are you laughing? It's too dramatic, huh? Well whatever the word is, I can go off at night by myself and really make music. But the thing is I can't seem to make it with the group. I think what's wrong is that music as an exercise is *disaster*. I think I've been too technical, too academic. I'm always advising, making signals and cues and stuff. But there's nothing there, you know? There's nothing in their eyes. It's like taking a symphony apart and naming rhythms and notes. There's no *feeling*. It's too cold. There's no *me* in that. And above all there's no *them*. You want to know what I've become? I've become an intellectual music teacher. It's a complete humiliation. I haven't found a way to give music to the group.'

'What happens next?'

'Search *me*. Hey, listen! I hear you've written a show. What's it like? Is it a masterpiece? Does it make the spirits *soar*?'

'It's about a pair of shoes.'

'Shoes, huh?'

'Andreas Katsulas' shoes.'

Brook grabbed the script after exercises. I watched him reading it from behind one of the Land-Rovers. He was laughing to himself quite a bit. If he had the same reading speed as me it could only be a good sign. As a matter of fact, he seemed pretty thrilled. He had a show.

'When do we rehearse?' I asked.

He looked at me as if I were mad.

'Rehearse? I don't think we'll rehearse. Let's see what happens.'

'That's good. We *won't* rehearse. We'll see what happens.'

'Now,' said Brook. 'Who are you casting?'

Casting? I mean, anyone would have done. But it was a beautiful question. Directors don't usually ask writers what they think about anything, except seating arrangements. 'We've cut the end, rewritten a couple of scenes. Nothing to worry about. By the way, I don't see why your entire family should have free seats *every* night. What about *my* family?' Well, I'm generalising.

'Who are you casting?'

I suggested Mirren for hag, Katsulas for King, Zeldis for one-legged man, Myers and Marthouret for ridiculous thieves. Agreed!

'Are you going to show them the script now?' I asked.

'Let's wait.'

'What for?'

'The show.'

'That's good. We'll wait for the show.'

'Why are you looking so worried?'

'I'm not. It's just that it might be a little late if we wait for the show. I could be *wrong*.'

'Let's see what happens,' said Brook.

After the previous show in Tamanrasset some of the audience, trying to make things better, went up to the actors and thanked them for the dancing. This was doubly embarrassing because there hadn't been any dancing. People frequently said the dancing was nice. But the reason dawned on us eventually—there wasn't a word in the local language for 'play' or 'acting'. Tamanrasset had never seen a piece of theatre and therefore didn't have a word for it. Theatre didn't exist. We were dancers.

And it created problems. If the group announced before a show that they'd come to dance, there would be a little misunderstanding. Yoshi Oida raised the point before we left for the come-back.

'When the people ask before the show why we have come, what do we reply?'

'There's no *easy* answer,' replied Brook. 'If they speak French the best word would be *fête*. We're a kind of festival. If we say we've come for *une fête*, it might hit the right note.'

'Maybe,' added Katsulas, who's a practical man. 'That might be okay for what we're going to do. But what do we reply when they've seen the show and say, "Yes, but what *did* you do?"'

Everyone laughed, for no one was tense, except me. I thought the Day of Judgement was at hand. So did Marva and Deirdre the two cooks. They were in a panic about an ancient Tuareg who'd been eyeing the camp for hours. Actually, he was eyeing the tuna fish. But we couldn't be sure. We'd seen too many John Ford movies. Was he planning a surprise attack? The stranger and his muchachos in the mountains? The truth is that anyone could have taken the camp and all its worldly goods at any time. If they'd wanted to. We gave the Tuareg a bowl of tuna fish as a peace offering. 'There you go', said Katsulas, handing it over. 'You likey?'

In case he didn't, Brook decided to leave behind a token fighting force. Daniel Charlot, the lonely and shambling French observer, would observe the Tuareg. 'I don't mind missing the show', he said. 'Truly, I don't mind.'

We met another stranger on the road, a middle-aged Englishman who appeared like a mirage to thumb a lift as we headed for the centre. He wore a thick tweed jacket with that proud and stubborn resistance to heat the true Englishman always displays when abroad. He looked exactly like Sir Ralph Richardson. Perhaps he was. Sir Ralph Richardson rides a motor bike and, it's said, often gets lost.

'You heading south?' the stranger asked me.

'To Niger eventually, if there's petrol. And you?'

'Ethiopia. Get there some day, I suppose.'

'Hot.'

'Bloody hot.'

'I expect it's hot in Ethiopia.'

'It's bloody hot in Ethiopia.'

'Thought so.'

'Where are you heading now?' he asked.

'Down the road. We're a group of actors.'

'Actors, eh?'

'Sort of.'

'Awfully decent of you to give me a lift.'

'Oh, think nothing of it.'

'Anyone mind the pipe? Frightful habit, but there we are.'

He smoked shag tobacco. I was sorry to see him go. 'Good luck', he said, waving good-bye. 'You'll need it.'

We didn't play in the centre. Brook had chosen a new playing area just outside, a dusty wasteland surrounded by mud hovels. We could not be cornered there. It was little more than an hour before dusk, a cooler time to play. The carpet was enlarged by a tarpaulin about fifteen feet square—there would be room to move.

We strolled around the back streets, smiling at strangers who didn't always smile back. Some were Muslims, distant and watchful, a little threatening perhaps. Veils are threatening. Children ran away when Yoshi Oida appeared. Then ran back again to take another look. Others followed at a distance, giggling. Zeldis was causing a sensation, though. Perhaps it was the flowing robes and frizzy blond hair. Lou always carries a tiny silver box of stones and beads. It means he always has a present for someone.

There were few people about. Goats strolled around. A woman

dyed leather bright green. A teacher whipped a child for not concentrating on the Koran. The child was staring at us.

This was a poor village. Yet a young Tuareg returned money to the photographer, which she had lost the previous day. He could not understand our astonishment.

'What are you doing here?' a stranger asked in French.

'We've come to entertain you. *C'est une fête.*'

'Oh, that's okay.' The stranger looked pleased.

A small crowd gathered, no more than twenty or so at first, gazing at us round the carpet. Tamanrasset was a town of different temperaments. Life was calmer here. As we sat and waited for the crowd to grow, Brook put a scrappy piece of paper down on the carpet. It was *The Shoe Show*. I was very busy nervously pacing about in an imaginary silk dressing-gown and gay cravat. You must forgive me. I was comparatively young at the time, and over-excited. The actors gathered round. 'You might like to try a little of this,' said Brook, conjuring the rabbit out of the hat. The actors buzzed and seemed to look at me with a new respect. Or perhaps I imagined it. I had a new identity. 'It's nothing much,' I said to Mirren, reading the script with her.

Brook didn't explain anything. Most of the actors only had time to glance at the piece of paper.

If they only glanced at the paper, what was the point of having a script in the first place? Well, I was to ask that question many times—but not then. Not in the nerves and excitement of my first night. Or first afternoon. I'm always having first afternoons. The first play I ever had performed in a real theatre was at lunchtime. It takes the gloss off things. I mean people were really hungry.

Still, this was no time to quibble. Peter Brook doesn't direct my work, as a general rule. But he seemed to be convulsed with laughter at me. He yelled across the carpet that I looked like a terrified author in the crush bar before curtain-up. He said he didn't have time to send me flowers.

I ignored him, for I knew there was a post office. He could have sent me a telegram. 'Wishing you every success. Love and kisses. Peter and the gang.'

Curtain up! Swados and the seal act were on. They took the opening music gently, building confidence. Sometimes the crowd laughed at the strange music, though hushed itself into concentrated silence. It was good. Things were working. Michèle Collison fights Natasha Parry in sound. Others join them, taking sides: gang warfare of a special kind. No one wins the sound battle. There is no breath left. The Babylon song follows and, though sung in English, strikes a chord. An actor conducts the group, now a sound orchestra, builds rhythms, creating a melody. Instrumental work follows, simple, calm, together, taking off. Into a crazy burbling sound, burble duets, a bizarre spectacle that has the actors laughing and the crowd in hysterics.

Why do audiences sit in darkness at the theatre? The whole convention seemed madness now. In the traditional theatre the actors don't even see their audience. And the members of the audience don't see each other. It's as if no one wants to meet. Whatever direction Brook's work took in the future I wouldn't believe it if a show of his ever played in darkness again.

'*Shoe Show!*' ordered Brook.

And Katsulas entered the carpet and placed his enormous shoes in the centre, his cartoon shoes. And Mirren was on her feet, bent double, ugly hag creeping and cursing her way round the fringes of the carpet. And I was so proud of this, it's ridiculous. But something dead on a scrap of paper had come to life. Life! And the crowd watched Mirren's every move because hag or no hag she's terrific to look at. And she found the shoes, grunting with pleasure. The crowd fell silent, watching. Veiled women peep round corners.

The old hag stared at the enormous shoes and everyone stared at the enormous shoes. She held them for a while. Was something wrong? She was taking her time. Slowly she put the shoes on. And then with a great shriek of triumph, Mirren grew and grew, and the old hag was young. Oh, fantastic! I just thought, fantastic. And cheered louder than anyone. No cute transformation this! There was violence there, and power. 'HANIKKA SHNIMIKKA SHNAP!' chanted Mirren, cribbing the words from a children's story she once read. 'HANIKKA SHNIMIKKA SHNIMIKKA SHNAP!'

107

And the rest of the actors struck up the band as Ayansola got his drum talking and Mirren strode and strutted round that carpet in the amazing magic shoes. 'HANIKKA SHNIMIKKA SHNIMIKKA SHNAP! SHNAPAK SHNIMAK SHNIMIKKA MAAAAAAAH!'

It wasn't anything you could join in. But the crowd were glad they came. And King Katsulas and a one-legged shoe polisher entered the carpet now on account of the fact that the two ridiculous thieves had missed their cue. 'This is what improvisation is all about,' I told myself. 'It's silly to have a heart attack.' But I couldn't believe what was happening on the carpet.

There seemed to be a rival Shoe Show going on.

King Katsulas was merrily cartwheeling round the place in the magic shoes when lovely mad Miriam Goldschmidt suddenly decided to enter with a rival shoe, which was dangling from a stick. I was following my script like the score of a concerto. I knew things had got a bit out of sequence. But I definitely didn't write the rival shoe scene. I was practically up on my feet slinging her off the carpet. Brook was helpless with laughter. King Katsulas looked stunned. There was a rival show dangling under his nose. But you could tell what was going on. She was a *wild* sorceress. All those wild sounds, she had to be. You could tell what she was saying. She was saying, 'You give me your shoes and I'll give you mine.' And it was so vivid and people were laughing so much I was already pretending I wrote it. I was the original inspiration, after all. But either way it didn't matter because I knew then that the show couldn't go wrong. We were laughing with the Tuaregs. Father de Foucauld was right. Laugh and the Tuaregs laugh with you.

The world comes later.

Well, in the end my precious script seemed to get a little lost in a thrilling tale about General Katsulas leading an army patrol through the jungle. It was a re-make of *The Snows of Kilimanjaro*. But what matter? In the simple beginnings to this journey there were simple failures, simple triumphs. The show had revived confidence. A start had been made. My début in Africa was a modest triumph. I may not have made it on Broadway yet, but I'm very big in the Sahara Desert. When Brook's critics say that

he no longer cares about audiences, they mean something different. I think they unintentionally mean that he no longer cares
about the 'right' audiences.

For myself, better a contented Tuareg than a miserable
European.

Spirits were so high after the come-back that Brook thought a
celebration would be in order. Several of us joined him on a
visit to the local *hammam*—steam baths. We took a Land-Rover,
bouncing and rattling through the back streets of the town as
men knelt in the sand, praying. It was dusk. A small boy guided
us for a small tip to a dark doorway. A sultan figure bowed and
scraped us inside. Brook clapped his hands, ordering mint tea.
But it wasn't exactly Arabian Nights. There wasn't any steam.

But there was water—water rediscovered! There was one hot-
water tap. As we stood shivering, Brook was reminded of Orson
Welles' version of *Othello,* a film shot mostly in a Turkish bath
in Morocco because the costumes didn't turn up. 'Wonderful
improvisation,' said Brook, soaping himself down as cockroaches
scattered across the floor.

Then we had the post-show conference.

'We must learn to *train* the audience,' said Brook, whispering
to a group of naked actors in his urgent voice. 'If you meet a
stranger, you don't pour out your heart to him in the first five
minutes. We must learn to build a real relationship. Did you
notice how quickly we were able to touch and disturb the
children? You see, they don't have television to create thick
skins. There's a lot to learn. Still, an hour of theatre without
sex or violence,' added Brook, who's no prude, 'is truly remarkable. Anyone seen the soap?'

Suddenly the girls in the group tiptoed into the bath clutching
tiny towels. We men had abandoned our towels. 'Hi, girls!' But
the girls preferred to maintain some decorum, taking to the
waters on the other side of the room. Only Miriam Goldschmidt
dared to cross the lines, slithering and shrieking towards us.
Things had changed a little since that first shy night in Algiers.

After a while Ayansola appeared. A hush fell. And I looked at

Ayansola. And I knew then that whatever any of us thought of him, he would always have the last laugh.

Oh Jesus! Ayansola had the biggest cock in the world.

The next morning, the petrol supplies came through. We left immediately on the hard drive to Agades in the north of Niger, beautiful, doomed Agades, 1,800 miles from Algiers. We did not know that Agades was about to suffer the worst famine and drought in living memory. Some of the people we met, and loved, can't be alive any more.

We crossed the final stretch of desert, the final void. I saw vultures circling the new world.

9

Mr. Brook isn't a man to go back on his word, though it depends sometimes what the word is. His pattern of work is very much like an improvisation. Anything can happen. It's eclectic. But there's one sense where it's possible to anticipate him—the need, it's more a compulsion, for work.

He isn't concerned with an outward show of freedom. Rather, with something deeper—what he calls 'freeing the dynamic process'. Such freedom, the freedom to create, comes only through the most intense and demanding discipline. In a very different context someone as unlikely as Noël Coward had the same idea. 'I like total spontaneity on the stage,' he said. 'After six weeks' careful rehearsal.' Spontaneity must be worked for. Hence, Brook's daily exercises and tough working methods of constant checks and reminders, obligations and duties, until a shared understanding takes their place. And Brook didn't see it any differently for life outside the work. Except of this, the strange new community of reluctant campers—the tribe who couldn't get it together—was the outward symbol.

When Brook warned me from the beginning that there was bound to be a series of 'confrontations', nothing was therefore more certain. And it happened on our arrival in Agades when he suddenly called the actors together, and let them have it.

The explosion had been simmering for days. For Brook, the attempt to create a real sense of community was central to the journey. Everything affected the work. Everything was the work. But the antennae hadn't been out enough. The crew was getting ratty, rattier than usual. People weren't helping each other out. We weren't sufficiently *alert*. Also the washing-up issue was getting out of hand. I used to have to hide in shame. I used to

III

pretend to be doing vital research into the history of glow-worms. But in the end only the work, THE WORK, would suffer.

'See the camp as an *extension* of the work,' Brook kept telling us. 'See it as an improvisation. Either it lives or it doesn't.'

But when we pitched camp just outside the centre of Agades, work wasn't on most minds. The final, bewildering stretch of the desert had almost finished us off. The actors looked tense and grey: exhausted. The crew, haggard and relieved. There had been danger in the crossing, soft sand, treacherous, swirling dust bowls, shapes like seas, thirst, nausea, cramp, sweat, sleep, by rotting carcasses, a tree, Godot's tree, there in the void, on and on until the first village, life at last, red earth, grass, crickets, women beating millet, a pulse, children smiling, open, trusting, begging black faces, blacker now.

The crossing had taken three days. The first sickness had begun—headaches, dizziness. The Leader said it came from eating sand.

Water! There was water where we camped. The crew knew of a camping ground owned by a mysterious white German where we could buy water. Also, pretty postcards. When we arrived there, the entire afternoon was spent in a demented ritual of washing. We showered from a bucket, washed hair and clothes, transforming the camp into a launderette. We were queer for water. Work was forgotten. Brook had left immediately for vital meetings with the Préfet. We were expected to begin work in his absence.

But when he returned three hours later, work had only just begun. Swados sat on the edge of the carpet, angry and helpless. Like Brook, work for her is a justification of life. The washing can go hang itself. There's work to be done! But the actors took the musical workshop casually, drifting along at different times. It was half-hearted. There didn't seem to be any energy left. It's often so when Brook isn't there, watching.

Andreas Katsulas, a stickler for punctuality—the eight-hour day, no more, no less—was angry too. And when Katsulas gets angry, everyone knows about it. He has this tell-tale side to him. He told Brook what was going on.

Katsulas tells tales.

Immediately Brook returned from the Préfet of Agades, he called the actors together. He was shaking with anger. He confronted them in silence on the carpet. His face was drained of colour, without a trace of kindness.

'I am prepared to stop this trip at any time,' he began. The force of it stunned us. 'I will stop it this minute if necessary! If I'm to be put in the position of a schoolmaster it would be intolerable. But if we cannot work together at every level there is just no *point* in us being here. This isn't a sightseeing tour. If there is anyone who thinks it is, then say so now and go home.'

There was a terrible silence: blood silence. The actors stared at the ground.

'There are moments when none of us will stand up to him,' Sylvain Corthay told me later in the journey. 'It makes me feel ashamed. A part of our relationship with him is based on fear.'

Brook sat absolutely still, waiting for a response.

You could hear that silence.

Eventually the other French actor, François Marthouret, broke it.

'I wish to say that I am not here on a sightseeing tour. Because if I was, I would come alone. But since I am the most disorganized, since I am the one who is always late, I will speak.'

Marthouret, as I've mentioned, would be late for his own funeral. It gives him a very endearing quality.

'Why *am* I late?' he asked, scarcely louder than a whisper. 'I know I shouldn't be, and yet I am. I try so hard *not* to be. I wish I could be like Andreas. I wish I knew his secret. Yet I cannot help being late. . . .'

His voice trailed away. For one moment I thought he might burst into tears. 'This man', I thought, 'is the greatest actor in the world.'

'But there is a far more important issue involved here,' he continued. 'Why has this confrontation arisen? I feel we must search ourselves to find an answer.'

Brook agreed, asking each member of the group to speak his thoughts. Again the actors sat in total silence for so long that an outsider might have found it unendurable. Brook's silences are famous, however, and it is prudent to join them.

This time Michèle Collison, the American actress, broke the ice. She speaks gently. 'In Paris we felt there was a balance to the work. We felt we could keep it contained. There was the work and our lives outside. But here we're still learning to live with each other. There's no escape. There's no place to go. There are no diversions. Each one of us is stuck with each other. Such a total involvement has never been demanded of us before. All sense of privacy has gone. To me, it's a terrifying thing.'

Natasha Parry, Brook's wife, who like some of the others in the group says little in discussions, added simply this: 'I think it would be a little easy to go into confessions of guilt. If I'm honest with myself I have to say that I don't yet feel a part of the journey. I find Africa very bewildering. At the moment I find the work very difficult.'

Lou Zeldis, who also spoke rarely: 'I agree with Natasha and Michèle, but I ought to say that a strong part of me *is* here for the trip. I want to see Africa. It's crazy to deny it.'

Bruce Myers, who wouldn't be late for his own funeral but might well lose the cortège, eased the tension a little: 'What I don't understand is why we've all gone completely mad about water! If you look at the crew you'll see they're servicing the cars. It's the first thing they do after each day's travel. They do their work. But the first thing we do is *wash*. Why have we gone insane over water? I've never showered so much in my life. Well, I just want to say I think we've got it wrong about the water.'

So each took his turn, for there wasn't a choice, as Brook sat in silence listening to every word. Was he being fair? The past three days on the road had left us sapped and dry with fatigue. We'd travelled nine hours each day. When camp had been pitched the work continued just the same. Improvisations, music, exercise, talk into the night.

Yet it was the same for Brook.

'The travel is exhausting,' said Helen Mirren, perhaps the most independent voice in the group. 'I find it incredibly difficult to adjust to the new conditions. None of us has ever really camped before. I don't find it easy to live together either. There's so much happening. Our energy is so dispersed. Every day there's something totally new and challenging. Yet I don't agree the work has suffered. I think there's been some really terrific work. The truth is I think we're all still learning to cope.'

'It's not enough to *cope*,' Brook intervened. 'Coping isn't a part of it. It is not enough to go back home with the feeling that we've got through an arduous journey. We must be equipped and disciplined enough at every level to work and learn. It isn't just a challenge. It's something far more than this. It's the nature of a super-challenge. It is for us the whole point of being here. Are we aware of this? It is the word that summarizes this whole discussion—*awareness*.'

And with that, the confrontation and the confession ended. Perhaps Brook's fury was a calculated move. He's a skilful politician. The outburst was to prove timely, in the scheme of things.

And yet I believed him when he said that he'd abandon the trip at any moment.

And Brook believed the Préfet of Agades when he'd told him exactly the same thing. The actors didn't know about this. But Brook did. The Préfet was threatening everything Brook feared most in Africa. He was refusing us permission to play.

At the precise moment Brook confronted the group, it looked as if everyone might be going home anyway. The Préfet, a powerful force in the region, wasn't fond of foreigners. Brook is quite fond of a battle, however. The stakes were high, and he doesn't give in easily.

When he began preparing the whole journey it was clear the group would be entering countries where there was intense suspicion of outsiders. The inner political situation of countries such as Uganda and Guinea made them closed to Brook. Mali was on our route but until only three months before we left, Brook was advised not to go there. By the time we reached Mali, the tide could have turned again. But he had permission to play in Niger—or so he thought.

He had already visited Niamey, the capital, to prepare the way.

That visit turned out to be a typical Brook situation. Expecting to be met at the airport by a Mr. Gerber of the National Assembly, a man recommended to him by influential figures in UNESCO, he found no sign of anyone to meet him and nowhere to go. But the owner of a battered taxi knew Mr. Gerber personally and took Brook hurtling through the back streets of Niamey until they arrived at a mud hut with a few chickens outside. Everyone said that Mr. Gerber was having his Sunday afternoon nap and daren't be disturbed. 'But I am his guest!' announced Brook. 'I've come thousands of miles to see him.' So in the end someone bravely went inside and out came a nine-foot giant with a face of thunder.

He was the wrong Mr. Gerber.

Eventually, Brook tracked the right man down after two days, and ended up with the President.

He stayed for dinner. The journey was arranged in a matter of minutes. 'There's no problem,' said the President. 'Rely on my word. Anything you want. *Pas de problème*.'

Perhaps the President of Niger did not know of the Mungo Park world of his Préfet of Agades. Still, the experience was to be a useful lesson in communication—the point of the journey. Different worlds were about to meet, and surprise each other.

When Brook arrived at the Préfet's residence the place was buzzing. They were preparing for the Independence Day celebrations. He peeped through a door and could see rehearsals in progress. Then he sent a message saying 'Le Directeur' had arrived. Since we left Algiers Brook had taken the precaution of sending telegrams whenever possible, informing the Préfet of our progress. Each telegram was signed 'Le Directeur'. Brook felt it had the right sort of ring.

But the director of *what*? The Préfet didn't know. It was clear from the first meeting that the telegram was all he knew about Brook.

Pleasantries were exchanged, names dropped, discreetly, not too many at a time. Brook said that he'd come personally from the President and the Préfet replied he was most honoured. He sat smiling with his council around him, a cool man in the heat, too composed for comfort. Brook explained what we were doing in Agades and that he'd just come to see the Préfet as a courtesy. And the Préfet replied he was most honoured. Several villages were even suggested where Brook might care to play. Bows and compliments followed, part of a ritual. A charming meeting, everything Brook could have wished. Then he mentioned the film unit. The Préfet's charm vanished instantly with his smile.

No country in Africa totally trusts a stranger with a camera. It's a permanent suspicion. There's too much to hide, too much to be exploited, perhaps. The film crew were from French television— an instrument of political propaganda in the past. It's why they couldn't shoot in Algiers. And it's why they were sent home when we reached Nigeria.

The Préfet would now require a little time to reflect on the entire matter. His charm had become honeyed. 'Monsieur le Directeur,' smiled the Préfet, showing Brook the door. 'I am sure you understand.'

When Brook returned the following day, the Préfet was a transformed personality. The beautiful game of hospitality and charm, courtesy and concern, was played out as before. But other qualities now emerged—cunning, hypocrisy, steel, danger —ice-cool qualities revealing none of the emotional weakness of the Western politician. This man would have wiped the Watergate tapes clean.

'Ah, Monsieur le Directeur! I have been thinking since we last met . . .'

And Brook said that he had too. He'd visited one of the villages the Préfet had recommended. It was a trifle too small for our purposes, fascinating though it was. There were about three people there.

'That's *exactly* what I've been thinking,' replied the Préfet immediately. 'As you so rightly say, there are not enough people. We have considered this very deeply and there are not enough people anywhere for you. We have this situation of poverty, you understand. Difficulties in the area, and so on. You see, Monsieur le Directeur, everyone seems to have travelled to the

117

South in search of richer land and we have thought, and thought, and there is no community around Agades that would suit your purposes. There's the sadness of it! We should hate to think of you, our distinguished visitors, going to all the trouble of finding a village only to discover no one there. Monsieur le Directeur, we must spare you from this at all costs.'

Monsieur le Directeur thanked Monsieur le Préfet for his kindness and asked his advice on the matter. Ah, but the problem solved itself! It so happened that a special group of artists would be performing in a courtyard as part of the Independence Day celebrations. There would be Tuaregs and Peulhs and Monsieur le Directeur could perform *with* them. It would be a 'cultural exchange'. The long journey to Agades would be fulfilled.

Once again Monsieur le Directeur expressed his deepest gratitude, only pausing to inquire what *alternatives* Monsieur le Prèfet had in mind. Particularly as the group planned such a *wide* series of events in the area.

'What I am proposing,' came the reply, 'is that this completely sums up in one event all you could wish to find here.'

Whereupon there followed two hours of mutual flattery and beautifully turned sentences as each complimented the other on his wisdom for seeing something so clearly whilst pointing out with an increasingly steely edge that the other's stand was completely unacceptable. 'Monsieur le Directeur,' the Préfet eventually announced with a sense of total finality. 'Perhaps I haven't made myself clear. Forgive me. But what I am saying is that in no circumstances can you play anywhere at all outside Agades.'

It meant that Brook had won the first round. At the very least the group could now play in the market-place.

Unless Monsieur le Préfet had made a deliberate mistake.

Brook seized his chance, however, launching into a long and great speech about the Third World and how tragic it is that all the emerging nations are trapped in the false choice of a return to folklore or a small step towards an imitation of foreign culture. 'But there exists another choice, Monsieur le Préfet! There exists the possibility of a *giant leap* forwards to a new culture of shared

118

human impulses that are nothing to do with the traditions of the past or with the traditions of the over-developed countries. This is why we are here in your country—to find the way with the help and encouragement of the fathers of the African states. But of course we will be honoured to play in the market-place of Agades. Yet is this why the fathers of the African states have given us such *high-level* support? You see, that's what must be on our minds at the moment. . . .'

Well, that left the Préfet cold. But Brook was in his stride: unstoppable.

'And so, Monsieur le Préfet, of course we will be honoured to play within the town of Agades. Yet as the fathers of the African states well understand, we have come through the desert on a journey that is to take us through five countries and whose whole purpose is to go into the villages as the *central* experience around which everything else, interesting though it is, amounts merely to *side decoration*. But what am I to say if I find that the central experience has not taken place in Agades? Alas, I will be forced to leave here with the impression of a very particular sort of *déception*. And this might indeed turn out to be a very bitter *déception* if the central experience we are searching for was accessible everywhere else *except* Agades. Because if we had realized that in Agades *alone* there would be this unfortunate lack of understanding, not only would we not have come on this route, but it is quite possible that we would not have come to Niger at all. We could have gone to another country that would have welcomed us more truly. . . .'

The Préfet was unmoved.

'Monsieur le Directeur, I am only here as an administrator of the regions. I have problems which you no doubt cannot share. I wish that it *was* possible to allow distinguished guests such as yourself to move freely around the area. Naturally, it is different with the filming. You see, filming is of no interest to me. We must prevent a lamentable error taking place on that level. But as for yourself, Monsieur le Directeur, I wish only that our problems in Agades did not prevent you travelling wherever you wished. That is the unfortunate tragedy of the whole situation. . . .'

It reached the point where Brook was beginning to think that he should settle for the market-place and move out of Agades as fast as possible. But what if the same thing happened all along the line? It might be that the group would never be allowed into a single village.

Brook decided to keep talking. It's something he does when told there aren't any seats left on a plane or in a theatre. He keeps talking. Something will happen sooner or later. Later, I think.

'Monsieur le Préfet, I need to ask your advice.'

'My advice? But of course, Monsieur le Directeur.'

'It seems that you must help me understand for the rest of our journey something of the workings of your country that I have thoroughly and completely misunderstood. I have always understood that in Africa the *word* of someone was what mattered most. I, as a foreigner, naturally have no way of understanding the elaborate workings of your bureaucracy. So I have simply understood that when your President takes my hand and says, "The country is open to you, you are my guests, you will go and see the Préfet of Agades who will make everything possible for you," I understand that this is Africa and the word of the President is good enough. Now, Monsieur le Préfet, I need your advice. Explain to me where I was wrong?'

In the niceties of this lengthy and diplomatic barter Brook had finally played his trump card. To have played it earlier would have been disastrous. No African's going to be pushed around by a white man. Also, people enjoy games. You play the game first.

But the Préfet didn't bat an eyelid.

'You *are* our guests, Monsieur le Directeur. As I have said, you are most welcome to play here. . . .'

Except as the Préfet talked, something must have been ticking over: 'Maybe the freak does know the President.'

'Nevertheless, I'll tell you what I propose,' he added unexpectedly. 'Under the circumstances I will telephone the President personally.'

Sweet victory was Brook's! The Préfet smiled. And Brook smiled. And the Préfet smiled again.

'Yes, I will telephone the President who won't, I have just this second remembered, be in. How stupid of me! It's the National Holiday. We might not be able to contact the President for *days*. Ah, what difficulties there are! And the telephone might not even work. Atmospheric conditions and so on. Life is so complicated. . . . In the meantime, perhaps you would care to see a little more of our city?'

Brook didn't have any smiles left. More courtesies, more bows, more thanks, and exit. 'Follow the customs,' goes the African proverb, 'or flee the country.'

But that afternoon, as the group prepared for shows that might never take place, a chauffeur-driven Mercedes came ploughing across the dusty track to the camping ground. It was the Préfet, beaming as never before.

'Ah, Monsieur le Directeur! How fortunate I managed to get the President on the telephone. . . .'

We could play wherever we wished. The historic events must be filmed too. No question about it. *Pas de problème.*

'Monsieur le Directeur, we want you to feel welcome here. We want you to see Agades as *chez vous*. It is all most unfortunate. Can you ever forget the first impression we must have given you?'

And Brook said why should he. For there was nothing to forget.

'And Monsieur le Directeur, may we look forward to your presence at the Independence Day celebrations? Naturally, you will all come to the party afterwards. . . .'

And that is what is known as game, set and match.

A little way beyond the camping ground was a small village. I walked there after the confrontation between Brook and the actors. I could hear the sound of drums, though they must have been miles away. I was happy to be alone, away from the camp. I walked through fields in the darkness, past a deep well drawn by oxen, as far as a group of oval huts woven from palm leaves and rush matting. The land was arid. Clusters of corn and millet grew, and pumpkins. The pumpkins could be used as bowls sewn with

121

leather when the surface split. Families squatted inside the huts. There were small fires, for wood was scarce. Babies coughed. A thin man, the head of the family, shook my hand. We couldn't speak the same language.

But he knew one French word.

'*Cadeaux*,' he said.

He wanted money. And I gave him some. He didn't seem humbled in any way.

I saw another man filing bracelets to be worn round your arms. He didn't mind me watching him. Nor did he seem surprised to see me. I envied his sense of calm. Nothing would trouble this man. He sat cross-legged, resting the metal for the bracelets on the heel of one foot. He filed the metal with great care and precision, perfectly. When it was finished he put it in a leather bag. And began again.

He did not ask for money. Perhaps he had no need. He seemed a free man.

When I returned to the camp there was terrific excitement. The confrontation was forgotten. Two sheep had been brought from the market and roasted on a spit. Rice gushed out of their bellies. The actors were ripping the limbs apart.

I could hear Swados in the distance, wailing at the moon. 'She ought to be locked up,' muttered one of the crew.

The crew sat drinking beer together, talking only among themselves.

The actors laughed, enjoying their unexpected feast.

From the forest surrounding them, children stared silently: eyes of another world.

I did not want to be with this group then. The actors looked greedy and unattractive, ripping the roasted limbs apart. What did I have in common with them, and they with me? Yoshi Oida sat alone, as if he were asking the same question of himself. 'Always the outsider,' he said to me. 'We are international group, but somehow I am still on the outside looking in.' And he laughed, without bitterness.

Later that night, Brook told me a little about this strange man who has been with the group from the beginning. He said that within the group Yoshi Oida stands apart as someone who's really sensed that there's something to be searched for in life, and something to be found. From the start of the work, he was prepared to let go of the very thing that made him—the whole structure of his Oriental personality, the Yoshi as seemed to be. Over the years, he's consistently and honestly tried to take to pieces his own super-structure. And something exceptional has happened to him.

'Something has opened and grown,' said Brook. 'But he hasn't lost his identity. The result isn't a Yoshi less individual, but *more*. Because the beautifully created image of Yoshi has been replaced by something more true. He's more himself.'

I said it must have been quite a struggle for him—and perhaps it has to be for anyone who tries to live in a group?

'Yes, and I wish I knew the answer,' Brook replied. 'It remains the one question every single person carries with him from the day he's born. How to live with other people? If you withdraw from life and become a hermit—in almost all cases you deprive yourself of everything you need the most. If you throw yourself into life in the wrong way, you can easily find it swamps you. The formation of a real group is as difficult to achieve as the real identity of the people within it. I don't think there's any set of rules. Nor is any group structure a model or ideal. All one can say is that it's through this whole question of the individual versus society that a living community might evolve. The question can never be solved. But I think it can make a group come to life.'

The actors ended their feast, throwing the scraps away.

Work was abandoned that night.

It began again at 7 a.m. the next morning. On the dot, sweetheart.

10

There's a very simple and beautiful tower rising out of the mosque in the centre of Agades. The tower isn't too high, overlooking the city. From the outside it looks quite easy to climb.

But the mud stairway inside the tower takes you by surprise. It twists and turns in a bewildering circle, narrower and narrower, towards the top. Just when you think the way is clear another turning appears. It's dark. If you rush, you stumble. You must take your time. The roof gets lower and lower, deliberately. You might be brought to your knees. You must be patient with the tower.

When you reach the top you can stand upright in the open. Sunlight dazzles you. You see the small dun-coloured city below. And you discover what you thought had been left behind. The city is surrounded by miles and miles of desert. You struggle up the tower only to discover that you're still in a void.

I took it personally. On the corrugated tin door to the entrance were stamped the words: 'Made in Britain.'

The group headed for the market place, huge nerve centre of Agades. A medicine man offered the beaks of vultures, ostrich claws, shells, skulls, bags of bones, magic potions in old tins of Nescafé. Camels were whipped, spitting anger. Sewing machines whirred behind makeshift stalls. Veiled women turned away from us. Children laughed, merchants pounced. *Cadeaux!* You're rich! Give! Buy! Silver, amber, cloth, suits, sweets, nuts and pens—BUY! Others watched. The red ribs of goats hung out on a line like washing. The carpet would go in the market-place.

Nearby a bar, a refuge, with faded airline posters, an electric fan, Craven A cigarettes, two white men whispering in crumpled suits.

A young Tuareg wanted me to buy his sword and dagger.

'But what would I want them for?' I asked.

'To fight battles,' he replied.

It was almost a deal. But most of us bought silver medallions shaped like a cross, a status symbol to those who've travelled through the desert to get them. The Tuaregs make and sell the crosses. Perhaps their lives are a shambles now, these former lords of the desert scraping a living off greedy tourists. Yet if you offer too low a price for their work, they turn their backs on you and walk away. With the Arabs this is a trick, part of the theatre of market life. But the Tuareg means it and does not return.

The actors gathered round the carpet in the dust and rubble of the cattle market. A vast, frightening crowd surrounded us. We were to perform *The Shoe Show*, in search of the miraculous.

Brook had worked on the show for hours in the morning, bombarding me with many ideas. He recalled a meeting he once had with Samuel Beckett. And the great Beckett told him that he couldn't write narrative. All he could do was build different scenes of what he called 'tension'. The tensions make the story.

But you have to be Samuel Beckett to do it.

I worked with Swados on a little music for the show, just talking. 'Can't you write me a sound?' she asked. 'You know, some really terrific *sounds*.' So I said, 'Nope.' She wrote a song for shoe-laces instead.

Myers and Marthouret, the two ridiculous thieves, worked on a comic routine involving Siamese-twin shoes, ghost shoes, climbing shoes, stuck-in shoes, lover shoes, genie shoes, goody two shoes, can't get rid of horrible shoes, until it wasn't funny any more.

How does an actor repeat something and give it life? It's a problem that haunts Brook. 'Perhaps the truly great actor only exists in films,' he told me. 'Because in films you do it only once.'

The super-challenge was about to take place. The crowd surrounding us was the biggest so far—as many as five hundred people shoving and jostling, screaming and laughing together round the carpet. Tamanrasset was chicken feed compared to

125

this. Nomads on camels peeped over the top—best seats in the house. Fights broke out as children surged forward for a better view. No way! The ideal number to watch a show was about two hundred. We were FULL. Stage door Tuaregs slapped the actors on their backs. 'Good luck! Good luck for whatever it is you're selling. . . .' We were soaked in sweat. The crowd spilled over us. The carpet began to shrink.

I sat next to Brook during the musical overture, quite a risky thing to do. He was joining in some of the songs now. But if you sat next to him you could easily be singing a different song to everyone else before you knew it. You could be singing 'Land of Hope and Glory'. It's incredible with Brook. Swados gave him a kettle-drum to bang. But the first time he went for the beat, he missed the drum completely. Then he hit the drum, but missed the beat. He liked the kettle-drum.

Then *The Shoe Show* sank without trace.

You know what they say. If you're going to have a disaster, make it big. Well, this was HUGE. In the bewildered crowd I caught sight of the German who owned the camping ground. He had an amazed expression on his face. It told the whole story. 'You mean to say you've come all this way to do *this*?' He just couldn't believe it.

'Change and develop with each audience,' said Brook. 'Or you're lost.' We were lost. Fortunately, one of the advantages of working in a group is that there's always someone else to blame when things go wrong. It wasn't me . . . Often I'd watch the actors struggling and fighting for inspiration and wonder what on earth I would do in their place. Get off the carpet, I suppose. Improvising in front of any audience can be a terrifying experience, particularly when people are booing and hissing at the time. It's an instant process of creation, as if a writer had someone reading his manuscript while he wrote it, but was forbidden to cross anything out. You can easily find yourself trapped in a nightmare world. But I think something else was wrong this time. I think it was the script. And I think it was the actors. Between the two, a dire combination.

For Brook, who can deliver the most thunderous criticism with the purr of a cat, the actors had failed to 'sense out' the audience. It's a rare quality, this wish to transform a performance through all the different rhythms and sensibilities of an audience. It's something the very best cabaret artists can do through sixth sense. If the audience is drunk—skip the preliminaries, move faster, change direction before it's too late. If there's a convention of businessmen out there—so the pace and material of the show will change again, unless they're drunk too. It's something Noël Coward could do without blinking. And it's why Brook's group train themselves in Paris before audiences as diverse as deaf children and psychiatrists.

But in this very different context of Africa, the diversity of the vast and agitated crowd seemed fantastic. The actors couldn't get on terms with it. Instead, they stuck to their own subdued pace —and lost the audience. How they came eventually to mirror the richness of the African crowds is one of the miracles of the journey. But in the market-place of Agadez, they were helpless. There was no real contact with the people: no involvement. We were just curiosity value. We were still 'The Freak Show'.

'Do you know what's wrong with the script?' Brook whispered to me after half an hour. 'We haven't got over the fact that the show is meant to be about shoes.'

Well shoes were definitely in the show. It's just that no one knew why. It was a mystery.

'Why don't you stop the show and begin again?' I asked. Somehow I don't think the audience would mind.'

'Not the audience,' replied Brook. 'But the actors would.'

Even in the traditional theatre Brook never interferes if a show's going badly. The talk and advice come after the performance. He doesn't even go backstage during the interval. He says it never does any good. The actors are in their own rhythm. Once the show has begun, it's too late. The performance belongs to the actors.

I watched my precious *Shoe Show* dying a noble death until another fight broke out in the crowd just behind me. About fifty people crashed on to the carpet. I have been buried by an audience.

'What do you know!' laughed Swados afterwards. 'We wrote a *flop*! Rogers and Hammerstein wrote a flop!'

'If you think the show was bad,' said Michèle Collison, 'wait till you read the reviews.'

As we left, a young boy, perhaps ten years old, sang a song for Brook. When he finished, the boy shot out his hand.

'*Cadeaux!*'

'But when I sang for you,' said Brook, teasing. 'I didn't ask for money.'

'Ah,' replied the boy. 'But I gave you pleasure.'

The conference took place at the camp during a meal of soup mixed with meat from the market. We gathered round Brook. I don't want to complain but there was a camel in my soup. . . .

Every move of the show was analysed, test-tube analysis: germs held up to the light. These can be long sessions and the minutiae a little wearisome. What's the meaning of life? It all depends what you mean by 'of'. But they're important to the development of the group, and Brook has a leech-like quality. 'The show really did prove how simple things must be,' he said eventually. 'There wasn't one point where we couldn't have had more energy. And there wasn't a single moment where we couldn't have had more danger.'

Those three little words cropped up in the conferences over and over again: energy, danger, simplicity.

Those and another, special word: 'JOHAKYU'. Brook would say that such and such a performance was stuck in 'HA'. Another didn't progress beyond the 'KYU' of 'JO'. But the 'KYU' of 'KYU' made more sense than the 'HA' of 'HA'. People would nod their heads gravely.

'JOHAKYU' is a simple and immediately understandable law that was written about and perhaps invented by one of the first great masters of the Noh Theatre, Zéami. Zéami's *Secret Tradition of the Noh* is a classic book that Brook often refers to. 'JOHAKYU' applies to the three stages that exist in absolutely any aspect of a theatre performance. You can apply it to a play as a whole. So that the beginning is 'JO', the middle is 'HA', and the end is 'KYU'. You can apply it to any one scene, or a movement, or even a word. And what this means at its simplest level is that it's a law according to which changes of quality can take place.

So that if, for instance, something starts in 'JO', that's the quality of beginning, setting forth, exposition: morning. But if a development is to take place 'JO' passes into 'HA', the state of development, activity: afternoon. Until 'KYU' is reached, the state of climax, apotheosis: evening. And you can apply it to anything you like. So that in relation to a movement a man gets out of bed as 'JO', he drives to the office as 'HA' and begins to work as 'KYU'. In a game of poker 'JO' is dealing the cards, 'HA' is the game and 'KYU' is scooping up the winnings. And you can break it up so that you can have the 'JOHAKYU' of 'JO', 'HA' and 'KYU'. You're having a polite discussion with someone and they're going round in circles. Well, they might be stuck in the 'HA' of 'JO'. You're having a row with your wife and she's throwing the best china at you. So you can say: 'I wish you wouldn't always start off in the "KYU" of "KYU", dear.' And your wife can say: 'That's the trouble with you, Arthur. You've no sense of adventure.'

But it isn't necessarily a matter of pace or speed. There's a rider galloping flat out across the desert but even though it's in full energy, it's 'JO'. Suddenly arrows start whistling from all sides and the rider leaps from his horse and shoots back. That's the central scene, 'HA'. Then everything dies down and he lies motionless, feigning death. In dramatic terms, his inner activity is 'KYU'. So there's an example of the external movement going on a downward turn, but the story is still developing in 'JOHAKYU'.

For Brook, Zéami's law is a useful shorthand for all those natural developments and evolving rhythms that make a successful show. Abuse the law of 'JOHAKYU' and you're lost. And when it comes down to it, that's just what was so wrong with the show in the market-place of Agadez. We were stuck in 'JO'. If you insist, the 'JO' of 'JO'.

The show never got off the ground.

Sometimes things can go so hopelessly wrong the only thing you can do is laugh. This is how you come smiling through. But now the actors had something to think about again. And now I had a show to rewrite. You must take these things on the chin, particularly with Brook. He bides his time. In fact, he pointed out that all of us were really applying to special experimental material the essential practices of the big Broadway musical. Because the Broadway musical is evolved on tour, tested nightly by different audiences and rewritten on the road. Then the show finally opens and the men in the monogrammed shirts come and take all the champagne away. Our aims and talk were high-flown but it turns out we were working on exactly the same principle behind everything Brook now rejects, at least in theory.

And that's the process that makes or breaks the awful, despised, hysterical, beautiful commercial theatre.

After any set-back Brook returns to work immediately and keeps moving. It's as if he wills and forces events to take a better turn. In the most extraordinary way imaginable, they were about to.

He organised another show to take place in Agades as soon as possible the next day—the first show outside a market-place. But the villagers in the fields somehow thought we were tourists. Perhaps we were, in a way. They were going to put on a show for us.

And so we became the audience.

The weather changed just before we left. The sand surrounding the city was blowing hard. Conditions would be difficult. 'You'll have to play for your lives.' Brook said to the actors, blinking through the sand. It was an uncharacteristic thing for him to say. I think he was trying to whip up a sense of urgency. The danger existed in the tough new conditions. Perhaps the simplicity would come in the performance. But the energy had to be dredged up from somewhere. 'Play for your *lives*.'

We left after dark, planning to light the show with the fluorescent lights from the camp or the film crew's powerful generator. A young boy guided the Land-Rovers along the dusty tracks into the fields. Brook had fixed the location during the day: a Tuareg village, farmers, goat men, makers of camel bags and shoes. We hung the lights between two trees, feeding the wires into the car batteries. I couldn't see any homes in the dim light. We were in a field of sand and stone: the empty space.

When we arrived a man and a boy were playing drums and gourds. We thought it a nice welcome.

We shook hands with the village elders, tall and lean in their robes and *cheches*. Veils give such men a sense of mystery: you meet their eyes. We smiled, shook their hands, and sat around the carpet. But the man and the boy weren't stopping on the drums. So we smiled and sat some more. But a group of women joined the drummers now. The women were bunched together in brightly coloured costumes, best outfits, singing and clapping for us. And they weren't stopping either. None of the villagers gathered round the carpet, not even the children. And then of course it dawned on us. We weren't expected to play, but to watch. We were the audience. They must have thought it a bit grand to bring a carpet to sit on.

Brook wasn't sure what to do. Do we begin? Do we wait? The singing might go on for hours. It was similar to American-Indian music, chants and calling sounds that last through the night summoning the spirits. People do not value what is easily come by, and the spirits take their time. The drumming grew more insistent, the women sang on. They clapped a basic hypnotic pulse round and round a circle as each sang and returned to the pulse. The sound grew louder, building. But as the actors waited on the carpet their eyes began to open. The pulse grew out of the skills of generations. From the pulse, sounds took life. The women were creating a perfect improvisation. The women smiled.

Hesitantly, Swados began to edge towards the women, and joined their music. They weren't offended. They helped her with the strange chants and rhythms, taking her with them.

Others ventured off the carpet to sing with the women.

The rest joined the drummers with their own drums. The Tuaregs were taken by surprise now, shrieking with delight at this unexpected audience participation. Their shrieks sounded like battle-cries.

And to our astonishment, the field was suddenly full of leaping Tuaregs. Without warning the men dashed into the centre of the field and started leaping up and down. It was a *dance*, a jumping-up-and-down dance. They rammed a walking stick into the ground and jumped up and down with such force the earth vibrated. I couldn't believe it. It was as if they were using pogo sticks. They were going crazy! They were taking off! They were FLYING! If a youngster had the nerve to join them, the men charged into the field and knocked the child's stick from under him. 'Out of the way! Let the *men* dance!' And the child scampered off. And the women kept singing. And the Tuaregs kept leaping into the field, jumping up and down on walking sticks.

And it was catching. A few of the actors were trying it out for themselves on the carpet. It wasn't too difficult to learn. But could they risk it? Perhaps it was a sacred dance, not to be tampered with. What the hell! They went leaping into the field, leaping up and down with the Tuaregs. And others were tempted now, high on the chants and drums, jumping so hard their feet cut and bled through their shoes. HAAAAAAAAAR! The Tuaregs went *wild*. Madness! They were trying to lift the earth. There's madness in the field.

On such occasions, the amazing inscrutable Yoshi Oida is without equal. Very nice, no doubt, to have travelled all this way to leap merrily up and down with the Tuaregs but one couldn't help thinking it wasn't quite the point. 'What did you discover?' people would ask when we got back. 'Oh, you know. Leaping Tuaregs. . . .' But without warning in the field of madness Yoshi Oida suddenly appeared with a specially tiny stick he'd found somewhere and was leaping up and down on his knees. Because he was the leaping midget. And the leaping midget was taking cunning little leaps back towards the empty carpet. And the Tuaregs, hysterical with laughter, began to follow him. Instantly, Katsulas sensed what was happening and went cartwheeling wildly round the field in the same direction. The leaping midget and the giant Katsulas were racing for the carpet! And the other actors caught on now—diving, rolling, tumbling, screaming and leaping across the field until the whole village began to follow. *Transformation!*

There's a new audience round the carpet.

'SHOES!' shrieked Bagayogo, holding them up because he was taking no chances this time. People were going to know this show

132

was about *shoes*. When he chooses, Bagayogo can stop the world. 'Hey! KARRRRAAAAAAAAH! KARRRAHAAAAAAAAH! TOTOTOTO-TOTOTOTOTO! SHOOOOOOOOOOOOOOOOOOOOOOOOS!' The Tuaregs began to laugh and giggle a bit. But Bagayogo looks as if he'll *kill*. And no one laughs any more, except Brook, who can't really stop. It's something he does when incredible things happen.

And they did happen that night. Through the most unexpected and extraordinary means the audience had pumped new energy and life into the actors. The wall was down. In its place, real exchange, real and precious sharing. Yet in the normal way, actors find this trust in an audience difficult to come by. Often in theatre it's an ambiguous relationship, full of fear and suspicion —perhaps it's veiled hostility. Faced with an audience 'out there', the actor feels judged. In return, he defends himself. It's Brook's favourite illustration for all the stifling tensions and difficulties involved in performing in public. In French theatre, you actually find the expression *se défendre*. The actor defends himself against critical judgement and assumed hostility through the role he plays. He wears it like a suit of armour: a costume. But in Africa the traditional pressures were absent. You could begin from zero. In this relaxed atmosphere perhaps a way might be found to prepare and soften an audience. Little by little, an audience might be brought to the point where a totally natural event takes place. The actor and spectator become partners. For both will have been transformed simultaneously.

And for the first time, something of that very special quality began to happen in the village of the Tuaregs. Brook's urgent pleas and conferences were beginning to reap a few rewards at last. The pace and mood of the actors matched exactly the outward sensibility of their audience. They took it from there. At times it was as if they were playing in a frenzy, switching direction time and again, risking more and more in an effort to catch all the moods and lightning responses of the people. In such a way, an actor conditioned only by traditional theatre audiences is stretched and challenged to discover skills that perhaps he thought did not exist in him. In the most vivid way the true meaning of words such as 'spontaneity', 'danger', 'events' and

133

'relationship', 'openness', 'meeting', such words, mere words, are seen in a different light.

At one moment during the show Yoshi Oida suddenly risked everything. He presented the shoes to a Tuareg in the audience, the village schoolmaster. In the West, perhaps at the circus, such a move might not be unexpected. The actor who singles out someone in his audience usually succeeds in embarrassing him for life. The popular comedian might put him down, particularly if he's a heckler. He'll come out with the spontaneous ad-lib that he's used over the years. The clown will get it right, sensing just how far to go. But for an actor to stop a show and suddenly involve the audience without any warning on either side might seem suicidal. In fact, it almost was. For the schoolmaster thought the shoes were a genuine gift. He was *clinging* to them. So the risky move swung events in a totally new direction. Unless the actors got the shoes back, the show would come to an early end.

Enter a crazed sorceress with a rival show.

And the crowd howled with laughter. They were laughing because they knew the schoolmaster's no fool. He wasn't going to be fooled by a sorceress. Spells, incantations, curses, every manifestation of evil and doom could not move this man.

Crazed sorceress retires hurt.

Enter two ridiculous thieves, about to appear more ridiculous.

The schoolmaster was now sitting on the edge of the carpet, beginning to look like a fierce and stubborn patriarch. King! The two ridiculous thieves pay homage, song of homage for the King! And the King bows graciously and says, 'But you still can't have the shoes.'

And the two ridiculous thieves retire hurt.

Enter a shoe collector, the one shoe collector in existence who might be able to tempt the shoes back.

'AHAAAAARRR! SSSSSSSSSSSSSS! SSSSSSSSSSSSSSSSSSSSSSSSSS! SHOOOOOOOOOOOOOOOOOOS! SHOOOOOOOOOOOOOOOOOOOOOOOOS! SHOOOOOOOOOOOOOOOOOOOOOOOOOS!!

And the schoolmaster coughs and looks to the sky.

Give! No! *Give!* No! Shrieks, threats, orders—*give!* GIVE! Say please. *Please.* Say please again. Please, *please* gives us back the

134

shoes. Okay. The Tuareg says, 'Okay'. And returns the sweet and lovely shoes.

Best 'KYU' of 'KYU' I ever saw. . . .

Well, perhaps the show revealed little more than a new sustained energy from the group. If a distinguished critic had parachuted in to see the performance, all he might have seen was a pretty crude form of popular theatre, I'm not sure. But he would have missed the essentials, as critics have been known to do. He wouldn't have looked at the audience. For there in space and time two different worlds had met, and joined each other.

'It was a marriage,' said Miriam Goldschmidt.

And it takes energy to make one.

11

Enter the crazed spirit of Groucho Marx.

We were taken by surprise, not expecting an African version. But why not? If Africans leap, they grouch. The spirit of Groucho was making a special guest appearance in an entertainment we saw before leaving Agades. The spirit was wise, pointing the way.

The entertainment was part of the Independence Day celebrations the Préfet invited us to. As darkness fell, we gathered in a small courtyard in the centre of Agades. Outside a baby giraffe stood mournfully behind a wire fence. Monsieur Ozoom took pictures of us stroking its nose.

Quite a crowd was packed into the courtyard: councillors, army men, important-looking officials and their overdressed wives. I'd seen them in the afternoon watching a military march-past when the General's jeep broke down slap in front of the V.I.P. dais. The General looked like Chaplin in *The Great Dictator*. His medals bristled with anger. Then he whacked the driver over his head.

I was sitting next to the irritable old Sultan of Agades at the time. The two of us watched almost everything with intense displeasure, including each other. When a horse without a rider was guided ceremonially past the dais, the old Sultan leaned forward in his billowing robes expressing some interest for the first time. The riderless horse belonged to him, sad symbol of lost power. He leaned forward on his walking stick and grunted.

Eventually, the Préfet rose to make a speech to the people lining the dusty main track through the centre. Times of difficulties . . . low supplies of crops . . . we must all *pull* together.

And so on.

The V.I.P. dais rippled with applause. But the people stayed silent.

136

The Préfet sat down again, carefully arranging his silk robes. He bowed graciously to Brook.

A few festivities followed: wrestling matches, games of chance, a bicycle race. It was a token affair, for the V.I.P.s and the distinguished guests gathered in the shade of the makeshift dais. The Préfet judged the Miss Agades competition. There were just six entries, young girls huddled together embarrassed before so many eyes. After lengthy discussion with his councillors, banter behind smooth hands, worldly sniggers, the Préfet awarded first prize to the one girl dressed in a Western outfit. He pecked her on both cheeks, presenting a small package wrapped carefully in brown paper.

It was a bar of soap.

Now the V.I.P.s gathered together again in the courtyard for the evening entertainment. The Préfet and party sat in the front row with Brook: guest of honour. After a while he was introduced to the audience as 'the famous director of a circus'. He giggled and looked pleased, taking a bow. Then the announcement was corrected to 'the famous director of a foreign post office'. Which didn't get a bow. At one end of the courtyard, a raised slab of concrete served as a stage. Three dim light bulbs hung by a thread. A curtain was slung perilously over a temporary line. Behind it we could glimpse a man in a blue robe, a Brook figure, offering urgent last-minute advice. People were dashing about, nervous behind the curtain. A stage, a curtain, lights, nerves, an excited audience 'out there'. We were back in the world of traditional theatre. But there wasn't going to be a play. Plays don't exist.

'Enjoy the delay,' said Daniel Charlot, the observer from the French government, strolling off somewhere. Charlot had worked as a teacher in Mali for two years and knew that nothing ever starts on time in Africa. African time is behind time. I think they've got it right in a way. But it means you wait. At last, perhaps an hour behind schedule, a boy dragged the curtain open.

Tuaregs danced and sang—followed closely by the director figure holding a microphone. Their voices crackled from a loudspeaker. The boy closed the curtain long before they had finished. No one seemed to mind. Not even the director. To everyone's delight an old magician came next, slashing a sword across his bare chest. He whirled round as he did it, like a dervish. The crowd cheered him. It was a fine display. The slashing of the sword made the sound of a singing saw. But did the blade touch his chest? Perhaps he made the sound with his mouth. As if sensing our doubts the old magician flung his sword to the ground, dashing from the stage to show it to the audience. The blade seemed as sharp as a razor. Every time the magician performed the trick you could have sworn the blade slashed his chest and made the singing sound. Still, Brook wasn't as impressed by this as some. In Persia certain Sufi sects can slice a knife through their necks and carry on as if nothing happened. In theory, their heads should fall off. Now if the magician had plunged the sword into his heart, Brook might have been mildly impressed. He doesn't please easily, particularly at the theatre.

The boy dragged the curtain closed and the Tuareg troupe appeared again, and again actually. The Préfet and party applauded politely as if in the Royal Box at Covent Garden. But in this betwixt and between world of 'culture' and 'art' the Tuaregs weren't the same as they had been in the open field of the village. The makeshift stage had cramped and confined them into giving a 'performance'. Their easy movements now seemed self-conscious and clumsy. Nothing flowed freely for nothing was natural, or so it seemed watching the shadowy figures from a seat in the distance. Perhaps in the name of progress the Tuaregs and their director had moved closer to Brook's world now—the world of Western theatre trappings and effects he had gone to Africa to lose. And yet something wonderful was to come out of the evening, and save it. The curtain opened on the new and magical world of that special group of Africans known as the Peulh.

Amazing, pretty, camp, vain and irresistible Peulh. Peulh is pronounced like 'pearl'. And it's apt because both are decorative, unique and treasured. The actors fell in love with them, getting a quickie divorce from the boring old leaping Tuaregs. The Peulh are accustomed to this. They like a little attention.

There used to be a theatre group in New York known as the

Playhouse of the Ridiculous. The Peulh must have been founder members. They roll their eyes and flash quick smiles on and off like lights. And that's their dance. It's an amazing dance, absurd: ridiculous. They clap their hands lightly, shuffle their feet forward, roll their eyes and flash their teeth, and the instant they appeared from behind the curtain the audience exploded with laughter, laughter of recognition. Particularly the women laughed and cheered. For the Peulh were a male troupe, delicate and pretty with powdered faces, making the ridiculous dance that said, 'Look how beautiful we are.' And they are. And they know it. Brook's actors sat forward in their seats, amazed.

But it wasn't just the incredible sight of the Peulh. Even in the poor conditions, they were making music, miraculous music that seemed to come from another world. Swados was on her feet the instant she heard it. She knew the Peulh sound went to the heart of everything she's searching for.

There in one sustained note, a sound held for so long we weren't even aware of a voice behind it, a sound pure and simple, effortless, it was as if the whole meaning of everything that is so unintelligible and mystifying about life had somehow been shown to us. From where or how, I didn't know. But it was there and it was as if the sound had a life of its own. The sound merged with others, vibrating. It was as if the sounds weren't human. They were beyond art, beyond culture, beyond everything except dreams. They were beautiful. They were beyond the human.

'Music', wrote Leonardo, 'is the shape and form of the invisible.'

The Peulh could capture the invisible, and held the secret.

Before the evening ended Brook was excitedly fixing a meeting with them. We would meet the following afternoon. It was to be the first of the unexpected exchanges held in private that were to have such a dramatic effect on the group. Perhaps the Peulh would tell us some of their secrets. We met them briefly that night but all they would do for the moment was take our hands and roll their eyes, like Groucho. 'How's *that* for love-making?' We rolled our eyes back. We must have looked ridiculous. I think it was the point. But yes, it was love.

The Independence Day celebrations finished at the Préfet's party round open fires in the grounds of his official residence. Fairy lights hung from trees. Whole sheep were roasted and ripped apart. The army guarded the entrance from the villagers. And the Préfet waltzed to a record of 'I Love Paris Every Moment'.

12

Of all the peoples of Africa the Peulhs are renowned as something very special. I'm certain they're on all the tourist brochures —hippies of Africa, not to be missed. Yet they remain outsiders, bright and aloof nomads: shy of strangers. They're a mystery even to Africans. No one knows where they came from. Perhaps they're of Arab descent, but others claim connections with Israel, and the gipsies in England are said to bear a resemblance to them. Some own cattle but keep moving on in search of the best pasture land and water. Others refuse to intermarry with the Hausa, retaining distinctive features—light coffee-coloured skins, narrow noses, thin lips, soft and straight hair—features that set them apart from others. They're a gentle and decorative people. And such people show the outsider only what they want to.

How could we build a bridge to the Peulh in one meeting? Within our own little community there were many who were still strangers to each other.

We were nervous of the Peulh.

Brook had arranged to meet them on neutral territory—an empty mud hut in the centre of a wasteland in Agades. It was where the Peulhs were camped before moving on, back to their own people or to another place. Twelve men and women were sitting quietly together on mats in the hut. There was no water or electricity. A teapot brewed on a small fire in the middle of their circle. The Peulhs had about them such composure and gentleness that we felt clumsy, crowding into the hut: intruders. They watched us, smiling. But the two separate groups were shy and hesitant of each other. There was only silence, for we couldn't speak the same language. The Peulhs ran their hands through our hair and clothes, and smiled.

Sometimes, two or three of them sang to themselves and pointed to the sky.

Outside the hut our own white Peulh, Mr. Lou Zeldis, was making sounds with two black Peulhs rolling their eyes together, dancing and laughing. With his trinkets and beads and vanity and camp, Lou Zeldis was a kindred spirit. He was doing the eye routine with the Peulhs and you knew what they were all saying. 'Aren't we *beautiful*! We're beautiful! We're all amazingly, incredibly, fantastically BEAUTIFUL!' as they danced, and swopped trinkets, and made eyes, and laughed, and pointed to the sky zapping sounds to the grateful spirits up there. Lou likes life to be fun, heaven on earth—paradise now! The Peulhs understood. You've never seen a man look so happy. You knew he didn't want to enter the hut.

The two groups were still sitting in silence, not knowing what to do. Glasses of mint tea were sipped. The women in the Peulh group began to laugh. One hid beneath a blanket. You could see the blanket shaking. The men seemed above the entire proceedings, preferring to admire themselves in tiny mirrors. They were making up their faces. They were grinding lime stones into the heels of their leather sandals. They used a sword for the grinding. The powder from the lime painted their faces in yellows and whites and reds. They drew a line from their forehead to the tip of their nose. They cleaned perfect teeth with a small twig, fussing and admiring themselves in the tiny mirrors. They were always fussing and admiring themselves in the tiny mirrors. Terrific to watch, this serious business.

The men looked much prettier than the women, which was the general idea. The women rub butter in the men's hair to make it smooth and shiny. Then they plait it into pigtails. The men wore prettier clothes than the women, poor, plain, unequal women. The men wore loin cloths made from goat skins delicately embroidered, strings of white beads, leather gris-gris, feathers, bracelets, arm bands and many shiny objects. The Peulhs loved anything shiny: magpies. One was decorated with the silver foil of cigarette packs. Another wore a fly zip round his head.

There was only one way a real bridge might be built between the two groups who could only stare at each other in silence or smile or exchange little gifts. And it was through music. Brook asked the actors to sing a song.

They sang the Babylon song, our anthem, to raise the spirits. But this was totally and marvellously ignored by the Peulh. The men just continued admiring themselves in the tiny mirrors.

Brook asked the actors to sing one of Bagayogo's songs as Swados played her guitar. But at the end, the men were still admiring themselves and the women were admiring the guitar.

More songs followed, a total of six, but each was met with the same glorious indifference. The Peulhs weren't moving. They weren't returning the music. How much Brook and the rest wanted it, music that took you into other worlds, told magical stories, music sung for love and joy—*give it*! Show us the secret! The Peulhs carried on admiring themselves in the tiny mirrors.

Perhaps we should give up. What right did we have to be there? Perhaps we should let it be. But Brook decided to take a different direction.

He asked the group to make a sound they had worked on during the research in Paris. He asked for an 'ah' sound—just this one basic sound that was to be extended and developed as far as it could possibly go. It seems an easy thing to do. Yet the group had worked on this one sound for weeks and months. It seemed like an awful moment of truth in Agades.

The group began to make the sound. The Peulhs were still staring into the mirrors. I watched the actors grow hesitant, uncertain whether to continue. But the sound stretched and grew— and the Peulhs unexpectedly looked up from their mirrors for the first time. The sound took life, vibrating. The Peulhs discarded their mirrors and joined the sound. Oh, it seemed miraculous! It was as if the Peulh were pulling the sound from them. They pointed to the sky.

Just as the unimaginable sound reached its height, or seemed to, no one would venture any further. Somehow it was frightening. The two sides had met and come together in one sound. And yet it was as if they were stunned and frightened of the discovery. Ted Hughes has written of the sounds far beyond human words that open our deepest and innermost ghost to sudden attention. Was this such a sound? For everyone making it, the Peulhs and the actors together, stopped suddenly and would go no further.

But now the Peulh offered an exchange and sang their songs. And they told Brook something very precious. He knew at last that he was on the right road in the search for a universal language. Perhaps we were only beginning to understand. But spirits speak there, in invisible worlds.

Why is simplicity always so hard to find? The Peulh music showed us that a universal language might be as simple as one note repeated many, many times. But you must discover the right note first. There's a catch in everything. The Peulhs could vary and enrich the sound, changing it in subtle ways, but the strength behind the sound isn't made through force. Somehow, the strength makes itself. With the Peulh everything seemed effortless. Even the sound itself seemed to have a wondrous life of its own. When you listen to the Peulh music it reaches the point where the music actually seems to make itself. The Peulhs were like human musical instruments. We were light years behind their 'simplicity'.

And yet the sound that reached and touched the Peulh from the actors had been no shot in the dark. Both Brook and Swados had talked of the possibility of one note that can become a source, the purest of essence. So much of the group's work was based on this. A sound might somehow be found that encompasses an entire feeling, and conveys it. And there's nothing revolutionary in any of this—as the Peulh and others prove—but it's why Brook was so excited during the meeting. He was certain at last that he was on the right track, for the Peulh magic cut across everything he's working towards in theatre.

Month after month at his centre in Paris, Brook found that the most powerful expression in sound and movement always comes through shedding more and more outward forms. It's an attempt to make the greatest impact using minumum means, and the Peulh had mastered it to perfection. What used to be the fashionable 'Total Theatre'—flashing lights, dance, song, action, happenings, everything converging to make a fuller theatre statement—is the external answer to the same problem. How to make the most powerful impact? The internal answer is an enriching process using minimum means: the empty space. And it's the best and most hazardous answer because it's like a razor's edge. It must penetrate in sharpness and depth. In theatre terms you must not even see the razor. Everything should appear to flow so naturally the magician shows the audience that he has nothing in his hands.

So all of Brook's exercises have been as narrow and restrictive as they could possibly be. One stick, one box, one movement, one sound, one letter—all are a background to the work that forces the actor into a more riveting way of acting. To watch something as apparently simple as a T'ai Chi movement, to watch it done effortlessly is to witness a dream. For months in Paris the group had worked on just one passage of ancient Greek, stretching it in sound and quality in a way that wouldn't be possible with everyday language. It can drive you insane. But the principle behind it was no different than the months, years now, spent struggling with T'ai Chi, or Yoshi's song in ancient Japanese, or one stick movement, or one of Bagayogo's strange electric movements, or the 'ah' sound—or a bird, a trickster, a slave, a corpse, a giant, a king, even a hag transformed by a pair of shoes. Each is a part of a very challenging process—almost impossible, it seems, for the Western actor to master. And yet there have been times in the work of the group when all cultural associations, all barriers of language and class have been swept away. In their place a new power and freedom: a spirit. Ted Hughes, not a pretentious man, an honest man, describes such moments he has seen in the work as 'that riveting near-holy or unholy experience where, as the Bible says, "a spirit passed before my face, the hair of my flesh stood up." '

I believed him now.

145

'Such moments can't really be explained,' said Brook after the meeting with the Peulh. 'Yet they're not accidental any more. They grow out of the work. The special moments no longer happen by luck. Yet they can't be repeated. It's why spontaneous events are so terrifying and marvellous. They can only be re-discovered.' But how to find them again? In the Peulh meeting it was as if the actors were hopelessly lost at sea and suddenly caught sight of a lighthouse in the distance. If only for a short while, they were certain they were heading in the right direction. But then they might easily lose their way again, might easily drown. In fact they did drown, lots of times. Western actors, bewildered, tired, complex, neurotic, seaching for simplicity and invisible power. How could we ever hope to capture the force and magic of the Peulh? And yet it was there in moments. And Brook believes anything is possible. The danger of drowning doesn't concern him. He has an inflatable life-raft. Also nine lives, like a cat.

'Have you ever watched a cat?' he asked me unexpectedly as we took the road back to camp. I replied a cautious yes. For we have three at home: Caesar, Mary and Jack the Pisser. 'We have a Burmese cat,' said Brook, sounding a trifle superior. But the unlikely conversation led to one of Brook's favourite theories.

He told me that if you watch any cat, it isn't just that his body is so relaxed and expressive. It's something more important than that. A cat actually thinks visibly. If you watch him jump on a shelf, the wish to jump and the action of jumping are one and the same thing. There's no division. A thought animates his whole body. It's in exactly the same way that all Brook's exercises try to train the actor. The actor is trained to become so organically related within himself, he thinks completely with his body. He becomes one sensitive responding whole, like the cat.

An ultimate example of this state is revealed in a film of Picasso at work. In one lightning stroke you can see how the tip of Picasso's brush captures his entire imagination. His brushwork can actually be seen as his thought-process. The same is true of the great orchestra conductor. After years and years of work, he thinks and transmits as one gesture. The whole of him is one. And it can be the same with the actor.

It's like tuning an instrument. Eventually the actor can become so highly tuned, his exercises actually seem to happen by themselves. And for Brook, the day that happens consistently within the group the actors will have reached the real possibility of the truth and force and vast simplicity of the Peulh.

In theatre terms, Brook was referring to that ideal state where there exists no time lapse between inner and outer reaction: impulse and action are one. The body, says Grotowski, vanishes and burns. But in terms of the human personality there was this further, terrible challenge—the overwhelming emotional presence of the African, the unified presence that had so shattered Jung's understanding of what it is like to be a European. For it still exists in the African villages, men and women still linked with nature and myth, natural artists making music and dance as a living reality, a way of life.

'It's too late for us,' I said despondently to Brook. 'Everything we see is lost to us.'

'But isn't that our whole reason for coming here?' he answered. 'To try to rediscover it?'

New shows now followed as the pace began to quicken—*The Bread Show*, *The Man and the Woman Show*, *The Drink Show* and others, until it would be time to perform the big piece, *The Conference of the Birds*. The week that had begun with threats and confrontations had brought unexpected excitement— a renewal of faith, if you like. The Peulhs had swung the work in a far richer direction and at last Swados could transform the music. Out went the traditional folk songs and set routines: charm levels of communication. The Peulhs, superior guides, had put the music in its place. Too timid! Too earth-bound! Perhaps that was why the Peulhs always pointed to the sky, laughing. Free the music! Swados would no longer be cast as the intellectual music teacher handing out instructions to lifeless eyes. The music would take a more dangerous line: total improvisation. If the actors could improvise a show, why not a song? If a song came from the actors perhaps they would begin to believe in music. From Agades onwards, the actors would create the songs for themselves.

It seemed a wild risk: madness. The group now faced the frightening responsibility of composing instant songs in front of an audience. Most of them could neither sing well nor play a musical instrument. They were facing ridicule. Ridicule goes with the job, however. And sometimes they get it. After two years with Brook they were hardened to the dangers of improvisation. But there were always more nerves and fear in the musical work where skills were only just beginning. Music never came naturally. How could they improvise a song? The Peulh, like the Tuareg, knew the secret. Just as they invented sounds and songs from a firm pulse of rhythm, so the actors would now try to discover this same hypnotic quality. It wasn't a case of imitating their songs. The actors would learn from the technique behind them. The pulse is a catalyst. The pulse might change, but you must never lose it. Everyone returns to the pulse always.

Things seem so simple, in theory. And yet one knew that nothing facing the actors could have been more difficult. Everything about the Peulh was simple and everything was deceptive. Their magic, we knew, came from the deepest resources of inner strength and certainty. Their lives were hard. Even their external prettiness was misleading. Some of the men had deep scars, ridges across their chests. The scars are a symbol of manhood and courage, the ancient tradition of Sharo, a ceremonial public flogging. The flogging proves that the Peulh is worthy of his bride. He must never flinch. He will demand more strokes. Even when he bleeds, he asks for more.

The pretty and gentle Peulhs flog and torture themselves. They push themselves to extremes. And they have gifts that no one else has.

Before we drove further south into the heart of Niger there was a final performance outside Agades. The carpet was placed under a tree to shield the actors from the hot afternoon sun. It seemed an idyll, waiting in the fields of a village nearby. But the village

148

was almost deserted. Each time we asked where the villagers were, we were told they would soon return. The group waited until sunset, singing and waiting for an audience. But the Préfet had been right. The people had gone in search of richer land. The famine was coming. The group was lost, playing its music in a field to no one.

13

It was as if we were travelling backwards when we re-entered the desert beyond Agades, and backwards wasn't convenient. Perhaps the nature of all journeys is like this, and any search. If not backwards: circles. The camel train moves through the desert at an even pace, yet its progress is as imperceptible as the movement of the hands of a clock. It seems it will never reach its destination. We forced and skidded our way through the final stretch of desert until we were drained and sapped dry and thought we would never be free of the void. It was the most exhausting stretch of all: soft sand, last cruel punishment.

We would return to it when the journey came full circle.

Now the map we carried was crowded with many routes and villages, tiny dots signifying life that would eventually explode and bring us to breaking point. Black Africa! We were heading towards the bush country of the Hausa, a less remote people than the Muslim of the north, more volatile and open, unveiled. Such people have their own sense of mystery. The earth came alive with beetles, crickets and technicolour lizards. You could hear snakes swishing. We slept among giant millet stalks, date palms, mango and citrus trees. Bird symphonies exploded at dawn, sounds I had never heard in my life. At last our eyes were opened on a new world.

We stopped at a nightmare village where vultures swooped from great twisted nettle trees and the banks of a river were filled with bones. In the stifling afternoon heat the villagers were dozing among their hens and goats, squatting in the dust and shit and rotting bones. Brook decided to give a short impromptu performance there.

Small groups drifted together round the carpet—the local Hausa merchants and their children, several Tuaregs passing through, the Arab drivers of a salt train, a group of Peulhs in earrings so heavy their earlobes stretched down to their shoulders.

To our surprise, others were indifferent and did not trouble to watch.

The actors were taking their time for the hot sun brings a slower tempo, and people were watchful here. Brook always maintained that nothing had a better effect on the actors than the stillness of the African audiences. The African doesn't have a Mediterranean temperament. He's capable of enormous energy, explosions, a simmering quality. But the African also possesses a great sense of stillness. This concentrated attention was the most precious thing to play to. A small audience, curious eyes round the carpet, watching in silence—the conditions were ideal for risks and experiment.

It was the first occasion that the set songs were abandoned. Old sounds, like old ideas, block development. After a short discussion it was decided to risk total improvisation. From a basic pulse set by Swados and taken up by the group, three new songs were created on the spot. Perhaps it was beginner's luck, I wasn't sure. But with little hesitancy or stumbling the actors held together and made their songs. We feared laughter, but they were appreciated. The songs were gentle, not ambitious: a beginning.

Swados was grinning from ear to ear, which could only be the best of all possible signs. I'd never seen her react that way to the music before.

The songs developed spontaneously into movement, a dance eventually. Until the dance gathered in pace and suddenly erupted into acrobatics—and I love it when they do that, and so does the audience.

Then two Sphinx meet and in movement and action one Sphinx poses riddles, and another answers. Yoshi and Bagayogo turn their bodies inside out.

A trumpet argues with a penny whistle. The argument grows fierce. Even a penny whistle has rights.

Two birds fight for a piece of string—the first bird sounds of the journey, which intrigue and excite the audience. People

151

laugh but the fight is serious. The sounds and movements are undecorative and strong: half-bird, half-human. The bird show goes well.

Then the actors rolled up the carpet and headed further south. They forgot their travel weariness, as they always did when a show was successful. And it was the best so far. Although the show was short and limited in scope the actors had played with terrific discipline and clarity. Things were beginning to happen. They might not have reached the higher levels but they were outside cultural reference, among the universal language of sound and action. Two days later when we reached the city of Zinder, we were invited to watch an open-air theatre performance. The play was a Hausa comedy about a baptism, a great success with its vast audience. But no one in the group could appreciate it. At first it came as a shock to realize that we didn't speak the same language.

Perhaps we should have returned to the nightmare village of vultures and bones. There were powers and tensions beneath the surface of that place. Another show there might have caught them and taken the work in a more ambitious direction. But Brook didn't feel the time was right, and kept moving.

'In Japan if you wish to find a rock,' said Yoshi Oida, 'we dig and dig and dig always in the same place. But Western people change the place if they cannot find the rock. In Japan, we will dig with our hands. But you will use a machine—to find the rock quickly. I search for truth yet I don't know what it is. Perhaps you can find it sometimes, if you're very lucky. Perhaps the Japanese way is silly—always the same hole, very very deep. Brook digs in many different places, sometimes with a machine, sometimes with a spade. But always changing. Which is better? I'm not sure now. But his *aim* is clear. So somehow I can say that he searches in the same place. His aim doesn't change, but the way is always changing. Perhaps he finds stone, not a rock. It doesn't matter. The way doesn't matter if you find what you're searching for.'

The convoy, a Juggernaut, came to a stop outside Zinder in the fields of Mirriah, one hundred miles from the Nigerian border.

There were now thirty-one members of the expedition. A young Gabonese called Odim Bossoukou, a cynical presence, had joined us in Agades. Although he studied ethnology at the Sorbonne, he had formed the first experimental drama group in Gabon and Brook was impressed with a film of his work there. He was a handsome man, a laugher, vain and sly. He would watch the work with the French observer and take away any lessons that might be useful in his own work. The two observers became pals, joint outsiders talking and laughing together, throwing knives at trees.

The five-man film crew had taken charge of one Land-Rover, which left the rest of us crammed and boiling in only four cars and the spare seat of the truck. We resented the film crew a little. Monsieur Ozoom used to spurt ahead of the convoy to film the happy scene. He liked to end with a shot of a wheel. Cut to the *wheel*. . . .

Soon six others, including Ted Hughes and the two Brook children, were due to join us. But where would they go?

More illness was beginning to break out—high temperatures, diarrhoea, coughing, nausea. Vitamin pills were prescribed, and salt tablets. We smothered our food with salt. Malaria pills now became a strict routine each morning. We slept under mosquito nets shaped like small see-through tents. Water was filtered through a purifier attached to the side of the truck, or boiled before drinking. The doctor, Bagayogo's French wife Marguerite, issued solemn warnings about the dangers of venereal disease. The Leader alerted us to the danger of scorpions. We had to shake our shoes out before wearing them. Check your camp-bed thoroughly each night. Never walk barefoot, and so on.

One night Brook was holding a lengthy conference about the need for another form of costume, when a scorpion suddenly appeared in the middle of the circle. What colour would the costumes be? Would they be a uniform colour or what? Would we design them ourselves? What would be the design? And who would make them? Would there be time to make them ourselves?

153

Maybe a market man could make them? Do we agree on that or not? But how *quickly* could a market man make them? And what cost would they be? What *about* the cost? On and on until someone suddenly leapt in the air screaming: 'SCORPION! SCORPION!'

It might have been me. I'm not certain, there was too much panic. 'Stand back!' ordered Bagayogo. '*Everyone stand back!*' Then he lunged at it with the heel of his boot. But he missed it. He practically broke his ankle. Others went for the scorpion but it fought, only to be beaten to death with the butt of a torch.

That was the only night in the entire journey when everyone slept close to the camp. Safety in numbers.

Brook was now holding many conferences outside the acting group—sometimes with the two observers or myself, or a talk to pacify the two temperamental cooks, or whispered discussions in steamy Land-Rovers with the crew. The crew-conference with Brook was becoming a nightly ritual of map readings and supply checks, hours of talk about routes and time-schedules, future petrol stops, the state of the equipment, the difficulty of border crossings—every aspect of the mechanics of the journey down to such niggling matters as revised washing-up rotas and disappearing coffee cups. The crew would emerge from these conferences looking cramped and weary. So did the film crew from theirs. But Brook didn't. He has enormous reserves of energy, and likes to keep on top of things. Directors like to . . . direct.

'You must write your book like Sartre's introduction to Genet!' he announced to me one morning over breakfast. Then he might hand out another directive. 'No frivolous material! Keep it *serious*.' A minute later: 'Don't forget to write about the cock-up in Algiers. . . .' Until he finally came out with a peach. 'Tolstoy! You must write the book like a Tolstoy novel!'

We camped for three nights in the picturesque fields of Mirriah, or Yasnaya Polanya as I came to think of it. It was Christmas, a time to relax perhaps. We pitched the huge marquee tent in a forest clearing and could eat there untroubled by the flies. Ayansola hung several paintings round the flaps of the tent. They were for sale.

Helen Mirren made Bacofoil Christmas decorations, tinsel patterns that hung sadly inside the marquee. She was in floods of tears, unable to stop.

Yoshi Oida gave volunteers an instant haircut with blunt karate chops that transformed their hair into the shape of a pudding bowl. We bathed in a narrow stream nearby. Washed clothes dried quickly on trees.

The Sheikh of the area sent several fine horses for us to ride. They had been offered to Brook when he visited the Sheikh as a courtesy, although we ended up paying quite a lot of money for the privilege. Also, the horses were as stubborn as mules and refused to start. Crowds of children grinned and laughed when this happened. The more we kicked the horses, the more the children laughed. I felt very English and absurd. I rode in the English style: back straight, knees tucked in, a sedate posture, just superior enough to worry the opposition. 'Come along, Neddy,' I pleaded with my horse. 'There's a good boy.' Eventually, the children explained that the horses would never respond if you kicked them. You could slap them or touch them lightly with a whip, which the children made for us from the branches of a tree.

Then we set off at a cautious pace to the cheers of the crowd. Brook led the way, wearing a special mottle-green *cheche* for the occasion. He was humming 'The Desert Song'.

Sylvain Corthay, an expert horseman, swaggered bareback through the forest. Normally a brooding figure, he looked freer now—confident of his fine skills. 'Best to keep in line,' warned Brook, though Corthay was galloping too fast to hear. He went down with sunstroke the next day.

Swados followed at a wild romantic canter, making the gestures of a circus performer exiting to applause.

Marthouret took risky diversions among herds of buffalo. 'Hello herds of buffalo,' he said.

Miriam Goldschmidt nose-dived into the dust. When he spotted the incident, Corthay galloped urgently past her to rescue the horse.

Katsulas jogged along chewing imaginary tobacco. He was

heading for a showdown, kill as soon as spit, hired hand, fast draw: one of the Magnificent Seven.

Myers, the world-famous mountaineer, wasn't at ease on a horse. He wasn't at ease on washing-up nights either. He said nobody was interested in washing-up except him. Anyway his horse bolted, setting off a chain reaction. Before I knew it, I had bolted past Brook whose horse gave chase galloping at a speed neither of us could control. 'WHOA!' Brook shouted behind me. 'WHOA!' I was pulling on the reins with all my strength but my horse brushed such nonsense aside, as if blowing on an irritating fly. 'WHOA!' I cried, feeling it wasn't the moment to keep up appearances. 'WHOA! WHOA!' Brook was still pounding close behind me. I thought, 'We're both going to die and everyone will laugh themselves silly.' We were both heading straight for the wall of a village.

But so were the horses. Within yards of the wall they suddenly veered away until we slowed to a breathless halt. I was clinging to the belly of my horse. Brook was draped round the neck of his. 'Useful place to play,' he said, looking up at the village.

Such diversions from work were rare. Perhaps because it was Christmas and thoughts might be elsewhere, Brook began to work the group harder than at any time in the journey. The first morning in Mirriah we rose at dawn when the bird symphonies were at their height and deafening. 'Learn from them,' said Brook.

We worked in a clearing in the forest or on the carpet set up close to the marquee. A *Romeo and Juliet Bird Show* was invented, taking the plot from Shakespeare and improvising the characters in bird sounds. Sometimes, the real birds were surprised and joined in.

The group returned to work on one of the shows they had made in Paris from Ted Hughes' poems, *The Ogre Show*, which was about Hughes' favourite character called 'Something Horrible'. 'Something Horrible' is always emerging. But like the performance of *The Box Show* in Tamanrasset, it seemed needlessly difficult and complex, and Brook abandoned work on it. He said it belonged to another life.

156

Instead, Brook continued to develop an idea he gave to the group three days after we entered the desert. We called it *The Bread Show*.

He placed a loaf of baked bread in the centre of the carpet and called for suggestions. Bread, like water, had a new significance for all of us at this time. Neither bread nor water had ever been scarce in our lives before. Placed on the carpet the bread became a powerful symbol. One's first instinct was to eat it. But slowly the first tentative idea for a show began to take shape. A man has a piece of bread. Another man wants it. The man with the bread will not part. What could be easier? And yet Katsulas found it so frustrating that he squared up to Bagayogo on the carpet as if to hit him—the only time I've seen such an incident in the group. The actors struggled with the theme of *The Bread Show* for weeks, as a child learns to walk.

How can one refine anything down to its most powerful source—essential action, essential sound, essential emotion? It might take a lifetime, it is so difficult. The actors try to build a simple dramatic relationship through a piece of bread. And yet they falter and stumble, apparently unable to perform the simplest of things. Mere external effects can be no help to them. Truth, a truthful life and vitality, bursts from the centre. It is never the other way round. But to arrive at the centre, the actors must undertake the most intense life of self-exploration. They must strip away their outward personalities, mannerisms, habits, vanity, neuroses, tricks, clichés and stock responses until a higher state of perception is found. To watch a piece of theatre performed truthfully is to see in a different way. Perhaps we awaken. We are shaken out of our everyday condition and we see life differently. Sometimes our lives are changed. But the actor must change first. He must shed useless skins like a snake. He must transform his whole being.

For some of us in our own lives it can be almost too frightening to contemplate, this abandoning of the outward circumstances of life. Find the essence! *Know thyself!* Even if we're prepared to undertake such an arduous search, how is it to be done?

When the actors struggled in Mirriah with the simple theme of *The Bread Show*, Brook introduced a new exercise into the work that was to be developed almost daily until the journey ended. I describe it now because it had a startling effect on me, as if I'd been struck by a thunderbolt. I felt that I had been shocked into a real awareness of the whole mysterious nature of essence. And yet at first the exercise seemed so easy a child could have done it.

Brook asked us to stand in a circle and make one simple movement in total silence. An actor begins to make a movement. He might begin by raising his arms backwards and forwards towards the sky. The rest of us follow him. Eventually, the actor next to him changes the movement, developing it slightly. He might turn it into a circular action. And the rest follow him. The next might take the shape of the circle and hold it still, rocking his body from side to side. Each develops the movement while everyone follows. The movement passes completely round the circle.

Apart from the demand for simplicity, Brook asked us not to look at the actor developing the movement. We were to watch the person directly opposite us in the circle. If the exercise was done in this way, each movement would flow more naturally into the next. But if one of us faltered, everyone faltered. It was an exercise in simplicity and awareness.

But when we began everyone got it wrong. The fact is that no one made a simple movement. When it came to it, the actors began to make the most involved and elaborate gestures, made to impress. The word 'simple' had been ignored, though no one intended to. Even for people as highly trained as these, their first instinct was to do what came most naturally—the complex. From the start, Brook had proved his point. It's more 'natural' to be complicated.

And it's easier.

As with the simple theme of *The Bread Show*, so the group struggled for many days with this one exercise. They were after the simplicity that comes from inner-relatedness, the lost state of childhood openness and natural conviction that's been blurred and distorted by externals and learning and 'growing up'. Some call this search, the search for the essential 'I' of your being. The source that can be found uncluttered by habit and diversion holds the key of life.

For the most part I had joined in the exercises feeling self-conscious and shy, a little cynical. Only the sight of Brook, who seemed to find them more difficult than anyone, gave me a perverse kind of encouragement. But it seemed that anyone could do this new exercise and I felt more confident than usual. Knowing that it would be my turn to develop the movement as it passed slowly round the circle, I secretly prepared a stunning routine. It was meant to be a circular arm movement made as if gathering air to myself. 'It's poetic,' I thought. And that's just it—I didn't trust myself to make the movement spontaneously. Even after several tries, I would always prepare something instinctively and felt relieved when my turn was over. It's easy to talk of entering a void until you've tried to enter one yourself.

A simple natural movement! And yet whenever I tried to do it, nothing happened naturally. Voices whispered urgent messages inside my head: 'Move your arm this way.' 'Do something interesting.' 'What about your legs?' 'Go faster!' 'Go slower. . . .' My movements weren't exactly flowing. They weren't what you might call the spontaneous leap of a cat. Far from finding any unity of expression I found a tangled confusion of distractions and thoughts. It was the same with another simple exercise of Brook's. All you had to do was sit in an upright position and think of only one thought. Yet within a minute or so, the chances are that you lose concentration. Other thoughts will soon crowd in, distracting. Your body, which was first upright and alert, will become slack. You might not even be aware of it happening.

In the simple movement exercise I found that, no matter how hard I tried, I always lost concentration. Even after much practice, I reached the stage when I began to make the movements mechanically. Against all my better instincts, I'd become a mechanism. On the other hand, whenever I tried to concentrate particularly hard I found that I almost always lost sight of the group making the same movement around me. They became a blur in the background. It was as if I couldn't even control it. If you try to concentrate on reading a book while listening to music, the chances are that you'll have the same reaction. Sooner or later the music will be lost. It becomes background music. But if the powers of human awareness were trained to their real potential, it wouldn't happen. I was learning to jolt myself out of my everyday condition. I had to remember myself.

Of course, it's easy to get by. Yet there were Brook's skilful actors struggling to make the same simple movements. And what then of simplicity and essence? 'De la vaporisation et de la centralization du *Moi*,' wrote Baudelaire. 'Tout est là.' But such a search might be painful. For what was imagined to be free and natural within you might turn out to be merely closed and warped.

Know thyself! Perhaps the beginning of all self-knowledge is to understand that we know so little. In one of the last letters he wrote to his wife before he died, René Daumal, the author of the unfinished masterpiece *Mount Analogue*, grappled with the mystery of essence and described the path he saw before him. Daumal was a pupil of Gurdjieff for a while, and this is what he wrote:

> *I am dead because I lack desire;*
> *I lack desire because I think I possess;*
> *I think I possess because I do not try to give.*
> *In trying to give, you see that you have nothing;*
> *Seeing you have nothing, you try to give of yourself;*
> *Trying to give of yourself, you see that you are nothing;*
> *Seeing that you are nothing, you desire to become;*
> *In desiring to become, you begin to live.*

14

One afternoon in the fields of Mirriah I was taking notes on the work when I felt a pair of eyes burning into me from a crowd of children. I looked up and saw a youngster, perhaps twelve or thirteen years old, staring at me with these great black saucer eyes. I would note something down and then whenever I looked up, there he was again. And each time he grinned such a terrific grin that I found myself doing it too. He pointed at my notebook. Perhaps he was proud of me writing so urgently in a notebook. I made a gesture back as if to say, 'These are really important and great thoughts in here.' And he laughed and yes, he did seem proud.

When the afternoon's work was over the children gathered round us as always, and the youngster came to say hello. He was a fine and strong boy, grinning at me in silence for we couldn't speak the same language. He seemed happy. But I saw that he was crippled down one side of his body. He dragged a foot and one of his arms hung limply by his side. But he could get about. And stood in front of me, smiling.

I thought that he wanted money, although he hadn't asked for anything. Most of the children knew the word 'cadeaux'. I wanted to give him something. I suppose I wanted to be good.

I emptied the loose change from my pockets and gave him all of it. But to my surprise, he wouldn't take it. I mimed back that it was okay. I wanted him to have it. But he still refused and followed me as far as the entrance to the marquee tent. The group was meeting and I couldn't ask him inside. To let one child enter would have meant a hundred. The same rule applied to sharing food with the children, although we cheated from time to time. I had to leave the youngster and pointed across the fields that he should return to his village. I had to work. But he stood at the entrance, smiling.

So I pressed him again to accept the money. And to my relief, he took it this time and left with his friends across the fields. And I felt good. I went inside for the meeting, and soon forgot about him.

The next afternoon most of us were sitting inside the tent, thirsty from the sun, drinking orange squash before work began again. Suddenly, I heard a row going on outside. The crew was ordering several children away from the camp. They wanted to relax in peace, I suppose. But when I went to see what was happening, the youngster I'd met had returned. And he wouldn't leave. The crew kept ordering him away, but he stood his ground.

When he saw me he came running towards me clutching a small cardboard box as if there was treasure inside. He held the box out to me, gesturing that I should take it. It was a present.

At first I was embarrassed to accept. But he insisted, as I had done with the money.

Inside the box was a bunch of bananas.

The youngster's name was Zuledini. I didn't know what to say. He pointed towards the surrounding fields beckoning me to follow him home. So I followed him for perhaps a mile through the forests and fields of millet along the banks of a stream by herds of oxen until we came to the schoolhouse on the outskirts of his small village. Fat checked guinea fowl scattered as a bell clanged and the children dashed out of the school for a break. Zuledini introduced me to the young schoolmaster, who spoke French. We talked for a while. I told him about our journey.

'But if you don't use language,' he asked, 'how does anyone understand you?'

'It isn't easy,' I replied, at which he laughed. But perhaps he might be able to see for himself. The group was to perform at the village the next day. And he looked forward to it.

'Why doesn't Zuledini go to school?' I asked.

'I'm afraid it's too late for him,' the schoolmaster replied, explaining he'd been kept away from school since he was crippled.

'But what will he do?'

'He says he will work the land like his fathers.'

'Can he read or write?'

But he couldn't.

'Perhaps he'll leave the village one day,' I said.

'It will be difficult for him if he does.'

'Do many people leave the village?'

'Yes, but they always return.'

The schoolmaster smiled at that.

Would he ask Zuledini what he enjoyed most watching the group work? Was it the bird sounds the actors made? Or the work with the bread?

The schoolmaster asked the youngster in Hausa. Then he translated it back into French.

'He says that he enjoys you the best.'

I must have gone scarlet. We laughed and shook hands and Zuledini took my hand and led me into the village. We walked through a maze of fences woven in palm leaves. Behind them women beat millet: their bodies glistened with sweat. They giggled when they saw me, the white man. They were beautiful in cloths of many colours and one invited me to try to beat the millet. An African always has time for a laugh. So I took a long and smooth pestle, made smooth by centuries of work it seemed, and did my best to copy their easy sensual movement. The women gathered round to witness the great event. Zuledini looked very serious, studying my grip on the pestle and nodding encouragement. But it was hard work and the pestle soon began to weigh a ton. I fumbled and lost the beat and the beautiful women shrieked with laughter. Then they returned to work lifting the pestle with ease.

The villagers lived in oval huts made from mud with roofs of woven matting. They're called wattles: cool and neat homes, swept clean. Small fires were used for cooking. Goats and donkeys strolled about the yards. Zuledini lived in a family compound of four huts and took me there. The men were working the land but I sat in the open with his grandfather, who was very old, dressed in a blue robe and fez, pinning my cigarettes behind his ears.

163

Others came to visit, sitting on stools in silence. Zuledini's mother offered me a bowl of goat's milk. I offered it to the others and it passed from mouth to mouth until it was my turn. But the group had been warned many times not to eat and drink outside the camp for fear of illness. I pretended to drink the goat's milk, cursing my timidity. The others knew that I was pretending.

We sat for another hour or so as Zuledini fetched more and more relatives and friends to meet me. Eventually I began to laugh, for I couldn't believe they were all so enthusiastic. Zuledini was practically frog-marching them into the compound. It was a relaxed and tranquil place to be. Time didn't seem to matter there. But I began to grow anxious. I thought I might be missing something important in the work.

I shook hands with everyone and Zuledini guided me back through the fields. It was hot now and the flies were beginning to irritate. I began to walk faster, setting the pace. I was convinced that I was missing something vital. I urged Zuledini to point in the direction of the camp and let me continue the long walk alone. I could go faster alone. But he stuck to my side and wouldn't leave me. I kept gesturing at him to go faster. But now he was slowing me down deliberately. He put his hand on my shoulder and stood in front of me. He was smiling but he wouldn't let me walk any further. He bent down and scooped up the earth in his hands. He gave me the earth. He ran to the fruit trees and gave me the fruit. He pointed to the sky and the land, the trees and the cattle. 'Look!' he was saying. 'Look how miraculous life can be.' And I, who was so concerned with awareness and being, felt ashamed and looked at my young crippled friend in wonder.

The final performance in Niger was at this village, the village of Gangara.

The village was transformed when we arrived in the Land-Rovers. Now there was terrific excitement and noise. Hundreds of villagers seemed to be crammed into the small dusty square. Many came from surrounding villages, eager to see the strangers who talked to the birds and fought over a piece of bread. A horseman in bright billowing robes of reds and greens and pinks

164

galloped into the fields, perhaps to round up the latecomers. There was such a powerful sense of occasion that I couldn't help wishing Brook had something prepared to offer, a *real* show. I watched the actors tense—fearful of vast crowds.

The village elders shook our hands. Children struggled for a better view. The elders screamed and waved sticks at them and the children observed the ritual of pretending to be frightened. No one would beat a child in this village. Drummers welcomed us with louder drumming than we had heard before: freer. Women with babies folded into the backs of their dresses shrieked and performed a great sexy dance. When the girls in the group tried to join in, the crowd exploded with affectionate laughter. The head of the *canton* and his fat and jolly councillors dressed in white silk bou-bous sat in splendid wicker chairs. Others watched, standing with pots on their heads. A blind man walked without a stick towards the carpet under a tree. The Chief presented Brook with a bowl of lettuce—the first village to give the group a 'cadeau'.

As we sat round the fringes of the carpet another act suddenly upstaged us with an exquisite sense of timing. It was an ancient griot, master of the vagabond art of storytelling and flattery. Dressed in brown to stand apart from the crowd he was yelling and pointing, screaming out tales and jokes that would be well rewarded. The griot certainly knew how to handle a crowd. We couldn't get started because of him. Eventually he turned to the group and addressed us with such extravagant gestures that we knew what he was saying. 'Silence! These people have come thousands of miles! *Silence!* These good and brave people have come through a desert to see us! We are honoured! And I personally will be honoured if they give me money! MONEY!'

You slap a note on his forehead, as is the custom. It sticks to the sweat, which is why I guess he didn't deal in small change. 'MORE! You're beautiful. MORE! You're wise and beautiful. MORE! You're *incredibly* wise and beautiful. . . .'

At last we could begin—but then to our amazement another act made its entrance. Four horsemen, singers and entertainers, professional rivals, unexpectedly made a magnificent entry.

Swathed in fine and ornate robes, they rode in drumming and singing a high-pitched chant as the griot began again to address the crowd. If it was a coincidence, it was inspired. 'Welcome, horsemen! And what a crowd I've got for you! Jesus, what a *crowd*!' The horsemen looked at us with disdain and carried on performing. But the village elders decided they must wait their turn. The sultans of the entertainment world were ushered round the back, looking deeply offended.

Now the show could begin! But with what? For nothing was prepared. The crowd fell silent.

Tentatively, the actors began a song which actually had a lyric. It was in Hausa. It meant, 'We are pleased to meet you.' I don't think Brook knew about this song. The crowd was listening to the words with a horrified look on their faces. The Hausa wasn't coming out too well. 'Meet pleased we to are, no *really*...' (Language can be a terrible barrier.) After several horrifying moments the crowd decoded the line, got the message and collapsed with laughter. So did the actors, who didn't have much choice. Brook was pink with embarrassment. The worst of all imaginable starts—but press on!

So the group improvised another song to a background of slow and rhythmic clapping—too slack, too little energy. The song wasn't moving. There was polite indifference.

Yoshi Oida ran into the centre of the carpet, trying to switch the pace, gain interest—before it was too late. The crowd came to life, for he looks a weird sight with his hair tied in a bow and his baggy white shorts down to his knees. He took a solo, leading the chorus in sound. But there was laughter again from the crowd. The sounds were strained and artificial. He tried harder, gathered pace, silenced the crowd—and lost them again. He was going too fast: nervous. I'd never seen Yoshi Oida nervous before.

The fat and jolly councillors began to look at their fingernails.

Brook ordered a group song, and acrobatics. Those faces in the crowd were expectant. They wanted *action*. And when the song went into movement the faces brightened and people cheered at last. Diving, tumbling, rolling, whirling round the carpet, all to the same basic rhythm and sound, I felt the actors

166

could do anything now. The poor opening had been saved. Brook signalled to Ayansola, trying to keep the pace going. 'Not,' I thought, 'the hopping routine again.' But that got cheers too. Ayansola came off pouring with sweat. The crowd was with us.

Now Zeldis went onto the carpet, playing a flute. The wrong instrument! Too gentle! He couldn't be heard. Marthouret joined him with another flute. Brook's face fell. The moment had been lost. The flute routine died. When it was over, no actor wanted to move.

Birds! ordered Brook. And a bird trio improvised a short story, a boy meets girl story. The birds fought over the girl. And it went well. The crowd was intrigued. Applause for the birds!

'*Shoe Show!*' ordered Brook.

It didn't look hopeful. I'd just rewritten the second half and Brook had done little more than talk it through with the group. Marthouret was given the free-wheeling role of trickster. He told me before the show that he hadn't a clue what to do. He looked frightened.

'I think this is the day I get the sack,' he whispered to me in the Land-Rover en route to the village.

'Nonsense, dear boy!' replied Myers, who liked to play at the old-style English actor. 'The little darlings will be in the palm of our hands. . . .'

They weren't. Inspiration was in hiding, and the show fell apart. It was horrifying. No one could understand what was happening. Not Marthouret, or the others, or the crowd, or Brook (least of all myself). There was the special comfort of an isolated laugh. But everyone was very bewildered. The kids were chattering to themselves all the way through. The councillors were slumped in their wicker chairs. One fell asleep. Brook was pouting: sure sign.

He looked angry.

Something was badly wrong with this performance. Fearful of the constant noise and movement of the crowd, the actors had retreated into a shell. They had built a wall, to defend themselves. It was as if they had slid behind the closed doors of their centre in Paris where audiences do not exist. For one moment

Brook looked so angry I thought he might break his golden rule and stop the show. But he didn't have to. A horse did it for him. It might have been planted by the insulted sultans of the entertainment world. But just as Mirren was transforming herself into a camel, a horse reared at the back of the crowd and sent many women and children spilling and screaming onto the carpet. The chaos lasted several minutes and fortunately no one was hurt. But we could abandon *The Shoe Show* now: a natural break.

'*Bread Show*', Brook whispered without much conviction. The actors looked drained. Their confidence had evaporated. And without it, they were finished. Perhaps actors are more fragile than most. Theatre is a world of extreme success and extreme failure. It's why only egotists and masochists become actors. But faced with rejection, they crumble. If this audience wasn't booing or hissing or walking out, as a more sophisticated audience would have done, it was no consolation. No, the fact that the people stayed and still hoped for something only made it worse.

Myers went onto the carpet to begin *The Bread Show*. Who would get the bread off him, and how? The crowd hushed and again those bright expectant faces fell. The people were let down again. *The Bread Show* was played out in a private world, too small and cluttered to understand, too slow and hesitant, no danger, no simplicity, no energy—a failure.

Whenever a show goes well there's a ritual of rolling up the carpet to song. Whenever a show goes badly the carpet seems too heavy and clouded with dust. The ritual becomes a chore. This time the carpet was rolled up in silence, and the return to camp was silent.

The show in the village of Gangara had been the most ambitious so far, and the worst. After the preparation in the peace and tranquillity of the forest in Mirriah, the actors were panicked by all the noise and movement, took the chaos for rejection—and retreated. But interest from a Hausa audience, particularly those overwhelming crowds we were about to face in Nigeria, isn't revealed through silent attention. That reaction belongs to the West, or the more distant audiences of the Muslim villages we'd visited. Here the interest revealed itself in the constant chatter and agitation, more a rock festival atmosphere, and only the ancient griot had the courage to handle it. For that man worked with the kind of frenetic urgency and power that *demands* attention. You felt that his pulse must have been at exploding point. But the pulse of the group's work was too slow and subdued for the occasion. They were frightened. Their tempo came from fear and habit—the habit of different performances before very different audiences. Once again that despised conditioning 'habit' had proved the inevitable block to development. Envy the man who can break with the past. He will be fearless. But I knew that if the actors could somehow learn to control an audience like the griot, they would be masters.

'It's getting like a bullfight,' Brook said afterwards to the weary group. 'The challenge is to bring the bull to a standstill. But the bull is different with every fight. If you don't see that, it will kill you.'

And that was all he said, for the moment.

It was Christmas Eve and we had a party of sorts. I knew it was Christmas Eve because Katsulas was singing 'Jingle Bells'. Also, there was a card stuck on the mosquito net inside the communal tent. 'Happy Christmas everyone. The crew.'

We had real Christmas cake brought with us specially for the occasion. And the crew did the washing-up. The film crew put up a little tinsel Christmas tree, and filmed it.

'Just when we were all coping,' groaned Brook.

The film crew came to the party in suits, as if visiting a Paris suburb. Suits and ties.

'Suits and ties,' snapped The Leader. 'No wonder we're *overweight*.'

Ayansola played his rock and roll record. He invented a new party game called 'List the people you hate'.

Fresh supplies of warm beer were drunk practically dry. But before long the actors gathered round Brook and the party of sorts turned into a conference. Everything returns to work always. It's all there is. The actors were still stunned by the terrible failure of the show.

'It wasn't just that we let the audience down,' Brook told them. 'The point is that we failed to live up to everything we stand for.'

'But how's it possible?' asked one. 'How is it that with all our work and training such a thing could happen?'

Brook hesitated at first, as if to reply might be too near the bone.

'All right,' he said eventually. 'Just this once.'

And he replied by way of a comparison, and everything he said was the more withering for it. He referred to a speech in Peter Weiss's *Marat Sade* in which Marat talks of revolution and the new age. Imagination can't break down any real barriers, he says. For each man betrays the revolution, however hard he fights. Each is so clogged with dead ideas that even the best of us are unable to control our own lives. Look how everyone wants to cling to something from the past, a souvenir of the old regime. This man decided to keep his painting. This one keeps his horse. He keeps his estate. He keeps his factories. This man couldn't part with his shipyards. This one kept his army. And that one keeps his king. Each preaches the cause of revolution and the dawn of the new age. Everyone fears the unknown.

'We stand here more oppressed than when we began,' says Marat, pointing at his audience.

'And they think the revolution's been won.'

The next day we crossed the border into Nigeria, the central point of the journey.

15

Everything in this journey had been a preparation for Nigeria: a warning. Now we were to travel almost a thousand gruelling miles from Kano, biggest city in the North, down to the magical birth-place of the Yoruba cult, holy city of gods and possession called Ife. When you arrive there, say the Yorubas, you have reached the centre of the world.

Between those two distant points nothing was planned. But such a scheme has its advantages. If you haven't planned anything, nothing can really go wrong.

And we began in Kano, renowned for its ancient walled city, its dye pits and mosques, its groundnuts stacked as high as pyramids and the vast market where public scribes still write letters for people unable to write themselves. I bought a short book there called *How To Be A Nigerian*, which begins with the wise words: 'It is not easy to write a book. First you have to get a book, then you have to write it. Thus has been my experience. . . .'

It's a terrific book and I often read it. The author understands the nature of truth. At any rate, he let me know what was in store for us in Nigeria—

'In the beginning God created the Universe. Then He created the moon, the stars and the wild beasts of the forests. On the sixth day, He created the Nigerian. But on the seventh day while God rested, the Nigerian invented noise.

No noise is ever quite like the Nigerian noise. If you were a good student of noise, you would soon find that the solid, compelling monotony of Nigerian noise is something companionable and exciting; and after a while, you really begin to miss this regular, unabated noise, such as when you are temporarily abroad for instance.

A successful European buys a house in the country and spends the greater part of his life seeking solitude and quiet. He climbs mountains and joins a country club distinguished for its silent fun; where members do not speak to one another unless it is absolutely essential, such as when a brooding club-mate is on fire and hasn't noticed.

In Nigeria you are regarded with suspicion if you seek soli-tude, climb mountains and have a house in the country. . . .'

It took Brook and the actors a very long time before they came to grips with this vital quality of Nigerian culture called noise. After fighting a losing battle for so many shows, the penny finally dropped. They invented *The Noise Show*. As far as I remember, everyone jumped up and down for three-quarters of an hour screaming their heads off.

We rested outside Kano, living for several days in the deserted campus of the university. But we'd stopped as much for the Land-Rovers as ourselves. The machines looked battered by the journey and would need a great deal of work on them. The crew could get spare parts in the centre of the town. But within a day the mechanic collapsed with malaria. He was white and bent double, unable to stop shaking. It was so severe he had to be hospitalized.

Almost every actor and all of the crew were now to fall ill or go down with malaria.

We lived in the student quarters, more like army barracks, luxury to us. Each day we could take cold showers where frogs croaked welcome and lizards scampered up the walls. They were quite harmless and it was silly of me to keep clinging to the ceiling. We ate English-style in the canteen: pots of tea, boiled eggies, hot toast, bottles of sauce, dear old meat and two veg. For the first time in my life I enjoyed hot custard and thanked God for the British Empire.

The first letters arrived from home. Ruth, my wife, wrote: 'By the way, why do you say a pair of shoes is getting everyone nearer THE TRUTH? Are you all right? Shall I come and fetch you or what . . .'

Several professors and dons met us at the campus, excited to talk with Brook and hear news of the journey. One was a cool Trinidadian, a black Arthur Miller figure busy setting up a new drama department there. Another was a youngish English professor called Crowder, an expert on Africa, a sunny presence chattering about various African languages, Armenian restaurants and Lord's cricket ground. I liked him. He asked me how England was.

'How *is* England?'

'England? Oh, the same.'

'Oh, *good*.'

Professor Crowder guaranteed our safe journey through Northern Nigeria, acting as surety to a suspicious government. But in Kano the film unit was suddenly refused permission to film anywhere in the country. They took the first plane home.

The journey was over for them.

But it was convenient for us. There was now room for the newcomers in the Land-Rovers. François Marthouret's wife had arrived by plane with the two Brook children, eleven-year-old Irina and the six-year-old running, jumping, standing, talking, lisping, leaping, non-stop, all-action Simon. The lad has energy. He looks like his father too, and sat on his knee when a conference was called in a small courtyard of the campus. Brook looked more excited than at any time during the journey. The words came tumbling out of him as he tried to encourage the group to greater effort and commitment. I was wrong when I thought the campus might be a nice rest.

'By no stretch of the imagination could we compare Kano with the village life we've seen so far,' he told the actors gathered round him. 'We're in a city bursting with life and vitality, a city on the make, an Elizabethan city—don't sit on my shoulders, Simon. They'll be expecting a *show*. And we must give them some *real* skill. We must do things well for the pleasure of doing them. It's particularly exciting because what's happening here is comparable to Greek drama—*please* Simon—because in Nigeria there's a fascinating mixture of buzzing popular theatre sometimes based on everyday life and sometimes on epic and

173

mythic local material. Put the orange juice *down*, Simon. And the unique fascination of this theatre is that it's spontaneously recreated the conditions of Elizabethan drama on the one hand and ancient Greek drama on the other. It's the beginning of a whole new culture, not commercialized or set, but in its first roots. So we must try to give them the best that we possibly can. We must give Kano a *real* show. Oh, *Simon. . . .*'

For the next five days Brook returned to all the intense and highly concentrated working methods of his research centre in Paris. It was as if an athlete had run several races in strange conditions, collapsed on his last outing and decided to return to the training ground. A recreation room on the campus was transformed into a work room: a laboratory. There the group worked behind closed doors for many hours each day, slogging through the morning until it was too hot to continue and Brook allowed a short afternoon siesta. He seemed to be working with renewed energy and excitement. There was a sudden atmosphere of urgency about him, as if everything hinged on this new work. Africa was out there, somewhere. But Brook kept working. We were still getting up at six in the morning. The group was building up to a show in the grounds of the Emir's mud palace where the first performance of *The Conference of the Birds* would now take place. But I knew that Brook was also training the group psychologically for the gruelling journey ahead of us.

These are some of the improvisations and disciplines the group worked on:

An actor breathes through a long tube. The breathing turns into sound, and calls. Many birds gather and follow the man on a journey. The birds set off, diving across the carpet like flying fish.

Katsulas sweats and curses as he practises bird movements ugly as a vulture.

'You know the way I should be doing this,' he says to Brook eventually, 'but you're not telling me.'

'I don't,' Brook replied. 'I really don't know the way. But I know one can be found.'

Hours of acrobatic movements follow: new tricks, badly needed.

174

Suddenly, Brook returned to Ted Hughes' *Ogre Show*, considering it for performance in Kano. The show is ripped apart and birds introduced, but the work is slack. 'Look!' snapped Brook. 'We haven't got time to waste in soft thinking. The action must be full of something that makes people *want* to watch. It's the whole core of our work. Here you are sitting in a circle. An African walks by. What does he see? Nothing very positive. It would be all right on television. It's prissy and cute in an English revue manner. But it could really take off! How can we heighten this story? How can we develop and sustain interest? It needs to be clear and strong. It needs to be brought to life! But if there's no exploration, nothing will be found.'

The actors begin again.

Trickster experiment: each member of the group plays an archetype trickster, trying to deceive the others. Brook said to them: 'Imagine in a truthful way something that isn't truthful.'

Extra-sensory exercise: the group makes tiny hand movements while their eyes are closed. Everyone tries to make the same movement, form of thought-transference: doesn't work out that way.

Research question: when the actors go onto the carpet it's possible to see how what passes for highly positive and original acting is really nothing of the kind. In fact, what's happening is a reactive process. As you watch the actors perform under the searchlight you can actually see how something worked on years before in Paris suddenly re-emerges in the middle of Africa. And it's an unconscious happening. In the heat of the moment, a set of memory bells begin to ring. Out of which comes a reminder of a half-forgotten poem by Ted Hughes, which sets off another reminder in another actor, which triggers only another mechanical response from someone else. Therefore, when does the reactive process stop and real acting begin?

Thought of Chairman Brook: how strange that in such an overcrowded profession so many Mrs. Worthingtons want to put their daughters on the stage. When asked his advice he always replies: 'Don't, Mrs. Worthington. Let them be directors instead.'

Universal acting problem: the group has a way of thinking

'intensity' equals 'smallness'. When an actor wants to perform something particularly meaningful, he will lower his voice almost without knowing it. On the other hand, comedy is almost always played loud. It's often so in theatre.

Experiment with the *Romeo and Juliet Bird Show*, fifteen-minute version, doesn't work. The actors seem stifled by the narrative. 'There you are,' Brook said to me. 'Theatre isn't about narrative. Narrative isn't necessary. Events will make the whole.'

I couldn't help replying that theatre isn't about a mangled Shakespearean narrative, with or without words, or birds.

'If so,' added Brook, 'the question has at least been opened. We may not find the answer. But something that was closed has been opened.'

Each day as the new work intensified Brook urged the group to search for greater directness, greater power. Try not to perform describable ideas. Avoid imitation. Watch out for divisions: mind versus body, thought versus action. Search for a way of performing that bursts from inner force: natural life of its own. During the constant workshops, Swados kept saying: 'Try not to *think* what sound you're going to make. Don't even try to make it. Eventually, the sound will make the sound. . . .'

Musicians often 'become' the instrument they're playing. It was so with the Peulh, except in their case the instrument was themselves.

Now Swados got to work on a vital development in the music. With Brook if something works or fails, you change direction just the same. But for different reasons. If it works, it's told you what you want to know. If it fails, it's told you what you want to know but it isn't easy to accept. The musical work was failing again. After the exciting meeting with the Peulh, the gamble of asking the actors to improvise songs for themselves followed naturally. It was a very challenging exercise, forcing them to expand their skills as far as possible. It's surprising: an actor who can sing is a rare phenomenon. So is a singer who can act. And so is an actor or singer who can dance. Such a being is usually known as Ethel Merman. But to ask an actor to compose a song on the spot is virtually asking the impossible. Brook often does this. It's part of his scanning technique. If you shoot for the moon, you might at least get lift-off. The actor is stretched and stretched to the furthest point: impossible mission perhaps. But in the process, his talent will expand. Still, even in the context of Brook's work the improvised songs were premature. Uncertainty and nerves had brought the actors to another crisis.

Now Swados began to compose for them, songs with melody and shape, stories, which would feed the group like the rough script of a show. The songs weren't set, nor were they completely open. But there was no half-way with such music. The actors were forced to go into it as they went into an improvised scene. They'd been given a base. Improvise off the base. Return to base always.

In the process, she entered a treacherous field: sounds that were written, like a language. The songs were for *The Conference of the Birds*. The sounds: bird language. The actors take such things naturally, squawking with delight.

Swados was using a strange lyric based on sounds that Ted Hughes had written for the group. They were, it was rumoured, taken from an almost extinct African language he'd found somewhere or other. Not easy to describe, these sounds. They were . . . unusual. Here's a brief example of one of the lyrics: Song of the Partridge. The 'translation' should be taken only as the roughest of guides. To ask the meaning of a sound is like asking the 'meaning' of music. That's what Brook told me. 'What does it *mean?*' 'What's the meaning of Beethoven?'

TUWONNYILAFWE NUFYAFOFUNWE
Often I find myself between stone and fire
MEGEHAAAAK
inactive and perplexed
O OBEK UKAHAH OKAHOONNIM
O my friends see how I live
AKAHUUUM BEIEEA KAYUM
Is it possible to awaken one
YEHEKEN

177

Who sleeps
GEEYA-ORGA KYEGYA-WYA.
on rocks and eats gravel.

Is it conceivable that beneath the structures of all language can be found the lost primal speech of the universe, God's speech, there, deep in sounds explored so far it's as if a spirit vibrates and speaks? All my instincts deny it. 'PHONEY!' screams the inner voice, embarrassed at this sham straining after 'Intensity' and 'Meaning'. Yet the Peulh silenced such a voice. And when I heard the first hesitant steps towards these tortured sounds and songs there was nothing like it, nothing so astonishing. Birds communicate with each other in gesture and sound, very pure. And the human?

During this breathing space in Kano, period of re-valuation, several old friends turned up out of the blue.

The sticks!

The batch that had been lost in the desert was replaced by a new collection flown in from Paris with all the urgency of a rare blood supply. They were more than old friends. They were lost identities.

Struggling in Kano to recover all their former disciplines, the actors now worked with the sticks for hour after hour on the disused tennis court of the campus. Their arrival was pretty inspired. They were Brook's strange answer to the unspoken question everyone asked him when the group first met in Paris. The unspoken question was, 'Why are we here?' From time to time this developed into, 'Why, oh *why* are we here?' But when the essence of Brook's work is a total lack of anything concrete or final, there can be no immediate answer. Unlike those ancient thrillers where everyone gathers round the mastermind to be told the solution, Brook couldn't give an adequate explanation. In fact, for many months there was no explanation whatsoever. Silence was imposed. And Brook said: 'Let there be sticks.'

In many ways it was part of the shock-treatment for which he's renowned. For instance, he often announces to well-meaning actors that the most vital quality in their work is insincerity. 'Be insincere', he tells them with a smile. For Brook, all that's over-emotional, strangulated, indulgent, everything that stems from the worst excesses of drama school training is frequently a false and sentimental understanding of 'sincere' acting. Told to act insincerely the stunned actor will then collapse in a heap. But he might begin to lose some of his actorishness. So the sticks worked in a similar way—though they cut far, far deeper.

As I watched the actors work with them, the sticks were used simply as exercises in rhythm and timing, agility, balance, speed, and that favourite word of Brook's, awareness. They were the group's common language. The sticks might be used to build an image of a machine so that they're whirled round like the blades of a combine harvester. Each actor must walk through the blades without a stick touching him. Or the actors might use them to balance on their heads, throw from hand to hand, or stretch the body on a rack. But Brook refers to the sticks as neither mechanical nor abstract, but highly personal, intense and emotional objects: human. 'Follow the sticks,' I heard him tell the group in a moment of apparent lunacy. Listen to them. They will lead you.'

How is such an incredible thing possible? It's no coincidence that Yoshi Oida, trained for twenty years in Noh Theatre technique, always leads the group during the stick exercises. In his hands a stick really does take on a mysterious power. It becomes an extension of his body. The more he works on the stick, the more fundamental it becomes. The possibilities become inexhaustible and many combinations are to be made. But it's also clear, and miraculously so at times, that the stick isn't intended to train just the body and the mind. Somehow, the stick can bring both into contact with ultimate reality.

Like all of Brook's exercises, the real aim isn't physical but spiritual. And in every Japanese art form from flower arrangement to master swordsmanship, the ultimate end searched for isn't a facility or technique, an expertise or even an art. The goal is spiritual. So the archer, trained for many years by his all-powerful Zen Master, aims ultimately at hitting himself. The target is there but in truth it's himself. And the master archer can hit the target every time. So certain is he within himself that he can even hit the target without taking aim. It seems impossible and yet hundreds of people have seen it happen. The archer takes his bow and aims the arrow at the target without consciously trying to hit it. He faces the goal but sees it as though it wasn't there. Then without aim or effort, without consciousness or will, without doing or not doing, the arrow hits the target. And 'it' will do it every time.

There's a beautiful little book, a classic called *Zen in the Art of Archery*, which cures one's natural scepticism. The author, Eugen Herrigel, describes the moment when he was so bewildered by his Master's instruction to 'aim without aiming' that he challenged him to a test. If his Master took no conscious aim, then he ought to be able to hit the target blind-folded.

The lights of the practice hall were switched off. It was so dark that not even the outlines of the target could be seen. The Master shot his first arrow and it hit the target. The second arrow was a hit, too. But when the lights were switched on, the pupil found to his amazement that the first arrow was lodged full in the middle of the black. The second arrow had splintered the butt of the first and ploughed through its shaft, embedding itself beside it. 'What do you make of that?' asked the Master. 'I at any rate know that it is not "I" who must be given credit for this shot. "It" shot and "It" made the hit. Let us bow to the goal as before Buddha!'

In a sense, the Master no longer existed. He had 'become' the target. And so Brook's actors struggle to 'become' the stick. 'Listen to it,' says Brook. 'It will lead you.' The group stand in a circle. Every other one of them holds a stick. An actor runs round the inside of the circle, catches the stick thrown to him and instantly throws it to the actor who does not have one. He does it until he can run no more, catching and throwing. But if the exercise is to work, the catching and throwing become one action with scarcely a split second between them. Ultimately, it might seem as if the stick is propelling itself. 'It' throws. 'It' catches. But of course it very rarely works out that way. The exercise more often appears self-conscious and clumsy. The effortlessness that flows from real organic power takes many years to discover.

How the supreme gifts of the master archer become 'spiritual' isn't open to the group. Brook is no Zen Master and Yoshi Oida's lessons are limited. But sometimes the actors do approach a pitch of such control and intensity that your eyes would be opened. And it's the point of the exercise. Another of their stick movements is based on Samurai swordsmanship. The actors practise a movement in which defence and attack should happen as one. Between perceiving the intended thrust and evading it, there shouldn't be a hair's breadth. The master swordsman will possess such miraculous alertness in all his senses that he actually 'sees' the blow before it is struck. But the movement is new to the group and they fail to make it time after time. It seems they will never learn how to do it and the likelihood is that they never will. But the fundamental principle behind this one tortuous movement cuts across Brook's entire work.

'It' defends. 'It' strikes. Even to begin to approach this ideal the actor must transform his whole being. Ordinary stage skills and vanity will not help him. He must lose his ego. His body must become air. The movement must flow so irresistibly and with such awesome certainty that it seems to happen by itself. Like the lightning brush strokes of a great painter, the movements of a conductor, the sound of a Peulh or the thrust of a master swordsman, the whole of him will become one. Such a state, reached without effort or conscious will, inevitable, a spirit, is called 'the artless art'. And for Brook it is the ultimate.

Yes, a stick can be 'human'.

But if there are a hundred stages to the ultimate state I would guess that the actors are not yet beyond the tenth.

As for myself, during this period in Kano I began work on two more shows. My diary says, 'Got up. Wrote a show. Had a siesta. Wrote another.' Several days later the diary says, 'I know when Brook doesn't like my shows. He doesn't do them. . . .' The first was called *The Man-Woman Show*, which was about Man discovering this thing called Woman. It was a male chauvinistic farce with tragic undertones. The second show was my millionth attempt at a version of *The Bread Show*. But it was hopeless. I wasn't getting anywhere because I couldn't discover how to write a play without using dialogue. Also, I didn't think I was being unreasonable. It's like trying to write a ballet. You might come up with a story or useful idea or a startling image, but so might anyone else. Without language, words, the very thing that enables the writer to make his special contribution, you've cut off his blood supply.

Whenever I talked about this with Brook, he replied: 'Ah, the Writers Union strikes *again*.' And maybe he's right. Perhaps writers tend to regard themselves as the absolute rulers of theatre, to be 'served' by director and actor alike. If you want an illustration of pain, you've only to glance at a playwright during rehearsals. He's the one holding the placard, 'My work is being CRUCIFIED.' But in Brook's non-verbal form of theatre it's difficult to see the playwright's function. The actor finds other means of expression beyond traditional language: his body and sound. The composer is central to the work. But the playwright?

Even if Ted Hughes' experimental approach to language in *Orghast* could be counted a success (which is debatable) no performance was ever a spontaneous improvisation, and couldn't have been. The new sound-language was written to be repeated. There was a script. But the moment you move into improvisation, written sounds must become irrelevant. Quite simply, the actor doesn't know what he's going to say. It's why even conventional dialogue is no use to him if it's written in advance. He's improvising. The writer might help out with a repertoire of sounds to be used in basic situations. But at best they'll be limited, perhaps to the lyric of a song. More often than not, the actor soon runs dry and ends up speaking gibberish. In terms of creating image or story, the writer has a clear role to play whatever the form of theatre. But I felt that sounds could come from only one primary source: the actor himself.

Also, I remembered the stunning performance of the ancient griot. Because he used ordinary language and it seemed the only possible way of getting on terms with such a vast audience. Slang, in-jokes, local references, argot—no sound could hope to capture their special quality. Perhaps that's a price you pay in non-verbal theatre. Perhaps another price is a less crucial role for the playwright. Or a different role: more a poet-musician.

I struggled on with the scripts, depressed by them and other doubts. As I watched the group work for hour after hour behind the closed doors of the campus the difference between theory and practice seemed immense. So much theory! So many conferences! One could almost write a book about them. The more Brook slogged on talking and experimenting and analysing into the night, the more dispirited I became. How strange it seemed that the best work was often done in private. What happened to them when they got in front of an audience? No amount of theory and analysis could help them, or so it seemed at the time.

I was once lucky enough to meet the great sculptor Henry Moore and remembered asking him if he knew how a work of art was actually created. But he replied that with much of his work he didn't know how it happened. Had he read Erich Neumann's psychological study of his sculptures? Neumann was Jung's favourite disciple. But Moore had stopped reading it during the first chapter. He didn't want to know what made him tick as an artist or how his art actually happened. Because if he knew, he might try to prove or disprove it. But there was one analytical book he had read on the creative process—Freud on Leonardo. Freud makes out that the childhood accident of an eagle swooping into Leonardo's cot and almost carrying him away explains all sorts of things in his development and art. But Moore pointed out that Freud doesn't say that if this had happened to another child it would have turned them into a Leonardo.

I remembered this and thought: 'Artists are born. Brook would have to be God to create them.'

'It's good,' I said to him after another exhausting workshop. 'The research is good. Yet I can't help feeling all this is sort of *hopeless*. . . .'

'Then tell me,' he replied instantly, 'if a man wishes to reach his full potential, what's the greatest obligation on him?'

Obligation?

'Who puts it on him?' I asked.

'He does,' Brook replied.

'He doesn't want an easy life?'

'He wants a fulfilled life.'

'Then the obligation', I imagined, 'is to try and find it.'

'But why do you say such a thing if you believe all this is hopeless?'

'In the hope that it isn't.'

'Faith,' said Brook.

16

Although we couldn't have suspected it at the time, the special performance in Kano was destined to go down in history.

It took place on New Year's Eve, which was nice. We would ring out the Old and ring in the New.

I was still aged thirty in those days.

The day before the show Brook kept working for nineteen hours. I counted them. It was definitely a record even by his standards. After exercises first thing in the morning, the group drove to the Emir's mud palace and worked there until the early hours the following day. We were closer now to the more traditional theatre world of urgency and excitement, costumes, deadlines, technical rehearsals, a *performance*. The group was to play in the open courtyard, big enough to hold as many as a thousand people. After all the weeks on the road it seemed an unlikely setting. Arc lamps had been brought in when darkness fell, transforming the open-air theatre into the bizarre and weary atmosphere of a film set. We were miles away from the natural life of the villages and perhaps I resented it. In this unexpected new world of tangled cables and bright lights, busy technicians and yawning spectators, I half expected to see a movie camera and hear Brook shout '*Action!*' He did in a way. But the day was clammy and endless, with little food except nuts and warm lemonade—a relief when Brook called a halt at last and we could sleep.

At the eleventh hour, he'd suddenly changed his mind about the programme. There would now be the most ambitious performance of the journey. First, a surprise move—extracts from Ted Hughes' revolutionary sound-spectacle, *Orghast*. Then the group would try the first tentative scenes from the big piece, *The Conference of the Birds*. All day and into the night the air was filled with screams and unearthly sound, frightening, from hidden worlds, birds and half-human creatures.

But the night of the performance, this gala evening, no one seemed to be turning up.

Half an hour before the show was scheduled to begin only a handful of spectators arrived, strolling into the grounds of the mud palace like stray cats. The loyal Professor Crowder was there with a few earnest dons, several students, clusters of bewildered children. The actors were slumped around the palace ramparts, forlorn figures chewing nuts in their spotless white costumes.

Eventually a young Hausa woman proposed marriage to Brook who, not wishing to cause offence, accepted graciously. '*Money!*' snapped his new wife, shooting out her hand.

One of the dons was an anthropologist from England, a round and furry man, like a Womble of Wimbledon. I whiled away the delay with him. 'Nigeria is the only country where I've seen people reading Shakespeare for pleasure,' he told me. 'Shakespeare and Tarzan.' Then he laughed. Yug, yug, yug. A coffee-percolator laugh, threatening explosion. 'Of course, you realize they'll boo you off if you aren't any good. . . .'

Not without an audience they wouldn't. Where *was* the audience?

I consulted my invaluable guide-book, *How To Be A Nigerian*, and there was the answer—

'When you summon a Nigerian, saying to him: "Will you please come in a minute?" he will say to you, "I'm coming." But in fact, he's not moving. What he really means is that he will join you as soon as he can—which may be ages. Therefore, the answer is a compromise between outright rejection and rushing over to see you.'

We waited.

But still no one came. Brook went into urgent consultation with Professor Crowder, who seemed amused by the misunderstanding. A Nigerian, he explained, only moves when he senses action. If you want an audience, you must begin a show without one.

It seemed more than reasonable at the time. You just save the

186

best bits till later. Brook was taking no chances, however, and sent out Ayansola to round up a crowd with his talking drum. Ayansola's drum speaks Yoruba, so the general effect must have been limited with the Hausas. He was up against a language barrier. Still, he did his best—whacking his drum with a sound and fury ferocious enough to wake the dead. 'LISTEN! I know you don't understand a word I'm talking about but *please* come and see the show, not that I give a damn personally. . . .' He was having a great time, private jam session, zapping the message to the people. And they began to drift along. And as soon as *Orghast* started, more and more people followed the sounds and shrieks echoing out through the ancient city.

And came to see the show.

The group hadn't performed *Orghast* since their visit a year before to Persia and the ruins of Persepolis. In Africa they re-learnt their sounds with the dedication of Shakespearean actors learning their lines. But the critics who gathered in Persia for the great and long-awaited event were outraged and staggered. Some accused Brook of pretension and false mystification, assessing the new sound-language as even more narrow and élitist than the conventional theatre. In search of a language open to everyone, Brook and Hughes had succeeded only in building another blockade. Others saw the experiment differently. For them, eyes had been opened on a dark dream-world of ritual and myth, awesome in its force. The extraordinary sounds tunnelled beneath the intellect and local cultures to touch and shatter the deepest sensibilities. Perhaps a universal language of theatre was in its beginnings. . . .

In Persepolis, *Orghast* was played largely for the sophisticated theatre intelligentsia and even those who didn't like it were respectful. But in Kano, the audience was this wonderfully vivid mixture of street salesmen and giggling children, of local characters and heroes, market women and withdrawn intellectuals, politicians, dons, singers and dancers, the rowdy townsfolk, an Elizabethan quality perhaps, but an atmosphere simmering with more possibilities than any these actors had known. It was simple.

If *Orghast* didn't work, it would get the bird. When Brook's actors launched into the performance, it was everything they wanted most and feared most: moment of truth.

And the audience laughed.

When they heard those dark primordial cries and shrieks for the first time, they laughed. Looking on the bright side, I didn't think it was a form of ridicule. I think they mistook the story of the fire myths of the ancient world for a comedy. Or *Planet of the Apes*. They were convulsed with laughter. They were glad they came.

Outside the walls of the mud palace a rival *Orghast* group wailed and cried making its point. Satirists! The real actors kept going. And so did the rival group. But within minutes the sounds within the walls began to stretch and grow and gain incredible force. Vibrating. It was as if the air was vibrating. And now that mysterious world of gods and spirits took hold of the audience. And silenced it.

Magic!

There was magic then.

And then there was history.

Just when Professor Crowder was whispering to Brook that he'd never known a Hausa audience so hushed and attentive, people began to double up with laughter again. Malick Bagayogo, playing the God of Darkness, had hit on a word. The word, it was more a sound that he sang, was 'Bullorga torga'. But the instant he said it, these terrible snorts of laughter started to crack the precious silence. At first they were stifled, as if the audience couldn't quite believe what was happening. For a moment I thought maybe Bagayogo's trousers had fallen down, or worse— begun to. But then he repeated the word and the place exploded. 'BULLORGA TORGA!' And now the audience was anticipating it, and sure enough the word came out again as if by remote control. 'OH BULLORGA TORGA!' shrieked Bagayogo, rising magnificently above the tumult. But that audience was *hysterical*. 'Bullorga torga', a word invented by Ted Hughes, happens to be very similar to the Hausa slang for cunt.

In the gravity of the moment Bagayogo was wailing on about

188

cunts. He couldn't stop. He repeated the dread word not once or twice, but five times. And the final time, he was so angry and defiant he dredged up every last ounce of energy to scream out the word with such amazing force that it must surely silence the terrible laughter. 'OH CUUUUUUUUUUUNT!' And so history was made.

When I asked Malick why in God's name he didn't get on to another word, he looked most indignant. *'Mais c'est dans le texte!'* The actor trained for so long in the arts of improvisation had stuck to the script. I think Ted Hughes would have been proud of him in a way. At any rate, Hughes had triumphed again. In *Orghast* language his word for light is 'hoan'. It was a completely blind invention but when the group went to Persia he discovered it meant ray of light in the Persian language of Farsi. His word for 'Woman of Light' is 'Ussa'. It turned out to be the same word for dawn in Sanskrit. And the famous 'bullorga torga'? When Hughes invented the word 'bullorga' he had in mind the word for 'darkness'—the darkness that exists inside a body. I don't know about 'torga'.

After that, we were friends for life with the people of Kano, and the first performance of *The Conference of the Birds* could scarcely go wrong. At first amused and astonished, the audience was eventually won over by the strange journey of human birds and gave the actors a fine reception.

Brook looked unusually happy.

After the show, the good Professor Crowder threw a New Year's Eve party for us in a mirage home miraculously spirited away from literary Hampstead where we wolfed down ice-cold beer and peppered *shashlik* so hot it leaves you gasping for air. 'All actors are the same', goes a line in a movie I saw one time. 'How do you know?' 'Have you ever seen them *eat*?' We all ate greedily, as if coming out of starvation diets. 'Any more peppered *shashlik* going?' 'And what *is* the essence of your work?' asked the dignitaries and dons. 'Any more MEAT?'

But the whole essence of the work was there in the shows that night.

Nothing revealed more of what Brook wants from theatre. For the two performances were a symbol. And a key.

The first year's work led to *Orghast*: first part of the evening.

The second year's work led to *The Conference of the Birds:* second part.

The first year was a search for myths and archetypes, sounds and forms that touched the power beneath the surface, call it 'the collective unconscious'. But the second year was an attempt to discover something much freer and simpler—a show that could achieve all that *Orghast* set out to, but with a simplicity that could be enjoyed by a child.

The crucial part of the spectrum missing from *Orghast* was the more exuberant and popular qualities of all the rough improvised carpet shows which led up to *The Conference of the Birds*. After the first part of *Orghast* in Persepolis, a critic asked Brook if there would be any laughs in the second part. (He should have been in Kano.) But Brook replied, 'No, in the third part.' The point is, there wasn't a third part to *Orghast*. In Brook's scheme of things, the third part was to be *The Conference of the Birds*.

For many people *Orghast* was quite staggering in its scope. But for Brook it turned out to be too narrow and restrictive: too 'high'. The lower levels were missing. By 'lower' he means simply the scope that never excludes the possibility of many different responses. It's the essence of his work. Theatre must encompass the vast range of the Elizabethan experience—an experience packed and bursting with high and low qualities, serious and comic, élitist and popular. Every one of Brook's theories goes towards this central aim: the quality of density. And the one question he asks more than any other is just this: how is it possible to make plays rich in experience? For Brook, it is the whole problem of theatre today.

The real lesson of the performances of *Orghast* and *The Conference of the Birds* was the difference between a closed form of theatre and one that's trying to be open to everyone. It's the difference between rarefied aesthetic traps of myths and Greek tragedy, of the High Seriousness which goes with ancient and new languages, compared with the power and naïvety of an image which might be as simple as a bird emerging from an ordinary carboard box. For in that apparently mundane action might exist such directness and force, the spectator is suddenly involved on all levels of meaning. Such a form isn't the prisoner of aesthetic pre-conditioning. If Brook can discover it, the form which gives expression to his ideal theatre will encompass everything from our deepest sense of myth to the slapstick of a circus. More important than anything, such a theatre would be open to everyone regardless of background or class. There might be a real chance that at last the élitist barriers will fall.

So where are you now, Tom Stoppard?

And the answer is alive and well and contemplating the realistic. (You see, we playwrights do what we can.) Except that for Brook it isn't good enough. Time and again he returns to his pet theory that the work of contemporary artists is a product of the diluted and less imaginative urban life of the West. In a society of so much social decay and chaos, all that theatre can really affirm is a world in darkness. Even a giant such as Beckett, though greatly admired by Brook, is seen to possess a narrow vision. For myself, the whole of life is in that man. But for Brook, the play that can bring new and irresistible life to theatre will be so rich and diverse in experience that the special qualities of a Beckett become only a single part. When you say to Brook that such a fantastic ideal is impossible to achieve, he replies: 'Of course.' And carries on as if you haven't spoken.

Even then, you can't be sure. 'The moment you arrive anywhere,' Brook likes to say, 'you limit the distance you might have travelled.' But in Kano, the way at least seemed clearer now— as if one had grasped the real meaning of the work for the first time. What seemed clearer than anything was this whole tangled area that is so difficult in our lives: simplicity. Somehow I felt that I understood what Brecht must have meant when he told Brook his real term for theatre would be 'Theatre of Naïvety'. Within the simplest of forms all worlds must meet. The simplicity must be transparent. Perhaps one could rename it 'Theatre of Innocence'.

Brook has a symbol for such a theatre. It's a circle. A cat, a child and a sage can all play with a circle in their own way, finding in it whatever they want.

But you must invent the theatrical form of the circle first.

Well, it took us 345,000 years to invent the *wheel*.

And that's the catch. It's natural to want results, results now! But the nature of Brook's work is to edge step by step towards this ultimate expression of life and theatre, and perhaps you might glimpse it here and there until you're suddenly thrown back into the dark where you began, and even further back, and the task seems hopeless. It's difficult to cope with. And it's known as 'Work in Progress'. The term—it's become devalued of late—conveniently forestalls all conventional criticism. If the goal isn't yet reached, nothing is complete. If nothing is complete, it isn't open to final judgement. And when it is open to final judgement, it's too late. In such a way Brook might end up like Voltaire on his death-bed when he was asked to retract his lifetime's work and philosophy. He declined with the words, 'It's a little late in the day to start making enemies now. . . .'

At least, it isn't difficult to see how this device of 'Work in Progress' goes against the nature of things. Brook would ask me constantly to be patient and 'suspend judgement'. But the man who can do that would have to be a machine, or a groupie. There were times in the context of Brook's long-evolving work when it was a real struggle not to judge a show for what it was. Not for what it might be, but for what it *was*. In Kano I watched the shows as if examining two different specimens through a microscope. And the results were encouraging: something invaluable about the whole nature of the work had shown itself. But in truth, the reverse side of the picture was very different. In the general euphoria that followed the performance I seemed to be alone in judging the first *Conference of the Birds* a bitter disappointment. It was as if another voice was saying to me, 'Wait a minute! It was *rotten*.' And when the voice is outnumbered, it nags.

The performance I saw wasn't of *The Conference of the Birds*. I saw something else, maybe *The Bird Show*. But the whole point of the classic fable was missing: submerged. The doubts and conflicts of the birds deciding to commit themselves to the long journey ahead of them, all the allegories and stories which answer them, the symbolic struggle across the seven valleys from the Valley of Quest to the Valley of Deprivation and Death, search for ultimate union with truth and God—none of it was there. The masterpiece on which a whole year's work was based had been lost. When it came to its first performance, the 'mysticism' of the birds had been merely imposed. The audience enjoyed what it saw. But without ever meaning to, perhaps without ever knowing it, the group had produced a fake.

Yet when I told Brook my view of the performance, to my surprise he agreed. This was the first shot at *The Conference of the Birds*—not the moment for his customary teach-in with the actors. Besides, they had played with great discipline. But in private, Brook came clean. It couldn't be denied that the performance had scarcely begun to approach the special qualities of the book. In time I would understand how difficult it was. But as always, he replied with a question. He wanted to know what I thought about the opening of the show.

The opening had been stunning in its power. As the birds gathered for the first time, there in sound and movement was something unique and riveting. But the opening lasted only two minutes.

'Two minutes,' I said. 'Could be less.'

'I *know*,' Brook replied, as if time wasn't the point.

'It took a year's work to get those two minutes.'

'In a way,' he replied cheerfully, 'it took two years.'

'A minute a year.'

'Yes.'

'And you're saying it's worth it?'

'Yes.'

'But why?'

'I think we've seen the future.'

Then he closed this chapter of the journey by telling me a short anecdote which illustrates everything he means by beginning again and progress. Perhaps the story is the more meaningful because it's true.

At the height of the '68 student revolution in Paris almost every theatre group in France was left with a great wish to change everything. But one director decided this was the moment to go from theory to action. Instead of staying in Paris, he decided to escape the whole climate of talk and revolution, and make a fresh start. He took his group to Geneva and for a year they prepared themselves for the task ahead. Each day, the actors worked in private on different exercises and self-examination until the time was right to take more positive action. They decided to build the theatre in which they were to work. They would build it themselves.

The project was costly, in the region of £150,000. But some of the group were wealthy and they pooled their resources, raising the rest of the money elsewhere. The design of the theatre was like a spaceship, a five-hundred-seat completely metal structure in the form of a giant dome standing on iron struts. It was to be a portable theatre, a modern travelling circus.

For amateur builders to undertake a structure of this ambition in wood and brick would be beyond almost everyone. But to attempt to build it in metal would seem impossible. The group was determined, however. And so they set about learning their new trade. After a further two years, they mastered every technique. With no help from the outside, the actors were able to build this magnificent steel and aluminium dome, their theatre. In all it took them more than three years to build.

Then they returned to France. In an area that's part of the thriving new industrial Paris was a wasteland, and there the theatre was erected again. But within weeks the entire group disintegrated.

Through the most wonderful showing of human qualities the actors had created something miraculous. But when they came to fill it with life, they had built a lie. And it destroyed them. The outward symbol of their dedication had gone so far beyond their real possibilities as actors that the building couldn't be used by them. The all-purpose, anonymous structure was too vast. It had to become a mere public amenity. Soon there was talk of other visiting companies, film and pop shows, until the small experimental group in search of a new future became more and more conventional. They became impresarios, left to animate the shell that had overtaken their ideals. The passionate undertaking had lost all its purpose. The achievement is undeniable and yet the catastrophe was inevitable. So anxious were the actors to make their unique contribution they succeeded only in digging their own graves.

For Brook, the story of good intentions illustrates how much more than meets the eye there is in all these questions of new beginnings. And it exists on every conceivable level. The man who wishes to transform his personality or build a group or break with The Old cannot take anything for granted. A real beginning again is something so difficult to grasp it cannot skip one single step, however insignificant it may seem. The most provisional and tentative theatre space would have been the true expression of this group's needs. To the outsider it would not have appeared impressive. But in time their theatre would have changed and developed, transforming itself as a tiny seed eventually takes root and grows. In the name of progress you can easily overreach yourself, easily fool yourself. The seed takes root slowly and its progress is almost imperceptible. You must take every care. The New that emerges from The Old will not happen overnight. Progress, the real progress that edges its way out of the unknown, never follows as easily as day follows night.

17

Now as we left Kano and pressed deep into Nigeria one disaster followed another until the way ahead of us was lost.

If the Zen patriarch answers a foolish question by whacking his pupil over the head, there's a more lethal response in his power—the power of silence. When the pupil really puts his foot in it the revered master turns his back and will not speak again. And in a manner of speaking, that's just what the audiences in their role of teacher-critic did to us now. They do it as gently as they can. But actors sometimes 'die'. How did it go? 'We *died*.' And their plays with them.

On the other hand, it's axiomatic in Brook's dogged approach to every aspect of his work that failure doesn't actually exist. I don't think I've even heard him use the word. Failure can be a positive force and the group learns from it. Failure is progress. This is what the work does to you. It makes you crazy.

Perhaps it's my nature, but I believe there's a more traditional side to failure. This is the failure that really fails. Within that there can be found no hope it is so oppressive, so hopeless. Perhaps in one sense almost all works of art are failures. Unable to reach the ultimate expression of his dreams and hopes, the artist falls short of them, destroying the very ideal he aspires to. But there's also the failure which is simply so strong and depressing, no good will come of it and no future can be seen. In this darkness people crack and despair, seeing no escape. And this failure awaited us too.

The shock of the first disaster was the more traumatic because it was so unexpected.

Throughout the journey there was no other occasion when the group felt more certain of success. It was a mystery in a sense. It's like the battle-weary boxers say, 'Everything depends how you wake up on the morning of the fight.' The group woke up feeling good. We had returned to the famous *Shoe Show* and thought it a world-beater. Hence the other boxing expression, 'What hit us?' But for the first time in the journey, work on the show had sprung to real life as the actors tried it out before a performance in the fields outside Kano. I had rewritten the scenario again, building the show around the marvellous comic talents of the American-Greek giant, Katsulas. He told me once that if you asked him to be serious about anything he couldn't resist sending it up. Brook wouldn't have forgiven me, but I was anxious for things to go well and said to Katsulas: 'Listen, and listen good. This is a very big secret. *The Shoe Show* is really a tragedy. . . .' I'm not saying it was a direct cause or anything but when the actors tried the new script, Katsulas had the rest of us convulsed with laughter.

Looking at the show as objectively as I could, I honestly felt it might have gone down pretty well almost anywhere. It always amused Brook when I used to ask him, 'Yes, but how would it go down in New York—or Rome?' You see, we were in the African bush and conventional rewards not quite the point. But the show had its moments now. It was basically for children and though a sage wouldn't have found too much in it, even a sage can laugh. The rough rehearsal was wonderfully relaxed and inventive and, yes, we felt good. I thought we couldn't really fail, which for the most part was the exact opposite of anything I'd felt before. Brook looked confident enough, whispering advice and jokes in my ear as the actors improvised new scenes and Katsulas played *King Lear* for laughs. Brook told me a tale of a Bunuel movie he'd seen in New York. It was about a shoe fetishist. But the fetish ruins the hero's life. He just can't get shoes out of his system. So one day he goes to the only man left who might be able to help him—the priest. 'Oh dear,' says the priest eventually. 'I wouldn't like to be in your shoes.'

Before the show I drove with Brook to search for a good place to play. He chose the villages haphazardly, though there were now several rules about size and playing areas and the number of people who might attend. Often a child would translate for us or guide Brook to better locations. One village was too large and noisy: too worldly. 'It's the Chalfont St. Giles of Nigeria,' said Brook, ploughing on through lush pastures in search of another village.

At one, a British-made machine was grinding nuts into peanut butter inside a mud hut. The owner was proud of the machine and showed it me. Then his wife took the liquid away in a gourd, carrying it on her head.

Another village was built by a busy road and didn't have a playing area large enough. One of the elders shook our hands and pointed across the fields. There we found a collection of hamlets walled with stalks of golden guinea corn. Within each hamlet lived one family, brothers and cousins and aunts, in four or five huts built close together. There was no natural centre, but we were led into the open fields where a great mango tree shielded us from the hot afternoon sun. We would play there. It was a marvellous rural setting away from the bustle of the city. There were silk and palm trees surrounding millet stacked like hay, for it was harvest time. The air was sweet. Like so many of the settings, this seemed the place to be.

When we arrived for the show a horseman galloped at top speed from hamlet to hamlet announcing our arrival. Others arrived on battered bicycles. A smart *shashlik* seller set up a stall in the hope of quick business. Children stared and ran, always ran.

What did we symbolize to them?

There were so few spectators that we waited for a long time under the mango tree. The sun was hot and sleepy. We were already swigging from water bottles kept cool by wrapping them in damp cloth, a desert trick. Several actors stretched yawning in the guinea corn as Brook filmed the scene with his ciné camera. But his young son Simon was pacing about, agitated. He'd been promised a part in the show and, anxious to start, blew farts on a trumpet. Eventually Ayansola tried to gather a crowd with his talking drum, but felt so languid it was as if his drum was talking in slow motion. Few people came. Beads of sweat dripped down my forehead as I blinked through the sun and struggled to keep awake.

No more than thirty spectators had drifted round the carpet, and remembering the maxim that Nigerians only move when they sense action Brook at last ordered the show to begin. But the gentle musical section which opened the show fell flat. Yet it seemed okay to us. Then the songs that followed were greeted in silence. What was going on? The actors looked blank, sinking. Swados was vaguely hysterical. 'I've made a discovery!' cried Brook after another song died. 'Music is the least universal language there is. . . .'

He meant the group was still rooted in Western culture or the new musical influences of the Tuareg and Peulh. But what matter here? The gulf between the actors and the small silent audience was as wide as a canyon.

'Acrobatics!' ordered Brook, as a captain keeping a stiff upper lip calls for the lifeboats when the ship is about to sink. One of these days, I thought to myself, we're going to hit an iceberg. That's what they thought on the *Titanic*. But as always happened the sudden eruption of life brought the first cheers and warmth from the audience, and expectancy. In such a way events can prove deceptive.

The crowd had now grown to more than a hundred, as if by magic.

The Shoe Show came next as Katsulas the Giant strode confidently onto the carpet. Maybe a gambling man would have shortened the odds of success now. Swados the Witch has a sixth sense about these things, foreseeing doom. But I thought at worst the show hung in the balance. It would go one way or the other, I decided. But then almost without exception everything in the show, every single event and happening, every improvisation, every sure-fire routine, every joke, every trick, everything, everything failed. I couldn't believe my eyes. The show we had thought so direct and simple was greeted with total and horrifying bewilderment. The same show, the universal language show that all of us including Brook had been so confident about, was the biggest disaster of the journey.

For Katsulas who was stuck in every scene, hard though he tried from time to time to make a dignified exit, the experience was shattering. It was to take him literally weeks to recover from it. Stranded on the carpet, it was as if he were living out the worst of all actor nightmares. Every actor dreams about forgetting his lines. He's alone on an empty stage, speechless. It's the same nightmare as the concert pianist playing the silent piano. But for wretched, dying Katsulas the dream had come true. As one scene after another was greeted not with derision or disinterest but with this terrible crucifying silence, he was helpless. Trying all he knew to hold the show together, the only reaction he managed to get from the crowd was the one that finished him. Without meaning to, this huge and gentle man terrified the children. No matter what he did the children always scattered, and ran away.

For a split second Katsulas caught my eye. 'You were *right*. This is a tragedy.' But then in the panic and desperation he did something amazing. He began to use language. Suddenly, he was talking and babbling in non-stop English. Unfortunately, we were in a Hausa-speaking village at the time. But Katsulas had returned to the only safety net that was left: words. In Brook's non-verbal theatre, he had reversed the actor's traditional nightmare. Instead of forgetting his lines, he remembered them.

'Anyone care to join me?' he asked the rest of the actors sitting stunned round the carpet.

As Yoshi Oida tried to help out I glanced in Brook's direction, but he was now in urgent consultation with his son. Simon Brook was about to make his guest appearance.

During the show Katsulas always tried to get rid of the shoes near the end, throwing them away over the heads of the crowd. But one of the actors always lobbed them back. Katsulas would throw them away again, and back they came. This time, Simon Brook would return the shoes personally. Brook was secretly directing him to do no more than walk slowly towards Katsulas and hold out the shoes. He mustn't say a word. Also, he mustn't get the giggles.

Ahead of schedule, Katsulas threw away the shoes. 'I want a

wee!' whispered Simon Brook, hopping up and down. 'Well you can't!' cried his father. 'You're *on*.'

Katsulas was looking up at the sky awaiting the return of the shoes. 'They'll be here any second,' he announced. 'Any second NOW.' When Simon Brook made his entrance, 'Oh, no!' cried Katsulas, nonplussed for the moment. 'Not *you*. I can't take any more. Go away! This is your uncle Andreas speaking. Go away and wipe that horrendous smile off your face.' Determined not to speak or laugh, Simon Brook had cemented his face in this vile twisted smile, a smile of pure evil. And the harder he smiled the more evil he became. 'GO AWAY!' But Katsulas fell silent. The young child kept walking slowly towards him, and held out the shoes. Suddenly, the unexpected event began to go far beyond mere charm. It was as if the child wasn't acting. Somehow we were compelled to watch, it was so truthful. And for the first time the silent audience responded and understood. The child in his innocence had done what all the others with their fine acting skills couldn't do. If only for a few moments he had shown us the nature of simplicity.

Then it was lost and he laughed and giggled now and danced in the magic shoes.

The Chief of the village, a dignified and frail old man, was introduced to Brook before we left. The Chief leaned on his staff and thanked us for our kind visit. Others laughed good-naturedly, as did Brook. The people of the village were as confused and embarrassed as we were. The Chief tugged at his white goatee beard as if there was little else to be said.

'Could you tell us what you have seen?' asked Brook, looking bashful.

The Chief paused to consult with several others.

'We have seen something about a pair of shoes.'

The sense of relief could be felt on both sides.

'We have seen shoes change people in some way.'

'In what way?' asked Brook.

'It is all I can say,' replied the Chief, 'and I do not think anyone else could say more.'

The Chief, we knew it, was a diplomat. Then he shook our hands and left for evening prayer.

I do not know why one audience should be so different from another or why some should seem so special. The people here were good and kind, and yet their reaction had been devastating. There was no malice in them. They weren't an obviously tough audience. They had never seen a piece of theatre before, and anxious to see it welcomed us with open arms. And yet the sense of rejection was the most total we were to meet throughout the entire journey.

Usually after such a disaster the group would have been utterly depressed and drained of self-confidence. Yet it was just as strange that it didn't quite turn out this way. With the exception of the shattered Katsulas the actors were unusually reflective, trying hard to fathom what it was that could have gone as wrong as this. Their energy had been low in the hot sun, the acting had been cluttered and uncertain—but none of the usual criticisms seemed relevant. The disaster had been of such a special kind that it was as if the people were offering a form of guidance. It often struck us this way. We knew that the rejection of the people cut deep into the work: too deep for comfort. And it's why failure might eventually be seen as progress.

What had gone wrong? Like the actors, I couldn't fathom why the show failed so miserably. Everything had seemed right. We'd never felt so confident. The show really did seem to work. Yet when it came to it, the harsh truth to be swallowed was the simple undeniable fact that the audience couldn't understand what the hell we were supposed to be doing. And what now of Brook's universal language? I just couldn't make the failure out. But Brook could. . . . Far from being discouraged by the reaction, he was the reverse. In fact he seemed to be fascinated by the entire disaster. It was irritating in a way. Everyone's hit for six except for this one excited little man who's saying, 'But can't you *see*?' Brook knew exactly what had gone wrong, and nailed it.

'Why are the shoes magic?' he asked me unexpectedly. It was the kind of Brook question that you know instinctively goes to

the heart of the matter. But it doesn't necessarily help.
'Pardon?'
'Why are the shoes magic?'
'Well, they change people. It's like the Chief says.'
'Yes, but why?'
'Because they change people,' I could only repeat.
'I know,' Brook replied again. 'But *why*?'
And the more I thought about it the more I began to think there's no sane reason on earth why a pair of shoes should change anyone. It was just the answer Brook was waiting for. And at last I understood.

We'd missed the obvious.

Attempting to create a universal language, the show had been built entirely round a theatre convention of the West. This is the convention which takes it for granted that shoes can transform people, bringing luck and disaster, the popular folk reference on which so many children's stories are based. I'd seen too many pantomimes. But the African villagers hadn't, or any form of theatre as we know it. The audience couldn't understand what was happening because it couldn't share the convention. How simple everything seemed now! In spite of all our attempts at directness and simplicity we were still skipping the steps, taking short cuts to dramatic effects that could have little meaning here. We were still trapped in restricted art forms that made sense only to ourselves, which is why the rehearsal of the show was a success and the performance a failure. Offer an audience a theatre convention it doesn't understand and the lie will be given to the convention. It will become what it is, no more than a device: a cliché. And so one begins again.

And exactly the same lesson was true for the actors. An old hag puts on a pair of shoes and is transformed into a princess. It's obvious: the shoes must be magic. But without explanation or the use of language the event becomes a puzzle to anyone unschooled in the make-believe process. Unless the actor can somehow establish something totally honest, real simplicity and directness will always escape him. He can't rely on shared assumptions. He will be forced to do something incredibly

203

difficult: create the assumption for himself. If he can do that, he will have discovered truth.

An actor tries to portray an old man and so stoops, walking with difficulty. We would recognize the character instantly. But the African villager might see something entirely different. Why should he see an old man? He might see someone making an interesting physical movement or imagine him carrying a heavy object. An actor at one moment walking upright stoops and coughs. But the African villager might genuinely believe he's been taken ill. Katsulas portraying a timid man transformed into a giant lunges at the audience, as giants tend to do. But the adults look bewildered and the children scatter. Perhaps they see a stranger in their midst who walks across a carpet and for no apparent reason goes mad. But whatever interpretation you put on the reaction, they can't really understand what's happening. And they're right not to. So the actor must break with his own habits and clichés, and begin again.

'Draw back to leap', goes the saying. But how far? At so many points in the journey I had promised myself never to take anything for granted. Enter a void. . . . It doesn't happen so easily and such promises become as empty as New Year resolutions, however well-intentioned. All of us were aware of the danger of convention and habit before the journey began, and none more so than Brook. Yet time and again we were trapped by them. What else could we have expected? What pain and sacrifice to reach the obvious! Yet the 'living knowledge' that Brook speaks of transforms theory little by little into a very different awareness. Then you really do begin to understand what it is like to enter a void and begin again. Perhaps it's an illusion, and yet the way suddenly seems clear. Almost without noticing it, too much had been assumed and taken for granted. We had travelled this far only to discover that we must return to zero again. We must go back to that first simple performance in the desert town of In Salah. But perhaps it would be a better beginning again this time. For there it had been a celebration of innocence and the void had been entered innocently.

'I don't understand,' said Andreas Katsulas after his sad performance. 'I'm a simple man yet I failed to communicate with simple people.' Was he really such a simple man? No, he knew it wasn't true. The real simplicity belonged to the people who couldn't understand him. And it belongs to the child.

Why was it, I asked Brook, that the only truthful moment we had seen came from his six-year-old child?

'It's extraordinary,' he replied, 'but a child can do something the adult actor finds so very difficult. It's impossible for a child to act in a complex way. What you receive with a great feeling of joy is the whole of his being completely believing and living every moment—not because he's told to, but because he can't do otherwise. It's why children are a tremendous challenge to the adult actor. Through experience and understanding the adult struggles to arrive at the same point the child reaches through innocence.'

It's the invaluable lesson Brook learned from directing children in his film version of *Lord of the Flies*. The child never switches off. In fact the child who's unaware of acting tends to do everything in a rush. But if you slow him down and tell him when to pause, he won't think about it or query it in any way. His eyes will be full of the life flowing through him and everything in him will give life to what he's doing. The irony is that Brook directed the children in the film by numbers. Look at the ground, count two, wait for a signal, raise your head, count three, turn your eyes. . . . Nothing would make the adult actor more mechanical. But the child is at his best. The moment he tries to 'perform' it becomes unattractive. But when he's not acting, when he's just being, then what you see is full and completely satisfying. One's in contact with something very precious—the image of life flowing.

'In a sense,' added Brook, 'there isn't such a thing as a gifted child. There are children who are in their natural state of childhood innocence. And there are children who at a very early age become non-children. The childhood state of oneness begins to die. The child has begun to grow into this inert, amorphous, ill-defined state of adulthood. But the adult may never fully realize what he's lost or what he's become. The actor who performs in familiar territory plays before people who reflect his own state. If the group were to perform before a sophisticated city audience the actors would most likely be seen as apparently normal individuals. But the moment they're not in tune with the audience, the moment something *really* disturbs them, everything collapses in a second. We see it in Africa time and again. The moment the actor doesn't receive the sort of response he expects, his true state is revealed. In fact it's a highly dislocated and complex state. It can reach the point where two actors facing each other in a state of panic don't actually see each other. Their eyes are glazed. But the eyes of the child are alive.'

It was Stanislavsky who wrote—
   'Theatre is long-hoped for, long-promised child.'

18

Swados was the second member of the group to go down with malaria.

The mechanic was still in hospital, unable to move. As well as going down with malaria he'd slipped a disc heaving baggage from the truck. The Leader would drive back to pick him up in four days.

Six of the actors were now suffering from mild fever or vomiting.

Brook had begun coughing badly: acute bronchitis.

The group doctor gave injections or pills when we pitched camp for the night. Others were unusually listless, sleeping fitfully in the cramped cars.

Each day the travel became more exhausting. The heat was stifling now and I began to dread the long silent hours spent on the road. One day Bagayogo awoke from a deep sleep as we drove through the bush. 'I am going to Oxford,' he announced in English.

'Of course you are,' I replied, glancing at the others.

'I am going to Oxford. Is there a doctor in Oxford?'

'Let's hope so.'

'That is most welcome. I am going to Oxford. What *is* Oxford?'

'The original Cambridge.'

'I intend also to go to the original Cambridge. Are there shoes in Cambridge?'

'Shoes?'

'I buy, you sell.'

'What?'

'I am going to Oxford.'

I turned to Yoshi. 'This man needs help,' I said in a whisper. But Yoshi was snoring gently in his kamikazi mask.

'I buy, you sell.'

'What?'

'Shoes.'

'Or you can get them in Oxford,' I said, feeling it best to humour him a little.

'I *am* going to Oxford.'

'Well there you are. You're in luck.'

'I buy, you sell.'

'What?'

'Shoes.'

'I thought you were going to Oxford.'

'I am going to Oxford. What *is* Oxford?'

'The original Cambridge.'

'I intend also to go to the original Cambridge. Are there shoes in Cambridge?'

'Masses.'

'Masses?'

'There are masses of shoes in Cambridge.'

'But I am going to Oxford.'

'Malick, are you all right?'

'I am all right. Are you all right? I am all right. It is a nice day. The sun is very cold.'

'*Hot*. The sun is very hot.'

'Is it?'

'Oh, terribly.'

'It is good. I buy, you sell.'

'What?'

'Shoes. I buy, you sell. I am all right, are you all right? I speak, you speak.'

'What?'

'English,' he replied, smiling broadly. 'I am going to Oxford. The sun is very cold. I speak English, you speak English. We are having English. . . .'

Stuck for a word he thumbed the pages of a dictionary.

'*Lesson*,' he said at last as the convoy rattled on.

Over the windscreen of one Land-Rover a notice appeared unexpectedly. 'Remember your lines when yer swinging from vines.' Mirren had pinned it up. I used to stare at it for hours. It was crayoned in capitals.

REMEMBER YOUR LINES WHEN YER SWINGING FROM VINES

'You know,' said Swados, pale and shaking with malaria. 'It's sort of interesting to feel yourself going out of your mind.'

Katsulas had started to do something weird. Whenever we pitched camp he secretly threw bits of paper around. He dropped them behind his back. This was a little unexpected because in his role of camp commandant Katsulas was exceptionally keen on a sense of order. He used to watch me trying to put up the lights. I knew what he was doing. He was doing a time-and-motion survey. But we were getting to him. He was changing.

'You might not have noticed,' he confided in me, 'but I've started dropping litter around the place. See, in a strange way it makes me feel a part of things. I've never dropped any litter before. But what I figure is why should I always pick up everyone else's? It really bugs me. So I had this idea. What about my *own* litter? Maybe I wouldn't feel so bad if I had to pick up some of my *own*. All I do is scatter a few bits, you know, here and there. Maybe it'll help. Maybe it'll stop me going crazy.'

His wife, Marva the Cook, wasn't feeling too good either. I had a suspicion of this because every so often she would leap in the air and scream: 'Right, that's it! That's definitely it! Andy, get your things. We're going. We're going *home!*'

'Why is everyone so exhausted?' Brook asked plaintively. 'Is it the food?'

'Right, that's it! That's definitely it!'

'Oh, *honey* . . .' Andreas would say.

Marva Katsulas wasn't a born cook. She used to work in the theatre, which is how she met Andreas. They acted together at Indiana University. But in the coolness, to say the least, which had developed between the crew and the actors she was caught in a conflict of loyalties, and it showed. You never quite knew where you were with Marva. Sometimes she would slip you extra

cheese rations and other times you just felt grateful to get anything. But not for Marva the rustling up of hot chow at midnight.
Bored by moans about meals and washing-up, sick of cooking for
thirty ungrateful people in blistering heat and rotten conditions,
Marva Katsulas was beginning to speak her mind.

'After all,' she said to Brook, though it was more a general
announcement. 'We're all experimenting with living happily
together—isn't that *right*, Peter?'

The crew smiled to themselves.

The crew wished the lot of us would take a royal flying fuck
at the moon.

En route to the next performance, François Marthouret's car hit
a child as the convoy drove through a small village.

The child couldn't have been more than three years old. He
ran out into the road. Seeing what was happening his grandfather
ran to save him, panicked and ran back. Marthouret slammed on
his brakes and swerved to a stop. But the child was hit.

Marthouret was blameless and none of the villagers blamed
him. He couldn't have avoided the child. The child was carried
back to his home where the group doctor examined him carefully. At first she feared a brain hemorrhage. But he was all right.
The car must have grazed him. Soon he recovered and was
scampering about again.

'Another few inches and I would have killed him,' said
Marthouret.

His wife was crying. Marthouret was the colour of death.

Actors, Brook mentioned to me one time, spend less of their
lives living in reality than most. They have less of it and resist it
more, preferring fantasy. If so, the sooner there was another show
the better. The sickness and tension belonged to the real world
and the accident had shaken the actors badly. Perhaps the
world of imagination would bring a cure of sorts, if only there
was the energy to reach it.

A performance took place that night.

The carpet was laid out in a nearby village under a twisted

lifeless baobab tree, a tree that's famous in Africa. It looks as if it has been planted upside down so that the roots become its branches. I was told that whenever you see the baobab tree it means that the village is old and evil spirits live in it. The first time I saw the tree its gnarled branches were crammed with hundreds of white birds, and the tree moved.

The men of this village gave us the clenched fist sign, pointing their thumbs at the sky. It was a way of saying hello. One man made the sign to me so I returned it. He said my beard looked ridiculous.

Dusk was falling. The women were in purdah, for the men here would not permit them to watch us.

The lights left behind by the film unit were set up on the roof of a house decorated with pictures of birds, fish, a man, trees, a donkey, a motorbike, a transistor radio, and six pairs of shoes.

Then the lights were switched on and the performance began with a new show, *The Walking Show*.

This consisted of actors walking.

Now actors may tend to resist reality but they don't usually put on a show about walking. If they did people might think they're crazy. I've seen The Living Theatre put on a show about blowing your nose, and in deadly seriousness or so it seemed. An actor came on stage and just kept blowing his nose. Perhaps he had a cold. But he kept at it. Eventually cynical elements in the audience, feeling a little audience participation was called for, joined in. There were amazing nose blowing duets. But a show about walking was new to me and this was in deadly seriousness too. In order to go back to a real beginning, Brook asked the actors to learn literally to walk again. In such a way, no dramatic convention could be taken for granted. The audience would gradually become involved and lulled into the transition of theatrical experience. The act of walking could be shared and slowly would turn into improvisation. And so under the twisted baobab tree many actors walked round a carpet.

This is how you come to feel yourself going out of your mind. You stare intensely at the carpet and think, 'Yes, there they are— *walking*.' Then perhaps you think, 'Is it me or is it everyone else?'

211

It's difficult to decide, so crazy is the sight of people putting on a show about walking. Sometimes people stand on each other's head and shout out, 'Huplah!' But these people are called acrobats. And perhaps that's it: you've got to get used to things. At first it seemed amazing to me. But I came to realize there's walking and walking. And I came to the point when I saw that not one of the actors could actually walk.

Like the universal language of the body, Brook believes there exists a language of movement that can be totally expressive of a state of being. If it sounds a lofty theory, any disciple of Martha Graham would say that he's absolutely right. In fact Brook greatly admires Merce Cunningham's ballet company, which stems from the innovatory work of Martha Graham. No coincidence then that the actor who always began walking on the carpet was Mr. Lou Zeldis, the one member of the group trained as a dancer. Tall and vague as a giraffe, you would spot him in a fog. If anyone could turn something as banal as walking into a creative act, Zeldis was the man for the job. He lopes on air.

So now Zeldis the Giraffe began to walk round and round, in search of the miraculous. He covered the carpet in about three giant strides, a slow-motion walk, gathering in momentum and excitement. Others joined him. Too soon! They were *running*! It's astonishing—but given the simple direction to do no more than walk, everyone was running. In fact, they were running before they could walk. Even Zeldis's fine sense of rhythm and timing was lost in the scramble to 'perform', show out: get a reaction and get it quick. The exercise, so simple on the surface, had proved no easier than the tortuous movements everyone struggled with each day: never to master. Panicking inner voices whispered, 'Do this, do that.' The wonderful invention that springs from all those natural evolving shapes and rhythms the best dancers produce spontaneously, as if by nature, was nowhere to be seen. How could it be otherwise? The actors weren't yet dancers. But in its place, the muddle and formlessness that reflects only a desperate state of confusion. For Brook, the simple flow of life was missing. And not for the first time, he had proved his point.

The audience didn't mind the chaos: quite enjoyed it, laughing good-naturedly at the absurdity of it all. There's nothing the actors could show an African villager about rhythm and balance, yet the crowds were always generous and never judged us harshly. Also, the unexpected sight of strangers tearing round a carpet could have been no more surprising than human birds squawking and crowing at each other. As the audience discovered. For *The Walking Show* slid nicely into *The Bird Show* as two walking men became two gossiping birds and another scraped a violin.

'What is this!' cried someone in the excited crowd. 'What *is* this!'

'It's monkeys!' cried someone else.

Monkeys?

'That's a crab!' 'It's a duck!' 'A canary!' shouted the crowd as Ayansola went thundering in on his talking drum.

'Quiet!' snapped Brook.

Ayansola had thundered in at the wrong time.

'Please, Ayansola,' pleaded Brook, placing a finger over his lips.

'Welcome to the club,' said Swados, never too keen on old Ayansola.

Ayansola bowed regally.

Then he spread-eagled himself over the rest of the drums. If he wasn't going to play, no one was. Swados had to burrow her way through.

'Let me *through*.'

'That's a partridge!'

'It's an owl!'

'It's monkeys!'

Monkeys?

'Shit and puke, let me *through*.'

'*Please*, Ayansola.'

And into *The Shoe Show*. But we'd forgotten to bring the shoes. At a pinch, we could have done *The Sandal Show* but no one seemed enthusiastic. Not enough impact, I suppose.

And into *The Bread Show*.

'Oh my God,' said Bob Applegarth, the stage manager, turning amazingly white. 'I definitely remember packing the bread. Hey, Mary! You seen the bread? It's here *somewhere*. Jesus, I hope no one's eaten it.'

Fortunately for us, and fortunately for the stage manager, the bread was found in the box of musical instruments. There were a few teeth marks in the bread—*small* teeth marks. Could only have been Yoshi Oida. No time, no time for investigations now.

A hungry man sells his clothes and all that he possesses for a loaf of bread. On his travels others steal the bread and deceive the man, leaving him with nothing. There might be a grotesque and greedy woman, a soldier, a bully, a clown, a charlatan, a killer, a slave. All cheat and humiliate the hungry man.

Others offer him gifts of imaginary food. The hungry man receives the gifts and returns them. They share the imaginary food.

So had developed the rough scenario of *The Bread Show* with Myers at the centre of every scene as the hungry man. I used to feel nervous for him. With Myers, anything could happen and usually in extremes. Perhaps there might be the biggest disaster or biggest triumph of all time. But it wasn't easy for him. Responsible for inventing five or six totally different scenes with any actor who chose to enter the carpet, it was as if he were a sitting target for all the ingenuity and skill they could throw at him.He has a very special quality of naïvety, more powerful than anyone in the group. That and a flair for comedy, sometimes black. But when his confidence evaporates, all hell lets lose and things fall apart. By temperament, Myers creates the working atmosphere valued by Brook most—a terrific sense of danger.

Now the circle of actors launched into the theme music of *The Bread Show*, which was called *The Bread Show Song*. It was an unusual song for the group because it had a lyric in English. 'Breadabreadabreadabreada/breadabreadabreadabreada/breadabreadabreadabreada/gotta get the bread. . . .' And that was the lyric. And Myers enters the carpet as the hungry man.

The carpet: Brook's X-ray machine. No one enters it easily. Without the help of costume or scenery, dialogue or script, an actor who enters the carpet cannot lie. Perhaps he cannot hide. Every inhibition, every false move, everything will be seen for what it is. Either the actor creates something worthwhile or he doesn't. Either the performance stays below steam level, says Brook, or rises above it. But the nerves and fear involved in the process are what the X-ray machine reveals. And what it revealed this time was more unbelievable than anything we had yet witnessed. Without warning, the actors were suddenly thrown into a state of utter bewilderment: nervous paralysis. For the first time in the journey, people jeered them.

Even Brook was thrown, staring in disbelief at what was happening on the carpet.

'What are they *doing*?' he groaned.

It was unbelievable. Only Myers was doing *The Bread Show*. The others were doing a show about hags, which was called *The Hag Show*.

From exhaustion or panic or sickness the group had somehow hit a collective mental block. Gotta get the bread. But how? They just couldn't think of anything. Unable to unleash one fresh idea the Pavlovian reaction Brook fears came into horrifying reality. In desperation one actor followed another, going back to the central image of a show first worked on six months before in Paris. It was based on a Ted Hughes' poem called *The Hag*. A roadside hag thumbs a lift on a stranger's shoulders and once up, will not leave him. And it has nothing whatever to do with bread.

But it might.

When the first hag entered the carpet and flattened Myers there were what the group calls 'interesting possibilities'. Why shouldn't a hag try to get the bread? Even a hag's got to eat. But when another hag entered, and another, and another, the bread was lost in the amazing scramble and it was time to throw in the towel. Besides, Myers could scarcely move any more.

'It's bad,' said Yoshi, laughing nervously. 'It's very bad.'

'What's the *point*?' said Marthouret.

'Why are we here?' wondered Corthay.

'What are they *doing*?' groaned Brook.

'Forget it,' snapped Myers, throwing the bread away.

Some of the crowd had begun to jeer.

'Write it off.'

'For Jesus' sake,' I said to Brook. 'Why can't actors *see*?'

'Why can't a woman be more like a man?' he replied.

We drove back to camp in silence.

'Why are we here?' Sylvain Corthay eventually asked again. He was just thinking aloud and the others stayed with their own thoughts. No one had openly questioned the reason for the journey before.

'You're wise,' I said to Zeldis. 'So why are we here?'

'Where?'

'Africa.'

'I don't know. I don't know why we're here. But if we were somewhere else, I wouldn't know why we were there.'

At the camp: ritual conference, ritual sick bay, ritual mosquito attack, ritual bird bath, ritual tinned food, ritual moan, ritual routines. Sleep in sweat: bodies laid out like corpses.

Travel again the next day when during a pee stop among the shea nut trees a stranger in white robes emerged from the bush and approached me smiling. For a small reward he offered me a peep at several photos through a viewfinder. They were of Rin Tin Tin.

Now we camped in the bush twenty miles outside the city of Zaria, the road to the Jos Plateau and eventually the long-anticipated Mecca of Ife. Brook chose another village to play and ordered an unprecedented move—the previous show that failed so miserably would be repeated.

'Let's set our watches,' he announced, urgently trying to get everyone to gather at the same time for once.

But no one wore a watch, including Brook.

Natasha Parry used to, but it stopped working.

'I got the *bread*,' announced the stage manager.

Then we left for the new village. But it turned out to be more

216

like a small town and the centre was bursting with the most frightening crowd we had met, more than a thousand people crammed into the dusty square spilling and tumbling on to the not-so-magic carpet. Oh Jesus! It would take only the most amazing performance to control such a crowd. Several locals, self-appointed body-guards, patrolled the carpet beating back the chaotic crowd as Hell's Angels guard the stage of a rock show.

Suddenly Brook's voice cracked in the uproar. He lost his voice. Now he went into elaborate mime more dramatic than any actor, whistling frantically for attention, like Harpo Marx.

Oddly enough, he seemed to be enjoying himself.

'The chairs are coming!' shrieked someone important in the vast crowd.

Chairs?

'Make way! Make way for the chairs!'

The body-guards lashed out at the chaotic crowd even more, though we tried to restrain them now. Things were getting out of hand. Brook was miming and whistling that he wanted the crowd to stay where it was. Distance creates barriers. But the guards wouldn't stop. It was hopeless.

'The chairs are coming! *Make way for the chairs!*'

It turned out the chairs were for the Emir. But the chairs never came. And neither did the Emir.

Suddenly, to the astonishment of everyone, Myers unexpectedly decided to go out on a limb. In the midst of the tumult he went and sat in the centre of the carpet, pointing at a wig and a comb he had with him. Even Brook looked surprised.

Very slowly and deliberately he put on the wig and began to comb it, the long black wig.

The crowd hushed in anticipation.

It took him several minutes to do all this, for everything was done with precision and great care.

Then he began to roll up his trousers.

Then he put on a dress.

And was a tart, the sexiest shimmying most horrendous tart you ever saw. And that crowd erupted with joy! And that was just the best thing I'd seen anyone do for ages. Maybe you can theorise about theatre until the cows come home but something as simple as an actor gradually and openly transforming himself into a woman turns out to be one of the happiest memories of the entire journey for me. Oh, I know it wasn't the howl of Lear or the quintessential collective unconscious of mankind that had been captured then. But it was something marvellous for all that and I do not think that you or I or many actors could have done it. For there in the centre of a crowd so vast and tumultuous was a form of magic.

One of the best pieces of theatre I've ever seen was an amateur performance in the clearing of a wood in London. Both adults and children were in the show, and in the audience. About half-way through, most of the cast suddenly appeared and sang a song, a very gentle song. And as they were singing, two children unexpectedly unfolded a huge notice. Written on the notice was the word: INTERVAL.

Well, I think the unexpected appearance of Myers and the wig and comb was like that.

But then, just as Myers the Horrendous Tart and the other actors began to invent a boy meets girl story, a non-verbal *Irma La Douce* story, the crowd crashed on to the carpet and stopped the show.

The momentum was lost and Zeldis began again with *The Walking Show*—but again the crowd got out of control, and the show had to be stopped.

Swados was yelling at the actors, trying to be heard above the uproar.

Frightened of the crowd, young Simon Brook was in tears.

A song followed but it couldn't be heard.

A bird improvisation fell apart.

Suddenly the old fears were returning. The actors began to retreat into a shell. For Brook this was a unique opportunity for the kind of exuberant circus performance that would stretch the group in a new direction and take control of this impossible crowd. But there was little energy left and fear had taken over now. Uncertain of the right response the hopeful start had vanished. Instead of rising to the occasion, the actors were destroyed by it. The performance went completely to pieces.

Three times the crowd crashed on to the carpet during *The Bread Show*, stopping the bewildered actors in their tracks. But all confidence and imagination had dried up again and no actor wished to enter. Perhaps it was understandable: the bull was out of control. But so was the matador and from his dramatic gestures and mime Brook was disappointed and very angry. Not for the first time the actors seemed to ignore the very existence of the audience, behind their shell, their world. Take control! But the show only ground to a feeble end, finally abandoned when the crowd crashed onto the carpet for the last time.

The carpet was again rolled up in silence, for the people quickly went back to their homes and work. A few children watched us pack up and leave, staring at us with distant eyes. The actors looked exhausted and sick and near to despair.

'Why are we here?' I said to Brook as we drifted away.

Unable to speak, he took hold of my copy of *The Conference of the Birds* and pointed to one of the fables inside—

'A man who loved God saw Majnun sifting the earth of the road and said: "Majnun, what are you looking for?" "I am looking for Laila," he said. The man asked: "Do you hope to find Laila there?" "I look for her everywhere," said Majnun, "in the hope of finding her somewhere." '

19

Wise old saying:
'People are never happy without a mortgage.'

To my surprise, we didn't move on after this latest set-back but stayed camped in the bush. Something was brewing. Three shows had fallen apart in quick succession and each time it was as if all energy and will had vanished. Was the illness to blame?

Brook and the group doctor drove urgently into the city of Zaria to consult with another doctor there. The outbreak of malaria was a mystery to us. Everyone had been inoculated against every conceivable form of sickness. Yet sickness was spreading, and exhaustion. Had the malaria pills been handed out too late? It was the latest theory. The Leader was responsible for the malaria pills, being the expert on tropical matters. But perhaps some of us were forgetting to take our daily dose. It was an easy thing to do. The pills were very small. Whatever the cause, Brook was worried.

As he left for the local doctor, we were given the day off and told to rest. Swados continued to work, seeing no reason to stop. Without warning, Myers went down with malaria.

But when Brook returned to camp, he immediately ordered a conference with the entire expedition. He had solved the mystery of the growing illness. Also, his voice had returned.

'Are we all here?' he asked, as everyone gathered round.

Marthouret was always late.

'This should be *perfectly* simple,' snapped Brook, just as he'd done at almost every conference since the journey began. 'It should be perfectly simple to gather quickly together for a meeting. It's something that should be *sensed*. Yet it never happens....'

Marthouret came running, full of apologies. The best excuse

I heard him make was 'administrative reason'. 'Sorry I'm late. Administrative reasons.'

'Where's Malick?' asked Brook, looking weary.

'Search *me*.'

'Malick! Malick!'

Eventually, Bagayogo emerged from behind a tree. 'Is there a *meeting*?'

'We sleep soon?' asked Yoshi, sounding plaintive.

'We no sleep,' replied Katsulas. 'We have *talk*. We no sleep for two hours.'

'Two hours?'

'At least,' added Katsulas, settling down in one of the comfortable chairs as if for an evening's compulsive viewing in front of the television set.

The actors sat in the centre of the camp, under the dim lights attached to the batteries of the Land-Rovers.

The crew stood together.

Brook was seated on a wooden stool six inches off the ground.

Then he produced the rabbit out of the hat and I think the rabbit was more astonished than the audience. None other than The World Health Organization was to blame for the mystery illness.

I watched the crew look to the heavens.

NOT THE WORLD HEALTH ORGANIZATION! Not WHO!

The local doctor in Zaria had traced the outbreak of illness to the camp's water filter. The water filter happened to be approved by The World Health Organization. Also, by the Leader. But the local doctor didn't trust water filters, no matter who approved them. He thought we were crazy not to boil all the water we drank. And that was the gist of this latest difference of opinion with the crew and not since Myers got lost up a mountain had feelings run so high. They were as high as an elephant's eye.

'But, Peter,' mouthed the astonished Leader. 'The water filter is approved by WHO.'

'There's no need to take this personally,' said Brook.

'But I *chose* the water filter,' replied the Leader.

And so it began. And so it would continue. And I knew that

everything from the history and design of water filters to the current credibility of The World Health Organization would be discussed and analysed into the night until, like the election of former leaders of the Conservative Party in Britain, a final decision eventually 'emerged'. One time the group was earnestly discussing the possibility and implications of making sandwiches for lunch. After maybe half an hour François Marthouret, who enjoys a little philosophy, said: 'We can't decide whether or not to make a sandwich until we are certain what a sandwich *is*.' And the group actually discussed what a sandwich is, or might be, or was in the good old days when there were things to put in sandwiches and bread to put them on. 'What *is* a fault?' 'What *is* a sandwich?' And you know what the answer is? 'Remember your lines when yer swinging from vines.'

The water filter won an overall majority. To pacify the militant minority it was decided that water would be boiled for those who wanted it. In which case who would boil the water, how long would it take, when would it be boiled and who would dish it out? Does the same person who boils the water *dish it out*? Maybe we should have a rota system? Do we agree on a rota system for boiling the water or what? By the way, how *is* the water? But the water was low, and getting lower. Strict rationing would have to continue. In the interests of extra hygiene one bowl of water was spared for the entire camp to wash their hands in before each meal. Vitamin and salt pills were increased. The malaria pills were doubled. Then the conference turned to that great raw nerve of the privileged classes, second only in its explosive velocity to the chore of washing dishes and the state of the international monetary market: boring food.

I know we were in the African bush and shouldn't have complained. But the world of the camp didn't belong to this world. It belonged to the *Good Food Guide*. Were we in Africa? I wasn't sure any more. I wasn't sure where we were. We weren't in Maxim's. We weren't anywhere any of us had been before. We weren't even in La Coupole. We were suspended in mid-air. A time capsule had taken us to a place far away from a life we had grown totally accustomed to, and there we discussed the merits of water filters and tinned pilchards and searched for a mysterious lady called Laila. The amazing thing is, we found her.

'I'm not a fussy eater,' Myers announced, walking into the mine field. 'But I really can't take any more of the food. It makes me *sick*. I'm sorry.'

For the moment I thought Marva Katsulas was about to go in for a primal scream. The crew tensed, as if for a stand-up fight.

'I would like to say,' began Malick Bagayogo, 'that in my opinion the breakfast is quite nice.'

This is how an intended compliment turns into an unintentional insult. Breakfast was the one meal that involved no cooking.

'Well I don't know what the hell you're all talking about,' Katsulas announced, taking us by surprise. 'I haven't eaten better in Paris.'

Which brought the house down, I'm afraid.

Katsulas looked as if he might explode, like his wife. The crew would explode shortly. Give them time. But as the conference continued and at last tempers began to cool, every face was still set in the identical look of exhaustion and I don't think even this conference was to blame. The whole strain and effort of the long journey was taking its toll. In the failure and disillusion of their work, the actors had lost their way.

Yoshi Oida, normally so flexible and disciplined, was in hiding: a shadow. The actor with the greatest commitment and staying power was losing the control that seemed to rule his life. In the work his voice had become shrill and sometimes his eyes would blaze with frightening anger. The rest were taken by surprise.

Helen Mirren, still depressed by life in camp and the high seriousness of the work, threatened, unhappy, was relaxed only in an African setting, perhaps with the children and the villagers or in the open countryside. There for a short while she was private and could be herself. It was different with the group. 'It's difficult to laugh any more,' she said to me and, though we have known each other for years, cut herself off.

Sylvain Corthay, brooding, silent, alone by choice, it was as if he had become an observer of his own group. I travelled in the

Land-Rover he drove. Often for five or six hours he never said a word to anyone.

Lou Zeldis, apparently asleep in all conferences, his mind blown by what he called 'bombshells to the psyche, arrows to the spirit'. He resented all the probing and testing and pushing that made up the character of so much of this journey and consoled himself with the fantasy of producing the future Hollywood version of it. Peter Brook was played by Erich von Stroheim and got to direct the movie. John Wayne played Katsulas. Alain Delon played François Marthouret. Diana Ross played Miriam Goldschmidt. Gladys Knight and the Pips played the crew. Mirren played Mirren. And the star part went to Vanessa Redgrave as himself.

François Marthouret, badly shaken by his accident with the child, listless, worried, down, had lost that lightning speed of thought which gave his work its special appeal. All his energy and confidence had evaporated. In the heat and dryness, his voice had practically gone. His face, normally sunny, looked strained and miserable. Things can change overnight with actors, but he felt like giving up.

Natasha Parry, fearful, perplexed, tense, an actress whose natural instincts for theatre were rooted in the *status quo* she had been part of since her teens, was losing faith in the journey too. One time I watched her rooted to the edge of the carpet yet willing herself to enter. She literally ran on, stopped in her tracks as if to go back, and forced herself to . . . act.

'What's an improvisation?' asked her young son.

'An improvisation is something you make up as you go along,' she replied. 'And even then you can't be sure.'

Malick Bagayogo, a stranger it seemed in his own land, an African with all the gloss and sophistication of years of living comfortably in Europe, it was only rarely that his work captured its former power, the invisible power. Sometimes this gentle and lost man could appear trapped on the carpet, unable to escape. Now his enormous talent merely seemed surface: a trick. But it wasn't so. It was Africa that had trapped him.

Miriam Goldschmidt, hating the regimentation of life in camp, throwing herself into every activity, excited, young, over-compensating, over-acting, she told me of her vivid dreams and recurring nightmares:

'The actors are trying to roll up the carpet. It is impossible to lift. No one succeeds in lifting the carpet.'

'There is a tree. Brook is up the tree. He says to the actors: "Everyone must take a branch." As they take one he shouts: "*Stop!*" All remain motionless for hours. She asks: "How long?" Which is greeted by laughter.'

'There is a town built of bones. Ferocious fat birds sit on the bones, eating bones. Along strolls Andreas Katsulas who asks the birds the way. The birds tell him the direction to take is along the main bone street. At the end of the street appears a bar where Yoshi Oida sits in a chair. He does not speak but slants his eyes. Katsulas asks him the way but receives no answer except the slant of his eyes. Frustrated, he beats his head against the wall and discovers a tiny window. Through the window he sees another town built of bones with ferocious fat birds.'

'The actors are listening to a story. Brook is telling the story, which he gives many titles to. Then in one moment he gives the exact title but warns the actors that no one will ever remember it.' At which point, the dream ends and Miss Goldschmidt woke up screaming the word: 'ERRUGA'.

Michèle Collison, the one member of the group who seemed to be taking most things smugly in her stride, the protector figure, Earth Mother! very little could faze or depress her. Along with Katsulas, she was the only actor never to fall ill. Whatever the strain of the journey, whatever went wrong with the shows—she remained consistently and miraculously sublime. The group is very much her family and everyone she is closest to in life is there. Only a sense of claustrophobia seemed to trouble her, that and the loss of privacy. She wasn't troubled by losing two sets of glasses and could no longer see straight.

'I guess I see what I want to see,' she explained, squinting vaguely in my direction.

'But you don't seem able to see much.'

'Oh, I *can*,' she replied 'it's just a different shape.'

'What sort of shape?'

'The shape of things to come.'

Bruce Myers, now hit by malaria, low, confused, deeply troubled by recent failures, he believed we were still no closer to the spirit of Africa than we were on the first day we arrived. He said that he had never felt white in his life before. 'I am full of fear,' he told me, and tapped his head.

Andreas Katsulas, the group barometer of doubt and frustration and much else besides, this outspoken and emotional man couldn't help bringing to the surface the exasperation others chose to submerge. What he called 'the mystical shit' cut no ice with him, or so he liked to say. He could be marvellously tactless: 'I'm sorry to throw a bomb into the daisy field but I really *hate* the way Yoshi sings.' And he could be marvellously funny, which made him feel worse. Also, there were times when you didn't quite know whether he was joking or not. But Goldschmidt's dream about him banging his head against a brick wall was apt. Katsulas was suffering from that rare fever known as 'Brookitis'. The giant barometer made in America and Greece was at an all time low.

Perhaps it was because of the day the children ran away from him, or the tribe who couldn't get it together in the camp, or the moans about the food, which hurt his wife, or his own simmering anger and confusion at the current sense of gloom and hopelessness. But all these different nerve-ends jarred and exploded as he raged in front of me, after his own fashion.

'Clutch my *leg*. I want you to get the thorn out of my paw. Not that you've got the strength. I've seen you with the lights. Jesus Christ! You never made the boy scouts and that's for sure. Have I told you about my secret plan with the litter? You know, dropping it behind my back while nobody's looking. For this whole trip I've been stuffing candy wrappers in my pocket. You see what's happened? I don't *care* any more. Who gives a damn? I'm *miserable*. I don't have high philosophical motivation. There hasn't been a week when I haven't wanted to quit. I want to quit now.'

'Why don't you?'

'I *have*.'

'But you're still here?'

'That's what I can't understand. I'm still here. Everything's a constant source of misery to me and I'm still here. What's *wrong* with me? I tell you, nothing's wrong with me. It's *them*. They complain about the food, right? They don't like the tins. Well I remember living off nothing but tins for a long time of my life. I wasn't poor or starved. I used to rummage through trash cans for text books the other kids threw away. I used to sell them back to the stores so I could make a little change. I got by. But I never took anything for granted. I never felt when the good meals came they came by *right*. I never felt people could be so blind and unaware. It's the *opposite* of the work. They don't respect the people who wait on them. I've *been* a waiter. I've been lots of things. What do they want—a maid? This is supposed to be a real community and they don't even respect the people they're living with. It's a *joke*. It's an intellectual dream. Listen, camping is *alien* to me. I'm playing a role. It's what I get paid to do. But I don't feel I'm earning my money the way my mother is in a hotel kitchen. I get paid to *discuss* things! Work to me is not being able to move at the end of the day. I can't say any more.'

He fell silent, The Big Man.

'You know the first time I acted?' he said eventually. 'I played a *bear*. I was five years old and could already do tap dance. I used to sing a song in Greek called "Athens How I Love You". Anyway, I was in *The Three Bears*. I got my first stage laugh. I invented a bear language. I talked like a bear. And you know *what*? It's taken me twenty years to get from talking like a bear to talking like a bird. We work with Peter Brook and we end up playing birds. I mean, what's *that*! I'm sick of birds. I *am* a bird. I can't stand it any more. . . .'

And for a little while longer he ranted on about the camp, the food, the actors, the community, the trip, the work, always the work, until I felt that perhaps he was exaggerating a bit.

So I said so. And he said, yes that was true.

I said you couldn't expect a real community to come together

227

overnight. Stuff like that. And he said, yes that was true.

I said no one complained about the food every minute of the day. And he said, yes that was true.

I said the camp functioned quite well, considering. Actors were doing jobs he would never do, really dirty jobs. And he said, yes that was true.

I said he always talked about quitting but never did. In fact, few members of the group were more dedicated to the work than him. And be bowed his head humbly and said, yes that was true.

'So what are you complaining about?' I asked.

'Who's *complaining*?' The Big Man replied. 'Nobody's complaining. You see, we Greeks have a wise old saying. "People are never happy without a mortgage." '

Then the expedition moved deeper into the bush and found The Village of the Loonies.

The loonies were wise.

20

At the last minute Brook suddenly switched the route.

Instead of taking the direct road to Ife he decided to travel through the highest part of West Africa—a tropical region, densely populated with strange hill tribes, that's known as the Benue Plateau. The crew, worried about petrol and water supplies and even our safety, objected strongly. Brook likes the unexpected to happen, however.

By then we were weeks behind schedule, not that it mattered. All of us had lost any sense of time.

When we reached the northern tip of the Plateau and camped there Brook bustled into the nearby city of Jos, a modern city made rich by the surrounding tin mines, surprising E. M. Forster world of retired Europeans, Rotary Club luncheons and laundered lawns. He met up with an obliging official from the equivalent of Britain's Arts Council who advised him on the new route. The official took a map and pointed south to an area marked 'Pankshin'. With any luck it would take us five or six hours to reach: *go there.*

We were camped in a deserted part of the Plateau among rocks sculptured by wind and storms. Few Africans spotted us, but two middle-aged English strangers did, appearing suddenly from nowhere as if taking a stroll in Hyde Park on a Sunday afternoon. I liked them instantly, The Odd Couple. Even from a distance they had about them that unmistakable Englishness which manages to transport England to wherever in the world the English happen to be. They were pleased they had found us, though off-hand about it in the correct manner. 'We were just out for a little stroll,' they said.

'And where *is* the master?' asked the husband, scanning the landscape.

'Ah!' said his wife when she spotted him. 'Mr. Brook, I presume. . . .'

As the convoy headed for the villages further south I could still see them walking together arm in arm.

'Good luck!' they called. 'Good luck to you all.'

The Village of the Loonies was really called Wuseli, which means 'Take it easy.'

So they do.

We stopped by the road through Pankshin and simply asked a stranger to direct us to the nearest village in the bush. He pointed along a rough track, which we followed until it came to a dead end. The village was a further mile away through the scrub and trees. We would have to walk to it.

Immediately the camp was hemmed in by scores of children anxious to see the unexpected visitors.

The elders from the village joined us for tea. Occasionally, they shrieked with laughter for no apparent reason. Others puffed furiously on pipes.

Warnings were given out about the danger of scorpions. Camp-beds crawled with ants. We dug a well in a dried-up river-bed and washed in the murky water. Tempers began to fray in the stifling heat. 'I hate them,' said Yoshi Oida, surrounded always by eyes. He had become The Yellow Man. Small, scarred women stared.

Within the group only Ayansola seemed relaxed now. Yoruba-land and Ife were getting closer: he was almost home. He'd started to throw rocks at me. Hell, it was only *fun*. No man could take you through a richer range of human emotions than old Ayansola, but ever since we crossed the border into Nigeria he had been a happy man. One night, the drumming we heard from the surrounding villages seemed to have a crack in it. This was because it was a record. Ayansola had found a new record for his portable record player: a Yoruba drumming record. The rock and roll number had been locked away, discarded.

Dogs howled at us from this village.

Brook arranged a short performance there before dusk that

evening. The following day the villagers had promised to show us one of their ceremonies.

The people here were farmers of guinea corn, beans, ground-nuts, cotton, millet, rice, yams and cassava. Like many of the places we came to, visitors were rare. The only white people to have been there before were doctors, agricultural experts and missionaries. The villagers had never seen a piece of theatre as we understand it, or even as Brook understands it. When I spoke in English to the young schoolmaster the only word he didn't know the meaning of was 'theatre'.

We chatted together in the crowded camp.

'Do you know who Hitler was?' I asked suddenly, surprising the two of us.

'*Hitler?*' replied the young schoolmaster.

'Adolf.'

'Adolf Hitler? Let me see.' And he thought about it for a few moments. 'Yes, I believe he was a warrior. This Adolf was a warrior who fought many battles.'

'Anything else?'

'Yes, I believe that he lost them.'

It was soon time to walk through the fields for the show in the village square. The villagers guided us along a narrow track in the half-light that comes before dusk. I could see several huts and wattles scattered among trees: not a large village. The carpet went on a sand football field by the small schoolhouse. A black-board was nailed to a flame tree. Perhaps fifty children and thirty men stood round us, keeping a distance. No women.

'It would be nice to do *Hamlet*,' said one of the actors rolling out the carpet.

'You see,' whispered Brook, 'they're still terrified of the void.'

'But what shall we do?' asked Katsulas, for nothing was pre-pared.

'Do what comes naturally,' replied Brook, waiting sternly on the edge of the carpet for someone to enter.

Swados began. She began to laugh. 'Oh dear,' I thought. 'She's finally cracked.' But I was wrong. She was her usual self. She'd decided to open the show with a laughing song. The lyric was the laughter. I think it was inspired by the laughing men of the village. And that whole village began to laugh hysterically! And to Brook's delight several elders dashed onto the carpet laughing in time to the amazing laughing song. Brook was urging the actors on, clapping and singing with them. And the show went well. It had seemed so long in coming. But the group was relaxed here and played for the fun of it, finding themselves again. There were songs and chants, staggered times, strange rhythms, sudden electric movements, flute duets, useless trumpet, crazed violin, a dance of sorts, with sticks and many birds. The actors were beginning to flow. It was good, this jamboree. The crowd yelled and shrieked whenever they saw the birds. You knew what they were thinking. They were thinking we were loonies.

'Well,' Brook said afterwards. 'It was a useful *start*.'

But the ceremony of the villagers was the thing.

The next morning, Brook and the actors were as excited as children. Perhaps the villagers here would open up a little of their secret world for us. Many people were to come from seven valleys to perform the ceremony—ritual celebration of earth and gods. Perhaps like the meeting with the Peulh, a way would be shown.

The Chief visited the camp: laughing man, tiny, toothless laughing man in huge plastic sandals and a battered old Western suit big enough for two. Others wore robes or skins, chewing on tobacco. When they drank tea with us the Chief and his men were most pleased, letting out great whoops and yells. We nodded and smiled back not knowing quite how to react. The Chief was still laughing. The yells grew louder.

Eventually, the call came that we must go to the village.

We walked slowly in the hot sun through the fields of pink and brown, green and yellow. 'It's just like Provence,' said Brook. 'Every Englishman ends up there sooner or later. They build cottages.'

The elders were still laughing and yelling.

Children held our hands. 'Do all your women belong to your chief?' asked one.

232

Some stared suspiciously.

In the doorway of a mud house a great bare-breasted woman spread her arms to the roof like the wings of an eagle.

Other women worked in the fields carrying bundles of grass on their heads: the bald women. Their heads were shaved.

But when we arrived for the ceremony nobody was there except an old man jigging up and down on the football field. Where were the others? They must have been taking it easy. The old man laughed and waved his nobbly walking stick.

We waited an hour or so and with little else to do a few of us kicked a ball round the dusty field with the schoolkids. Brook was furious at this, dashing out from under a tree. 'If you want to go down with sunstroke,' he yelled. 'Let it be on your own head. . . .'

After another hour we drifted the mile back to camp, hot and disappointed. Perhaps there had been a misunderstanding. Perhaps we should move on. Brook decided to strike camp but we would wait for the ceremony until dark. The chief and his merry men joined us for lunch, giggling.

Then at last the call came that the dancers were ready. We took water bottles and sun hats with us this time, trekking slowly through the fields. The old man was still jigging up and down outside the schoolhouse. But several others had joined him now. The entire village surrounded the football field. Schoolbenches had been set out for us: important visitors. The tiny Chief sat chief to chief with Brook. He had a blue robe over his baggy suit now, clutching a paper flag of the kind you might buy as a souvenir from seaside resorts. He waved the flag.

And the ancient bearded men began the ceremony.

They made the sound of car hooters. They blew on antelope horns, which sounded like tuneless blasts on a car hooter. They blew on them haphazardly, as if in a traffic jam. While they did this they shuffled around chaotically to one drum. Also, I noticed they seemed to be in fits of laughter. And it went on for over an hour like this—hoot, shuffle, hoot, shuffle, hoot, shuffle—until I could feel myself starting to laugh, I mean, nothing seemed to be happening. Maybe we had expected something spectacular as in the travelogues. But the ancient men just jigged round

233

laughing and making the sound of car hooters. Hoot, shuffle, hoot, shuffle, hoot, shuffle. 'They're loonies,' I thought to myself. We were as nonplussed as audiences must have been watching us. Maybe it was a form of revenge.

I looked closer.

I saw a man dressed up as a monkey, with an orange fez on his head, swinging from the branches of a nearby tree. *Monkey-Man!* He was blowing a policeman's whistle as he swung from the tree. The elders were still shuffling and hooting around but I noticed that one of them had a long cotton tail dangling between his legs. And if one of them didn't have a horn he blew on the end of his walking stick, making the sound of the horn just the same. And slowly, very slowly, that village was going *wild*. And a little millet wine helped, no doubt about it. Blows the roof off. 'Not too much now,' said Brook, knocking it back. Shuffle, hoot, shuffle, hoot, shuffle, hoot. Everything, everything to the rhythm of the crazy horns.

I felt a tap on my back.

It was the tail-man blowing his brains out through a hollow tube. Each time he blew, he jerked his shoulder forward. I didn't know what to do. So I risked it, smacking a shilling onto the blade of his shoulder. The tail-man laughed and danced away across the fields.

Another offered us bits of his grey beard.

The schoolmaster arrived, swaying slightly.

The monkey-man leapt from his tree to pay homage, homage to the Chief! The little Chief waved his flag. The monkey-man danced. Chief's clown! And pranced up and down like a monkey. Nobody was allowed to blow his whistle.

Now the old women of the village joined the circle of elders, beautiful, bald women with sagging tits, some with babies wrapped in the back of their dresses, laughing and pissing down their backs. The women clapped as they danced gently with the men, but soft hands could not make their sound. Sound of two pieces of wood slapped together. Others were pregnant: dancers in the womb.

All blew their horns and sticks at the little Chief! The tail-man was still blowing hard through his hollow tube. Of course! One of the actors had done the same thing in the show the previous night. And now they shuffled and danced up to us, whispering sounds and rhythms. And you returned the sounds. And talked. Too serious! they said. Too intense! they said. You knew what they were saying. 'It's a nice day. Take it easy. *Relax*. Okay?' And when you returned their sounds, they looked as if they could kiss you. It meant you understood. But if you got the rhythm wrong with the monkey-man he wouldn't indulge you like the others. He cursed and left. 'Come on! Come on!' they called us to dance. So we ventured into the circle of dancers, laughing. Shuffle, hoot, shuffle, hoot. Take it easy! they said. Keep the pulse! they said. Then you can hoot! And it went on for hours with the village of the loonies, the village who dance in trees, elect a silly chief, miss their noses with warpaint, fall off horses, collect paper flags and policemen's whistles, make slapstick love, forget the names of their gods, make new ones up every day, forget they exist, forget misery, laugh, laugh at the discovery of themselves, at every limb and waggling tongue, everything is funny, everything.

They accompanied us back to camp still hooting and dancing through the fields and along the banks of the river. Street band! Razamataz rhythms, roots of jazz, there in the crazy hoots. Approaching us in the opposite direction, another tail-man! The other half of the tail-man dancing team had finally made it. He went wild with joy. He was *fresh*. Children danced. Elders hooted to the heavens. One proposed marriage to Swados and when she turned him down with regrets, gave her a shilling. He gave his money away—like the others. For all of us received a present. The Chief gave us fifteen shillings and three live chickens. Brook returned the money but kept the chickens. Shuffle, hoot, shuffle, hoot. I was really sorry to leave.

The people were wise.

They understood the wisdom of craziness.

21

We left the village and found again the main route through the
Plateau. But the village had brought us luck.

Brook spurted ahead of the convoy, searching for a new location to camp for the night. He disappeared into the bush. But
when he emerged again he was in a terrific state of excitement.

He had found the perfect setting.

Built into one side of a deep valley was the village of Dungung.
When the people of the village first came to live there they found
a tree in the rocks which was called the Gung Tree. The tree
yields many fruits. And so the people settled by the tree to
multiply as the fruits. The name Dungung means 'to multiply'.
We camped among the rocks on the opposite side of the valley,
facing the narrow twisting goat path that led into the village.

Immediately Brook changed all future plans, sensing the time
and place were right to quit the road for a while. We would
stay there four nights. At last all the pressure and anxiety of
playing on the road would be freed. For the first time in the
journey the actors could relax a little, playing more than once in
the same village. There would be a chance to build something,
maybe. Would we always feel separated from the people?
Sometimes, miraculous times, it wasn't so and yet the fear that
we remained outsiders never left us. Perhaps it could never be
different. For all our good intentions we came like wealthy
prospectors into the villages. Such picturesque settings. Pastoral
idylls! You had only to see a child fight for the scraps of food we
threw away to have such an illusion shattered. Were we just
tourists of a special kind, urban romantics and intellectuals in
search of 'the simple life'? Whenever a show failed we must have
been all of that. Yet here and there a show or unexpected meeting
transformed the stereotypes sometimes, miraculous times. The

African will always welcome a stranger but on these occasions there was never fear of remaining an outsider, forced to by the circumstances of life. In a few moments a bridge could be built, imagination shared! Friendship! Life! Unless we stayed in Africa for years, the only real way we had of touching the people was through the shows. It was why failure brought such emptiness. But perhaps here in the few days spent in Dungung there would be a chance to understand more of the land we came to. If only for a short while we might free ourselves of the neurosis that comes with being a European, tense and clumsy, eager to please in a black country. Take it easy. It had been good advice.

Dungung was a beautiful village.

'Why Africa?' Brook said to us when we arrived. 'You will never have a greater opportunity to answer the question, "Why are we here?" You will never have a greater chance to learn and understand. We must use our eyes every second of the day. Because if there is a real Africa left any more, I think we've arrived.'

As luck would have it the Chief of the village was just about the most beautiful man any of us had seen in our lives, even in the movies.

When he came to visit us with his councillors he towered above them, serious and dignified in his robes, very gentle, tall and supple as a willow tree. 'My God,' whispered Michèle Collison as the rest of us tried to keep cool. 'Look at *that*. . . .'

The vision bowed to Brook, who was looking thunderstruck, and spoke in Hausa as the school-teacher cleaned his spectacles and translated into English:

'We are a peaceful people and we see that you come in peace. We welcome you.'

Touched by this, and not knowing quite what to do with the three live chickens, Brook presented them to the Chief.

A little explanation about why we had come:

'We are a group of actors. We are trying to discover a new way of communicating without the use of language. May we perform at your village?'

And as always happened, the Chief replied that he was most pleased. And as always happened, no further questions were asked. It never ceased to amaze and delight Brook—in Europe and America the agony of trying to explain and justify the nature of his work never ends. But in Africa it was totally accepted within seconds. In the West, the intellect rules and dominates. But the African goes about understanding differently, and bides his time.

Then the Chief and his councillors and the three live chickens left for the village.

A clearing was found in the rocks of the hillside where among snakes and goats the group exercised with sticks and unearthly sound, like witches. 'Are the snakes poisonous?' I asked one of the schoolchildren watching us. 'No,' he replied cheerfully, 'they strangle you.'

The village looked inviting, as all private worlds do. Could I risk entering? I left the group, walking across the valley and up the twisting goat path. I felt uneasy. Too many eyes stared. I was intruding. Eventually, I saw an old schoolhouse and peeped inside. A crowd of young children leapt to their feet instantly. 'Good afternoon, sir!' they yelled. They were well trained, in the English style. But the schoolmaster wasn't there for the moment and the children were too young to understand much English. I wasn't sure what to do. I said hello, but they just stood and stared. I must have looked a strange sight. 'Hello!' I said again, smiling hard. But they kept staring. 'Well if we can't speak to each other,' I said in desperation, 'then sing us a song!' At which they smiled and relaxed at last. *Song*—they knew the word and the second I said it that whole puzzled, polite, uneasy class of schoolkids erupted into this amazing song. And that was nice, I have to admit. The desks were bouncing. They sang lots of songs.

'Sorry,' I said to the schoolmaster when he returned. He said, 'Why?'

When I left the schoolhouse one of the villagers, perhaps thirty years old, quick like a ferret, beckoned me to follow him. He wore a ragged shirt and baggy old shorts. He walked barefoot.

238

The little toe of each foot was missing, though it didn't seem to trouble him. He wanted to show me round the village and I was glad to follow him.

We walked for miles through the fields where homes of mud and stone were scattered: none had a door.

Inside one was an empty Heinz Baked Bean tin. It must have been taken from our rubbish tip. It would find a purpose.

The rooms were dark and cool: uncluttered. Beds were made of smooth slabs of stone. My new friend laughed and showed me the knives he had made himself, a bow and arrow, a Bible. The village must have been converted to Christianity, though I learned there are still pagan ceremonies. No one would say more.

Over the entrance to one home the words in Hausa, which mean: 'God never sleeps.'

On the wall, a notice in English, status symbol of sorts: 'Care for your hair with Claricer. Claricer scalp investigator stimulates growth and keeps dandruff away from your hair. Use Claricer regularly and give your hair that glossy look that all of your friends envy and admire. Care for your hair with Claricer.'

We passed a circle of stones: a meeting place. The stones were shaped like toadstools.

Whenever there was a rock on the route through the fields my new friend put it carefully to one side, however small it was. There was a neatness about him, a sense of order: pride. Everything he showed me was done with pride.

As we walked he introduced me to many people: women beating washed clothes on stone, men returning from work in the fields, elders sitting on wooden stools among hens and goats. Strong people: strong and truthful lives.

The greeting would last a minute or so with everyone I met. 'Sanu!' 'Sanu kade!' 'Kade sanu!' 'Sanu kade . . .' The same words went back and forth, half-speech, half-song: ritual exchange. It just meant 'Hello!' But such a greeting means that you can never be curt to anyone. You must take your time to say hello.

When the greetings were over we drifted into silence. Silences can be awkward. And yet, when people are unable to speak the same language, they do not matter.

239

I was offered millet wine as the villagers laughed in anticipation. They know its effect. The wooden bowl was passed from mouth to mouth, like a joint.

We met the schoolmaster returning home before dusk.

'The houses don't seem to have any doors,' I said to him in English.

'Why are you surprised?'

'Well, maybe people can steal things.'

'Some have doors,' he said.

'But they're open.'

'But it's hot. And what would people steal?'

'Things, I guess.'

'But crime is unknown to us.'

'Doesn't anyone even pinch anything?'

'Yes,' replied the schoolmaster. 'But only for fun.'

When it was time to return to camp I wanted to thank my friend for troubling to show me his village. I felt awkward now: the tourist. I was embarrassed to offer money, particularly as it was getting short. Still, it would only be fair to give him something and I offered two pounds. He refused, gesturing that he couldn't accept it without offering a gift in exchange. He gave me a small leather bag and four fresh eggs. He returned some of the money. The bag was old.

Then he guided me across the fields back to camp. But when we arrived he wanted me to show him round the camp: our village.

He looked at the canvas beds, the nylon sleeping bags, the plastic plates, the steel knives, the aluminium chairs, the electric lights, the hissing kettles, the crates of warm beer, the stock piles of tinned food, the bustle and noise, everything he looked at with the same envy as I had looked at his world.

As always, we exercised early in the morning on the special movement that passes from one to another around a circle. An actor makes the simplest movement possible. Without looking directly at him, all follow. The next develops the movement, as all follow him. Until the movement is complete.

And for the first time, it worked. It *worked*! Nothing was

forced or complex. No one strained after outward effect. Somehow each movement flowed so naturally and spontaneously into the next it was as if one wasn't even aware of making it. It was as if our minds and bodies had vanished. And it seemed like a miracle.

'How did such a thing happen?' I asked Brook.

'What makes a spirit?' he replied, and laughed. 'If we could explain that one movement, we might know the secret to everything. All one can say is that something triggered us towards the most stunning simplicity. But it didn't happen by accident. It was worked for.'

That day the group looked as if it had shed a hundred years. For in the morning and afternoon two different shows were performed in the village and long stretches of them both worked marvellously. And glimpsed Brook's ideal theatre: spontaneous events. There, captured, were those long sought-for qualities of openness, simplicity, danger, special moments of intensity that seemed so spontaneous it was as if spirits were at work, playing. Sometimes it might last for only a few moments, this feeling that something unique had been caught at last, and then it was gone. For ever? The shows were little more than public workshops, stick work, song, the best musical work ever done by the group, and many birds: birds travelling, birds searching, birds lost, birds drowning, birds fighting for survival. The work was building up to another try at the big piece, *The Conference of the Birds*.

'You know,' said Zeldis afterwards, 'it's getting really irritating not being able to fly.'

The following morning, Brook and his wife drove all day with their children to the airport in Lagos. It was time for young Simon and Irina to return to Paris, incredible to believe they would be home in only a few hours. In his absence, Brook asked Myers to take personal responsibility for work on another show, *The Ogre Show*, which would be performed that night. Pleased and flattered, Myers accepted the job as the group's new boss. He found out later that Brook had given the same job to everyone else.

241

For myself, I had a meeting with the vision: The Beautiful Chief. 'Can you get us a *date*?' asked the girls. In the search for truth: escort agencies . . .

The Chief was waiting for me, sitting on the smooth rocks of the goat path that led into his village. Everything about him had such simplicity and goodness it was impossible not to feel a little awed in his presence. Yet he laughed easily, a man without a trace of self-importance, relaxed and friendly, curious to meet me. His name was Godunyilwada. Once a year his people cut the grass that is used to thatch the roofs of their homes. Before weaving the grass, the leaders pray to their gods. He was born on that day and so his name means 'A man born on the day the grass was cut'.

'It is nice to talk to you,' he said when we met. 'But you see, I am a little thirsty.'

A *hint*.

I dashed back to camp and returned with several bottles of beer, which were greeted with sounds such as, 'Oh, you shouldn't have troubled' and, 'Beer—what a surprise!' Everyone was laughing. The Chief drank his from a small glass, nodding appreciation.

The schoolmaster translated for us.

'Would it be impolite to ask your age?' I asked the Chief eventually.

'Why is it impolite to ask a question?' he replied. 'Why is it rude to ask someone's age?'

I replied that it was sometimes so in the West, particularly with actresses.

He smiled and went into discussion with his councillors, working out his age. He couldn't be certain. Perhaps he was forty-five.

'Older than you,' he said.

'But I feel a hundred and three.'

'Why? You are young.'

'But you are content. I walk round your village and everyone seems so.'

'To you we do,' replied the Chief, 'but we're not content. It isn't so. You see, quite a number of things worry us.'

And he named three: the crumbling school, the state of the crops and the low supplies of water.

'The people worry. A man who lives in the world has many problems.'

'Forgive me. My observation was stupid. It is just that life seems simple here.'

'To you, perhaps.'

'Then if you could leave here for a life in the city, would you?'

'I am sure he wouldn't,' said the schoolmaster.

'It is too late for me,' said the Chief. 'My parents forbade me to attend the missionary school. They were suspicious. And so I have no education and could not survive in the city. I have many children too. And those of my dead brothers.'

'Have you ever been in a car?' I asked.

'Once, once I went in a car.'

'What was it like?'

'*Comfortable,*' the Chief replied, and laughed again.

'Would you like one?'

'If I get it, I should be happy.'

'Do you think you ever will?'

'By what means?'

'Your children will become rich and give you one.'

'If there's life,' replied the Chief, 'there's hope.'

'Do you have many children?'

The counting went on for some time as he consulted with the others.

'I have nineteen of my own. And you?'

'One.'

'And how many wives?'

'One.'

I was beginning to feel depressed.

'One, at the last count,' I added. 'But in the West it's fairly normal.'

'I don't believe it,' said the Chief, looking shocked.

'How many wives do you have?'

'Seven, at present.'

'If there's life, there's hope.'

'Right!' replied the Chief.

'But don't your wives get jealous of each other?'

'No woman can live without jealousy.'

'That's true.'

'But it isn't a problem for the man. It's *their* problem. The women should not trouble the men with such matters as jealousy.'

'And nor,' I added, 'should the men trouble the women.'

The Chief paused to consider the matter.

'Perhaps,' he replied, looking cautious.

'But how can you give the same amount of attention to each of your wives?'

'I don't. It is not possible. I love them all. But I tell only one my secrets.'

'Which one?'

'That is one of the secrets,' replied The Cautious Chief.

But now he had a question for me.

'Are all the women who come here with you married?'

'No,' I told him. 'And those who aren't have asked if you would be kind enough to meet them.'

'Why should they wish to meet me?'

'Well, I think they can't resist temptation.'

At which everyone exploded with gales of laughter.

'But are they *mature*?' asked the Chief.

'How deep is the ocean, how high is the sky?'

'What does *that* mean?' asked the translator.

'I'm not sure. I'm just giving the message.'

'But which one of them would agree to stay behind in the village?' asked the Chief.

'I can't say, I'm afraid. It's quite a *step*.'

'To ask for the love of a woman is difficult.'

'Not always,' I replied, waving the flag.

'But in our case,' explained the Chief, 'even if the woman loved a man with all her heart she would never admit it.'

'Then how would the man ever know?'

'Someone else would tell him.'

'Well I'm doing my *best*,' I said.

And again the Chief and his councillors roared with affectionate laughter.

'Please, what did you think when you first saw us arrive?'

'Every year, European people come here in vehicles and stay in
the same place that you sleep. They disappear over the far side
of the valley. But they never speak to us. They arrive and disappear. We thought you were them. I was disturbed. But when
I learned that you came in peace, we welcomed you. My father
was the first to accept the white man in this area. He foresaw that
they would come one day. And while he was alive, they came.'

'How did he know they would come?'

'He heard sounds.'

'Do you hear such sounds?'

'Yes, I do.'

But he would say no more.

'And when you see our plays, what do you think?'

'Some of our sons have been overseas and they tell us of the
white people who sing and dance. And now we know it is a fact.'

'Why do you seem surprised?'

'Because we did not think it was possible for white people to
use their bodies as Africans do. We did not think they could
speak with their bodies.'

'It is the whole point of the work.'

'Well, we welcome you. If my father accepted the white
man, why should I turn him away? I do not mistrust you. But in
the past the white man has not always been accepted. It is true
that time kills all things. If not, you would never have met us.'

'Why?'

'Because we would have run away,' replied the beautiful Chief.

That night the actors waited for Brook to return from Lagos.
Then they crossed the valley into the village and performed
The Ogre Show. Here's just a short extract from the first part—

> A box enters, breathes and makes sounds.
> Birds approach the breathing box.
> A spirit warns of evil.
> One bird, an idiot, ignores the spirit and opens the box.

Ogre leaps out and kills. The ogre becomes a bird, eating the bird.
And returns to the box.
The ogre gives birth to a baby ogre.
In time, the baby ogre gives birth to a baby ogre.

And that was the first happy scene from the show. Based on several of Ted Hughes' strange and perverse poems, it had always seemed needlessly complex whenever the group worked on it before. Somehow, what were thought to be direct and simple images in Europe never seemed so in Africa. But for the first time a new clarity and power was caught here too. Maybe all one is left with after any play is an image. The story and plot, the author's finely honed lines, often they're forgotten soon afterwards. But a particular image might live with you for life. Perhaps Beckett is like this. But under that massive tree in the village of Dungung startling images were discovered, as if a new form of theatre could be glimpsed struggling to emerge from that vile world of ogre-monsters. Something was happening, all right. That other ogre-monster called Mr. Brook was looking unusually pleased.

But at the conference after the show, he talked to the actors of their true role. 'Reach out more into the imagination. Try harder to reach into your own world of experiences and fears. We're beginning to touch on it, beginning to find it. Avoid the mini-world of indulgence and interpretation. The true role of the actor must be creative. Open it up, as writers do. It's *there*.'

Then he reminded them that when the group was first formed at the height of the '68 revolution in Paris, the most popular student slogan was '*L'imagination au Pouvoir*'.

If so, Long Live Imagination!

The following day, the day of *The Conference of the Birds*, a messenger came from the village asking Brook to go to the Chief.

When he arrived at the village, the Chief and his councillors were sitting on wooden stools around the tree where we had performed. One man held a ram on a lead.

'I am sorry,' said the Chief. 'I cannot feed you all. But we would like to give you something. We would like to give you this ram.'

Nothing so wonderful could happen to us, a gift as generous as this from people who had no need to give us a thing. When the outsider sees in the African qualities that seem lost to his world, perhaps it is moments such as this which convince him of the truth. Touched and moved, Brook accepted the gift, calling on all the others to come and accept it with him.

We returned to the camp, taking the ram with us.

But that innocent ram was to lead to more problems than could have been imagined. For once accepted, the question arose as to what to do with it. Do we kill the ram? What do we do with the ram? 'All right, everyone! Gather round now. We're having a conference.' The conference of the ram.

The ram was tied to a tree, chewing grass: indifferent to its fate. The ram must be killed! But others fought for it. To Brook's surprise and exasperation, quite a few argued emotionally against killing it. One thing to eat a ram, another to kill it. '*Ridiculous*,' snapped Brook. But we *know* the ram, others argued back only making things worse. I mean, we didn't kill the chickens from the Village of the Loonies. Why pick on a ram? Why not *give* it away? We could put it in the back of the truck. We could take it *home*. 'Or we could give it back,' snapped Brook again. 'Kill it,' argued Sylvain Corthay, keener than anyone. Corthay had volunteered for the job of slaughterer. 'It's only right,' added Miriam Goldschmidt, 'we must learn to live off the land.' 'Live off the *land*,' groaned Mr. Royston Bennett, the camp master. 'My God but there's hell to pay when there's not enough Rice Crispies in the morning.'

Well I was enjoying this conference, particularly as Brook looked in danger of losing the vote. 'I vote against killing the ram,' I said when it was my turn to speak. 'I vote against on the grounds that I'm en route to becoming a vegetarian.' Brook rose above that. But then Mr. Lou Zeldis, who is a vegetarian, spoke. 'I vote against. I think we should give the ram a crown of thorns and let it roam free in the forest.' At which Brook looked as if he would hit the roof. 'Alternatively,' added Zeldis, 'we could paint it *blue*.' At which Brook looked as if he would hit the sky. And so he put a stop to such nonsense, guillotined the debate and ordered the ram to be killed. 'It's right,' said Corthay, asking for a sharp knife. 'I feel this is a special moment. I feel it will help the work. . . .'

Help the *work*? For myself, I didn't mind them killing the ram really. But for the life of me, and the life of the ram, I couldn't see how the work would benefit. You might as well kill a few relatives in order to play *Hamlet* a little better. 'Sorry, dad. But you always said you wanted my name in lights.' One time before the journey, I talked with Brook about the difference between theatre and ritual. He was discussing the vital distinction between ceremony in theatre and ceremony in religion. In the rituals of religious ceremony you kill animals, you kill people: blood sacrifice. But for Brook, theatre must always draw a distinction. For theatre always imitates. And he gave me a startling illustration.

At the end of his controversial play about Vietnam, *US*, a butterfly was burnt in full view of the audience. But it wasn't a real butterfly. Brook held passionately that the job of the actors was to burn a fake butterfly in such a way that everyone in the audience would be convinced they were burning a real one. In fact he took the argument to absurdity, though he was forced to by an amazing row which could only happen in England. When they saw the production, dog and butterfly lovers everywhere were outraged and called in The Royal Society for the Prevention of Cruelty to Animals. So Brook secretly told them the actors were really burning a piece of crumpled paper but if they ever dared to reveal it, he would substitute a real butterfly. Therefore to his delight, if they respected the life of a butterfly they had to accept the shame of not protesting.

Thus theatre imitates and animates life. Still, I couldn't help thinking it was only a butterfly. Wasn't Brook taking life a little seriously? 'No,' he replied. 'We're not qualified in the name of something as vague and spurious even as art to take anyone's life. We can shout and protest and do many things, but we can't take anyone's life—starting with the life of a butterfly.'

And a ram? Too late, too late for Brook to change the course of events now. The emotional debate had swept the issue into a setting no actor belongs. Actors *always* over-dramatize. The killing of the ram had become a form of theatre. The slaughter had turned into a sacrifice.

No one outside the acting group troubled to attend. And three actors chose not to either: Yoshi Oida, François Marthouret and Mirren. 'If you feel hungry and want to eat,' Mirren said to me, 'then kill and eat in honesty. Do not kill to bring anyone closer to their work.'

There weren't any scenes or anything. They ate the ram with the others afterwards.

Corthay led the ram into a clearing among the rocks of the valley. There, Katsulas and Bagayogo tied its legs together and hung it struggling from the thick branch of a tree. Brook and the rest gathered quietly: mixture of morbid curiosity, excitement and nerves. Corthay had slaughtered animals before. In his youth he killed the sheep of his family's farm in the south of France. When he was three years old he used to watch fascinated as his brother killed the sheep before delivering meat and wool to the local merchants. To keep him quiet, his brother always threw him the bones. He broke off the legs, peeled them and threw him the fresh bones to eat.

'My uncle's a butcher,' announced Katsulas, tying the rope round the ram. The others began to laugh nervously. Swados appeared with the bread knife over her head like a scene from *Psycho*. 'He's a butcher in St. Louis, Missouri.'

Then Corthay took the knife.

Made the shape of a cross on the head of the ram.

Kissed the cross.

And slit its throat.

Blood gushed over him, and the other two holding the ram down.

The others turned green.

The ram twitched violently, wounded only, fighting for life. The thrust of the blade could not have been clean. The ram was still strong. The ram was refusing to die! Horrified, some began to laugh nervously again. Brook quietened them sternly. Respect for the ram! But it would not die! What eternity passed before us then! Was the ram unaware that it was being sacrificed? That was the term used. Not 'killed' or 'slaughtered', but *sacrificed*. And to which deity? asked the ram. And receiving no reply, would not assist. Again Corthay plunged the knife into its throat and again the ram fought back, struggling and twitching, gasping for air as blood spattered. *But it would not die!* Used animal, degraded, innocent victim of this fake ceremony, resisting inevitable death, defiant, cursing, mocking ram, it fought for a more worthy end than this. *Die!* But it gasped only for more air, choking, fighting still until in one magnificent effort it gathered up all life that was left, sucked in the air with its whole being and *farted* it out in the faces of its stunned audience. Again Corthay went for it. But the ram only farted its final farewell. Oh sweet, slaughtered, lovely, farting ram. You saw it all.

Then it was skinned, disembowelled, chopped up, boiled and eaten.

When we left the valley the following day to continue the journey, it was by coincidence the holy day of the year when all Muslims are called on to sacrifice a ram. It's called the great day of Eid-ul-Adha, the day of symbolic sacrifice when a father offers a son to his Maker. Along the road in the fields and the backs of homes many Muslims gathered together to make their sacrifice. Sometimes hundreds of people could be seen, meeting and praying. But amongst them, without drama or piety, the ram was slaughtered swiftly on the earth and then given away. The rich give to the poor. Everyone sacrifices a portion of his wealth, sharing the celebration feast with those who are without means. Trying as best they could to share the customs of Africa, several actors killed a ram. But amongst them, no one shared his meal with a single villager.

Before the evening meal we crossed the valley for the final performance, *The Conference of the Birds*. As before the whole village was there, perhaps 400 people: same number as the first day.

Many ideas had been discussed, trying to sustain the idea of a voyage. But the actors decided against too much preparation, preferring to live dangerously during the performance. Such a risk means that anything can go wrong for no one knows in advance what might happen. In the book of *The Conference of the Birds,* the birds who make the journey do not know what might happen to them either. Their leader has told them of the seven valleys they must cross to find God. But the way through the valleys they must discover for themselves. Only the reason for the journey is known.

The actors gathered round the great tree of Dungung, and began. And *exploded.* Never since the journey began had there been such frenzied outpouring of energy and movement, wild surrealist expression of dreams and hopes, high as if on drugs, calling, screaming to each other, amazing as dervishes, near anarchy from insane spirits, forcing new images into life, in a travel dance, these birds on the move, to drums, sound, gesture, violent and crazed journey through sun and fire, desperate voyage through voids and valleys.

'What's happening?' I asked Brook.

But he was laughing too much to answer.

22

Then the crew walked out.

All communities, however small, need their fall-guy. It helps people survive, making them feel strong. But the crew were weak. And they'd had enough. It was different when the actors hit all-time lows. They could always be sustained by the work outside themselves, the grand illusion maybe, but it kept them going. From the depths of near despair the whole atmosphere of the group had been transformed by two villages: village of love, village of craziness. But without interest in the work, without diversion or relief, slogging through rough and stifling conditions, exhausted now, demoralized, sick of having their judgement questioned, sick of being the fall-guy, the crew felt trapped in an alien world. They felt used.

All of them were ill now.

The Leader, leader in name only, a lonely and insecure figure, a man to whom a sense of authority meant everything, had dysentery.

The Camp Master, powerless in his own kingdom, incensed by damaged equipment and the battering the Land-Rovers were taking, tired and strained, fussing over every lost tea cup and filched tomato like Captain Queeg—he had malaria.

The Cook, reduced to tears, unable to cope any longer, had malaria too.

The Mechanic, still shaky after a week's hospitalisation for severe malaria and a slipped disc, collapsed again bitten by a scorpion. 'I expect it'll be a lion next,' he said with a smile. He was a gentle and popular man, easier than the others. Opposed to the walk-out, he didn't involve himself. But the rest of the crew would make their stand—the Leader's last stand.

So the journey, reason and essence of which was to discover

new and powerful ways of making contact with people, hit a supreme irony. 'But don't you understand?' said Zeldis when the crew finally gave up on their rules and regulations, their rigid formats and chains of command. 'We've *won*.' But as the others nodded happy agreement, they got it wrong. They'd lost. The sad situation was never transformed. The camps within camps never met.

'If you could only *see*,' Brook would implore us.

But to the astonishment and anger of the crew, Brook had made a dramatic change in route again, intending now to travel through the potentially dangerous area of former Biafra.

The crew, lacking a sense of poetry, did not wish to die yet.

Although we would only touch the area, high-ranking officials had warned Brook in Paris that since the end of the Nigerian Civil War banditry might still exist there. If he wished to go they advised him to take every care. The cries and sounds of a Brook show echoing out through the forests might be misinterpreted. Perhaps the experts thought they'd start another war. Still, he took the precaution of abandoning work on a piece of music called *The Gun Symphony*. Which led to the story about the time he was ambushed by bandits in Southern Spain and tied to a tree. It could only happen to Brook. He managed to escape but the local police arrested him at gun-point. They thought he was one of the bandits.

'So you see,' he explained, 'people get the wrong idea.'

No matter. Rather than keep to the dull route into Yorubaland, Brook preferred to ignore the crew's advice and head out of the plateau through the thick forests of the south. Also, it was difficult to believe there was any real danger. The civil war had been over four years.

'Lives are at stake!' the Leader liked to say, handing out warnings about rabid dogs and murderous strangers in the night. At times it was as if he had a greater sense of drama than any actor. Unaware of danger, we didn't fear it. But throughout the entire journey the Leader lived in fear that something was always about to go desperately wrong. If just one Land-Rover was seriously damaged this overcrowded and overweight

253

expedition would have been in trouble. Two of the cars were so badly battered they would be sold as scrap at the journey's end. If we had got lost in the desert it's possible we might have died, singing as we went. It happens, I suppose. But for the weary crew this latest change in route was the final straw. The Leader knew nothing of the area. The roads would be hazardous. Food and water supplies were running low. An estimated million Biafrans were wiped out by a Nigerian government supported in the war by Britain. All the cars carried British number plates.

The crew confronted Brook in private.

The Leader made his stand.

Three hours later we climbed back into the Land-Rovers, and left for Biafra.

We had almost forgotten what it could be like on the road, cramped for hours, thirsty, boiling: silent. The long drive of the first day descending the plateau practically finished us. The way was lost many times, twisting and struggling through dust bowls and rough tracks leading nowhere. The crew sweated and cursed. Sudden blanket heat and dryness hit us: air hissing from a balloon. The heat was suffocating, yet we couldn't see the sun. A mist was over our eyes, like a cataract.

Sign on a lorry: 'No Condition is Permanent.'

We crossed the Makurdi bridge into former Biafran territory. Brook had gone ahead of the convoy, travelling faster alone in search of a possible place to play. But to our surprise, border guards stopped us on the bridge. Passports were demanded, as if entering a foreign country. The Leader went white. On the bonnet of his Land-Rover a mad man hummed and laughed.

We were forced to stay in the cars, stewing for two hours or so. The guards seemed young and excitable, searching us. The river beneath the bridge was silent.

The two Africans in the group were ordered out of the cars.

Bagayogo and Ayansola, nervous now, had been singled out.

'What are you doing with these people?' snapped the most threatening of the guards.

'We work with them,' Bagayogo replied. 'They are a group of actors.'

'How can you be sure?'

'I know them.'

'Don't let them use you.'

As we set off again, a motorbike followed us. It had been following us since the day we entered Nigeria.

But once across the bridge we couldn't find Brook. He'd disappeared. A search party went off but returned without success. Where was he? Was he lost? Was he in trouble? Had he, maybe, by any chance, not that anyone even wanted to think about it, but had he been *killed*?

No, he was looking for a Mr. Ubu. Mr. Ubu, a local contact, lived in the nearby town of Gboko. He lived in the Government House. But when Brook finally got there they'd never heard of him. This was because he'd gone to the wrong place. He'd been directed to the Rest House. But they hadn't heard of Mr. Ubu at the Government House either. Where *was* Mr. Ubu? Many meetings, many searches: many false trails. So Brook set off in search of a schoolmaster recommended to him during his visit to Jos. Many meetings, many searches: many schools. Until at last the schoolmaster was found and he directed Brook to the home of the Chief. But the Chief wasn't home. Nor at his second home, which was being built. Nor in his office. And if he wasn't in his office, everyone advised, then he *must* be in the bar. But he wasn't in the bar. And the whole town was most surprised now. Brook searched on until, miraculously, he found him under a tree swigging a bottle of Nigerian Guinness.

The Chief turned out to be a powerful man in the region, a fixer, a Gboko Godfather. No trouble, a performance could take place immediately. Do not worry about an audience.

Soldiers hemmed us in as we waited for Brook to rejoin the convoy at the cross-roads into town. Tivs: said to be the toughest fighters in the Nigerian army. They demanded money, teasing and goading. They put the evil eye on you. 'If there's trouble,' said one to Marthouret, 'you must escape quickly.' But to me he said, 'How *will* you escape?' That had me thinking. I did not like the look of the Tivs. They reminded me of Ernest Borgnine.

On one side of the road a strange group of dancers performed in a crowded market-place, waving toy guns. They wore dark glasses and shiny watches, pointing to the watches with the toy guns as they made undulating movements around a drummer. Two women were dressed in white shorts and shirts, patrolling outside the circle like policemen. All the dancers were women, pointing to their watches with toy guns.

The dance had been invented to cool tempers after the civil war. The watches mean that time runs out.

The Very Short Show

The show for the Gboko Godfather was to be watched by no more frightening crowd throughout the journey, and no show collapsed so quickly.

Therefore, I can be brief.

More than a thousand Tivs were waiting for us when the convoy drove into the fields.

The actors froze, as if they'd seen a ghost.

'Keep the engines running,' said Katsulas as we parked the Land-Rovers.

The group knew they couldn't master such a crowd. In Brook's scheme of things, nothing succeeds like failure. But there had been no preparation or discussion beforehand. There wasn't even a show. Or an idea. After respectful greetings with the Chief, Brook sent the actors out for the most dangerous test of all, near suicide mission before a crowd as vast as this: total improvisation.

No need to put the carpet down! The crowd had created its own empty space, forming itself into the shape of a frightening arena fifty yards square. Who would have the nerve to enter? And with what? No one was moving. Brook stood staring, impassive in the crowd: human X-ray machine. The actors were glancing nervously at each other. The crowd fell silent, waiting for something to happen.

Then Zeldis risked it, walking slowly round and round the vast, silent arena. Gradually, others joined him. It looked hopeful. Maybe the group would take off where the last performance ended. Tigers walk in such a way before they pounce. . . .

Suddenly they accelerated—taking the crowd completely by surprise. The actors quickened in pace, as if about to strike. But something was badly wrong. Too fast! In fear and doubt they'd slipped back into an old trap. They were *running*—and running so fast that the stifling heat could only dehydrate and finish them. Out for sudden dramatic effect, willing and forcing ideas into being, impatient, panicking, the actors had lost their heads. Amazingly, they were tearing round the field at such speed it was as if they were trying to run a two-minute mile. Madness! The crowd cheered but the group was out of control. They were running themselves into the ground. In the sweat and heat the arena was too big and the pace too killing. Within minutes all of them were burnt out.

The X-ray machine switched itself off.

Nothing, one knew it, would be discovered that day. The exhausted actors, embarrassed and shaken, struggled on as best they could. The audience looked blank, or laughed, or turned away. Katsulas, group barometer of collective frustration and disaster, could only curse and swear his way through. At which several Australian missionaries in the crowd upped and walked out. 'Mary! Paul! Matthew! Swear words! That's it! *Swear words!*' You could almost hear the seats slam.

No conference followed, breaking an unwritten rule. An elementary blunder had killed the show and everyone knew it. Or as Brook liked to say, 'Never begin in the KYU of KYU.' You might end up a stretcher case. Besides, there wasn't time for a meeting. Another show mercifully followed ours: exotic local performers, monster human puppets and dancing men made of straw, exciting warrior drummers and ritual displays which transformed the dead atmosphere and had the crowd roaring. What life was there! And yet for all that one sensed something within it was missing. For all the natural vitality and fine skills of the performers, the life that was revealed to us had begun to die.

It's bound to be so. Life changes, becoming modern. The

I

influence of twentieth-century life and orthodox religions destroy the traditional arts. Africa's fine, ritual pottery is replaced by imported tin. The art of indigo dying slowly gives way to cheap chemical dyes. The everyday beauty and craftsmanship of cooking utensils and furniture are destroyed by mass-produced objects: conveyor-belt production. A nation of proud woodcarvers produces 'airport culture', or fights for survival against the odds.

So the performers we saw had been made decorative and spectacular, becoming 'entertainment'. Modern influences were taking their toll. Perhaps before long those performers would be 'discovered', to perform in the big culture houses of the West or those of the African cities. In fact, one of the groups had already visited an arts festival in America. But the natural art and traditions of a community had begun to wither. Soon the community itself will die. People cry, 'Luddite!' But something that cannot be replaced will have been lost.

For ever? The Gboko Godfather showed what he thought of our own attempts at an answer. The Chief made Brook an offer he couldn't refuse. He presented him with six eggs.

'That's interesting,' said Katsulas as we left. 'A village of hundreds gave us a ram. A town of thousands gave us six eggs.'

Each day the Leader stepped up the pace, anxious to reach Ife: centre of the world.

A sense of urgency and excitement overtook us.

New land opened up, land of pea-green rivers and rain forests, of coconut, cactus and grapefruit trees, foliage so thick it was more like a jungle.

At night you could hear termites feasting on leaves.

Women streamed into the markets carrying calabashes on their heads, waving and blowing kisses as the convoy sped on.

By the roadside they splayed their legs apart, peeing like giraffes.

Always we bought fried beans and nuts in the markets, never meat. The group doctor advised against it. But Bagayago, proud of being African and thinking himself immune, ate meat once. Then he retched up. He'd eaten a rat.

Sign on a shack: 'Truth is Life'.

One night where we camped in the forest I followed the sound of drums and a guitar grating through a loudspeaker.

Men danced with each other, arm in arm.

A leaflet advertised 'The Progressive Union'.

Each day we drove for nine hours, crammed sweating and stinking in the cars until the light went or the drivers were too exhausted.

Bombed-out villages followed, shells: Ibo country of the conquered and dead.

We found a clearing where it was possible to camp in a yam field swarming with beetles and mosquitoes. We flattened the red earth and slumped, eager to rest. In the forest eyes stared: children's eyes. The children were too nervous to approach. As always happened, songs were sung. And suddenly, the music produced seemed exceptional. The songs were of a quality no one had ever reached before.

And the children approached.

They wanted to take us somewhere. They asked if we would go to a ceremony taking place nearby. So we followed them for a mile or so through the forest, guided by torchlight. But when we arrived at the destination there wasn't a ceremony as we understood it. But a funeral.

The children sat us on stools in a clearing surrounded by giant palm trees. In the darkness a village elder tuned a drum by chopping pieces of wood in two and tying them tightly to the drum's side. His matchet scythed straight through the tiny pieces of wood without hesitation. Then he played. And shadows danced and sang.

Not sadly.

And asked us to sing our songs.

From where or how I could not be sure, the group created a song so gentle and perfect it was as if everything in this journey had come together in a second, and lived.

Strangers met in the darkness, joining each other.

As we drove on to Yorubaland another event was to stun me almost as much as that wonderful meeting.

Against all expectations, against the grain, Brook suddenly

started to perform. No one could quite believe it. It was as if a statue had come to life.

The only time he'd ever acted was forty years ago. He acted in a school play, making a dramatic appearance. He stood proudly on wooden battlements, and announced: 'We surrender our city to you. Our expectation hath this day an end.' Loved it, apparently. But somehow he was never asked to act again.

Brook's surprising appearance on the carpet was therefore quite a step, not to be taken lightly. For all his experience and love of theatre, acting comes so unnaturally to him wild horses couldn't drag him on to a stage. He would advise them against it. Yet in Africa he suddenly plunged in at the deep end like a novice swimmer. It was as if he were lost in a world of his own. Watching him perform, amused at the curious new image of himself, bashful, awkward, excited, happy to be tasting an experience he'd avoided for years, the results can only be described as unusual. But such a step, it was more a leap, went beyond an impulsive dare with him. Something essential to a full understanding of this man had begun to free itself.

The convoy stopped for the night in the bush, a day's drive from Ife. And the moment we stopped, we were surrounded. Not by bandits, though. *Children!* Scores of children came running, surrounding the cars and the weary actors, yelling and laughing, eager to glimpse the unexpected visitors. Some of the kids were naked. We could scarcely move for children.

Normally we went through the dull routine of pitching camp as soon as we arrived anywhere—setting up the kitchen equipment, the tables and chairs, lights, water filter, camp-beds, mosquito nets, everything in its place before darkness fell. When the journey first began it took us almost two hours. Nowadays we'd got it down to about twenty minutes. Katsulas, the camp commandant, would start going for the world record. Swados would be perched on the roof of a Land-Rover unloading kit-bags onto people's heads, like Molotov cocktails. Myers would be very busy inventing some new washing-up system, such as all eat off the same plate. This cartoon activity. . . . But when we arrived this time, Brook unexpectedly skipped pitching camp for the moment. Instead he sprang out of his car, leading the crowds of children into a nearby field. To everyone's astonishment he was blowing on a flute. Brook, usually so prudent, had decided to perform.

It was doubly astonishing because he wasn't exactly an expert on the flute. I'm not so sure he could play it at all. No matter! No one was judging him. And the delighted children swarmed round and followed. Pied Piper! He was blowing so hard on the tiny flute it looked as if his head would come off. Also, he was jumping up and down....

Release from the road! Cramped cars, silence, weariness, tension—freedom in the wild happening! The rest of the group quickly grabbed drums and flutes and joined Brook, running, screaming, jumping, jumping up and down like the leaping Tuaregs of renown.

The Noise Show.

Couldn't go wrong.

Brook took the lead, building up duets and movements and chaos. He was taking on that vital quality of Nigerian culture, which is called noise. The show might not have won the Best Musical of the Year Award, but you couldn't ignore it. 'That's it!' yelled Myers, screaming with the rest. 'THE LOST CHORD!' You learn something new every day. Noise isn't noise until you've really tried. Still, Brook isn't that crazy. Before long he would exit from the carpet leaving the actors to slide into more serious improvisation, something they do best—gradually lulling amazed and unsuspecting strangers into such a pitch of involvement they're watching a real show before they know it. In such a way, order comes from chaos. Open transformation! It's the one part of acting that fascinates Brook more than anything. The actor's ability to change and transform completely into another person. Was this what Brook was after for himself too?

I was convinced of it. The Brook who suddenly cut the ground from under himself and tried to perform in Africa could no longer be regarded as the masterful director of his own work. In search of his real potential, he'd become one of its guinea-pigs. It was clearer than ever now. He was trying to enter his own

261

void, like his actors. I didn't think he wanted to be an actor. But I think that deep within him, he was in search of something more essential to his life. He had become a man who longs to wake up on the other side of his identity. In that sudden, manic plunge into performing in public I knew now that Brook the intellectual was trying desperately to kindle the very thing within himself that he wants from actors: a true creative flame.

Acting isn't the answer for him. To perform in public takes an enormous act of temperament, perverse kind of courage, and Brook just doesn't have it. He's come by a different route. He told me he wasn't sure whether he has no natural wish to act because he hasn't got the talent, or he hasn't got the wish. But even a brief try at performing could give him an insight into that side of his nature which has been submerged over years and years of directing other people's lives. A greater creativity and balance were there to be found within Brook's doubts and uncertainties. In time his own deadening habits and conditioned reponses might be lost, as a chain smoker cures himself. Such an man won't emerge a 'new' being. He will become more himself. Through struggle and longing, he will have found himself.

Brook had been destined to make a more ambitious appearance on the carpet earlier in the journey, but chickened out. He was supposed to play the role of a wise bird king who brings two warring bird families together in peace. But when the moment came, he didn't make it. Because the wise bird king, being wise, knew his limitations. 'Well why don't you try?' he said to me afterwards. Excuses, excuses. I just didn't have the courage. But from the way Brook reacted that time to the prospect of appearing on the carpet, I knew he didn't have the courage either. And yet here he was, making his amazing début as the leaping flute player of the African bush. And he was to risk a real try at acting eventually. When the group went to California and the campesinos of San Juan Bautista, he put himself to the test in a performance of *The Conference of the Birds*. He played a charlatan. Everyone plays charlatan.

We entered Ife the next day.

23

When the convoy entered Ife, weaving its way slowly through the narrows streets of the shanty town, Ayansola suddenly ordered his Land-Rover into the lead.

As it overtook us I could see him grinning to himself in dazzling new robes. He was tuning his talking drum.

He leaned out of the window of his car and thrust an arm into the air to stop us.

So we stopped.

Then he got out of his car and walked several paces ahead. And turned, waving us to follow him.

So we followed.

He walked ahead, took hold of that claw he used on his drum and split the heavens with it. Jesus! The crowds came running to greet him! Oh, the joy and power of his drumming now! King! The rest of us were ignored. From the homes and market stalls the people mobbed him. *King!* He took the greetings and applause, as of right. He looked just about the happiest man there could be on earth. Ayansola was where he wanted to be.

He was home.

Now we were thrown into the whole sweep and force of this legendary world of gods and ritual, cults and mystery we had never experienced in our lives before. According to Yoruba myth the creation of the world took place in Ife. It's a holy city, ancestral home of all Yorubas and cradle of mankind—black or white.

There's a supreme God. Yorubas call him Oladumare. But hundreds of gods are part of him, divine offshoots: cult of many gods to suit many people. Yorubas mostly worship these, renewing their faith each day through song and dance, drumming, divination, offerings and ritual. In spite of the inroads made by Chris-

tianity and Islam, the cult still remains a powerful force in religious life—and is a way of life. It affects everything, for in the
process of deity worship the people actually take on the character-
istics of their god. Shango is the god of thunder and his worshippers are likely to be emotional, quick-tempered, extrovert. Shango
punishes quickly but doesn't bear grudges. Eshu is a trickster god,
fate, creative and destructive, identified by missionaries with the
devil. Ogun is the symbol of iron, patron of hunters and soldiers,
powerful and strong.

It's a fascinating cult which accounts for a rich and electric
culture—often mistaken in the West for black magic or voodoo.
And it's the source of so much of the natural vitality of the people
who worship their gods with a mixture of love, abuse, awe and
humour. Black Americans in search of their roots have traced
their ancestry back to Yorubaland. Cult centres have sprung up in
New York. It's a highly tolerant and appealing religion which
carries with it neither the guilt-complex of Christianity nor the intense self-sacrifice of the East. More than anything perhaps, it's a
cult which stresses the unity of life and the universe: harmony.
Regardless of space or time, the past and myth are linked to life as
lived. Myth, like the dead, is seen as part of a fuller reality. Reality
becomes Whole.

For Brook, this new and exciting world was another way of
expanding the known and comfortable areas of our minds into
a greater sense of awareness. A people capable of moving so freely
between the real and the imaginary, the concrete and the mysterious, goes to the heart of the group's search. Yorubaland, we
knew it, would be a place to return to. But perhaps in a short
time something could be found, something which might push the
work into a direction we had never even imagined. And there was
one vital part of the Yoruba religion which fascinated Brook more
than all of this: the potentially dangerous cult of possession.

It can be a risky and frightening field for the outsider, and
easily misunderstood. The stranger who plays around with
possession might find himself in dangerous territory, as if one
had taken an acid trip for the first time. But Yoruba possession in
its purest form owes nothing to the more violent and traditional

forms practised in Haiti—or Dahomey, the next stop on our
route. The cults of possession outside Yorubaland would have
taken us little further than the mad-house. They're the exotic
forms of voodoo which often result in crude hysteria or a kind of
fit. The individual possessed in this way no longer exists as himself. It's as if he's sleep-walking. But what's so fantastic about
Yoruba possession is that it does the reverse. At the height of
deity worship, the Yoruba reaches the state when the force of his
god enters his whole being. But consciousness isn't wiped out.
In fact all capacities are tuned and stretched to their highest
levels of awareness. The individual isn't possessed in the way
that a man loans his house to a friend. He invites the friend to
stay with him. He receives him. It's an extraordinary phenomenon
of change and it was precisely this quality which fascinated
Brook so much. Yoruba possession is a supreme form of acting.
Like the actor, the medium or the spy, it's another area of life
where man transforms himself into another person.

The Yoruba remains himself. But he 'becomes' his god. So
the actor takes on the challenge of a role which is greater than
himself. The role is his god. The actor stretches himself to his
fullest height until the role he plays enters every pore in his
body. He 'becomes' his role. Then we witness something which
happens so rarely in theatre. The actor will be completely at
one with the role he plays. He understands exactly what he's
doing. But he will be possessed.

We knew that we might never be allowed close to Yoruba
possession, for cults value their secrets. But if we could only
see something of it, we would have seen an ultimate—the form
of possession considered to be the most mysterious and powerful
in the world.

As in Kano in the north, we headed now for the vast university of
Ife and camped there. But the modern campus turned out to be
completely shut off from the chaos and vitality of the town, a
sprawling suburban showpiece of wide avenues and tree-lined
routes, of identical gardens and identical homes: newly built
toy town entered through a toll gate as if from one country to

another. This soulless European monster seemed bigger than Ife itself, threatening it: schizoid creation.

It would be our base.

We camped in the forest within its grounds. But this 'natural' way of life had its set-backs too. The only clearing available to us was by a swamp. Ants in your hair, ants in your pants. Bull-frogs belched and croaked all night from the swamp. The noise was incredible, nerve-racking, as if that insane invention called the frog was preparing to march on us. Mosquitoes, snakes, bugs, sweat, nausea, sickness: malaria. 'I can't take any more of this,' groaned Myers, unable to sleep at night.

Myers had gone down with malaria for a second time.

The sick bay was growing worse.

Swados had a serious ear infection, unable to hear properly: going deaf, like Beethoven.

The stage manager was so ill he had to be hospitalised. He'd lost thirty pounds in weight.

Two newcomers arrived, looking hesitant. Sally Jacobs, the designer who's worked most with Brook over the years, arrived by plane from California. With her came a man called Steve Benedict, a man who ought to have a detective series named after him. A cool presence in his buttoned down shirts and lightweight suits, Mr. Benedict turned out to be a powerful figure in the Rockefeller Foundation. He hands out money. And is therefore a very popular man.

'You know,' he said to me after two days, 'before I came to Africa I thought I'd hate camping.'

'And now?' I asked.

'Now I *know* I hate camping.'

He was a nice man. He took on a sort of Kissinger role for Brook, fixing this and that, shuttle, shuttle, here and there. He used to drive around in one of the Land-Rovers before he hit a tree.

The crew left immediately for nearby Lagos. They could relax there for a few days, recovering from exhaustion and illness. The mechanic chose to stay behind.

Brook called a conference: important news.

266

Our stay in Yorubaland would be linked closely to Ife's sister city only a few miles away—Oshogbo, home of a sacred forest, one of the wonders of the world to those who know it.

He was relying on help from his contact in Yorubaland, a renowned white European in these parts called Ulli Beier. He was the one man any stranger would head straight to see, for few men have done more to revitalize the contemporary arts in Nigeria and few Europeans have such intimate knowledge of its traditions. Physically strong, middle-aged, unkempt, handsome, watchful of us, this formidable man would try to get us into the secret world of the cult.

It was help not to be taken for granted.

Before we left for Oshogbo, Professor Beier drove me to see the sacred forest there. But to his astonishment and rage, a group of American tourists were strolling round the shrines and temples. They must have been driven there by coach from Lagos. They were the only tourists I was to see. Compared with an area of Africa such as the Dogon, Oshogbo isn't yet too well known and tourism is strictly forbidden in its sacred forest. But there were the Americans, taking many photos, blue-rinsed and eager. They recognized the bearded figure of Ulli Beier. 'We've read your books, Professor!' called one of the ladies, running over excitedly to meet him. Click! She was stopped in her tracks. 'You have no business here,' said Professor Beier, quite calm at first. 'Get out.' Jaws dropped open. 'You're very *rude*, Professor!' risked one man, beginning to assert himself. For one moment I thought Beier would pick him up and sling him in the sacred river. 'All of you take your cameras and get out of here!' he yelled. 'GET OUT!'

Which they did.

The countries of Mali and Togo were now out of the trip. There was no longer time. Time! It had never been mentioned before. Time was running out.

Brook had also received word that the political situation within Mali had changed dramatically. It would be difficult to play there now, possibly dangerous. The news meant little to us. Yorubaland seemed like another country. But for Bagayogo it was a terrible blow. 'If there's trouble in Mali,' he murmured, 'they will kill my brother.' His brother was the Chief of Police. Bagayogo wouldn't be returning home.

I kept looking out anxiously for the familiar brooding figure of Ted Hughes, now due to join us. And sensed the shock outcome, as the others did: he wasn't turning up.

Brook, bitterly disappointed, faced the group.

Hughes had written a letter of apology and sent some new material for *The Conference of the Birds*.

'How can a man in England involve himself with what's happening to us here?' asked Katsulas as the rest received the news in silence.

'The man who invented T'ai Chi is even further away,' replied Brook.

The subject was closed.

I felt exhausted, bleeding from mosquito bites. The group looked strained and fearful now, as if no one knew where they were or what awaited them at the centre of the world.

24

No sun diety exists in Yorubaland. The sun is tedious, unworthy of a god. The sun is always there. Killer! The heat and pressure had become almost unbearable now. Yet to my amazement, Brook stepped up the pace of the work more than ever. It was as if he were making a last effort: desperate attempt at a break-through.

Each morning the work slogged on in the palm groves of the forest until the humidity was too stifling and the group could scarcely move or think much more. Each evening we worked in the open-air theatre of the university working till midnight, or beyond.

In the boiling afternoons: intense pressure of a different kind. The group split up for the first time in the journey. When not working, each of us would try to discover for ourselves what Brook called 'the spiritual world of Ife'.

It seemed an impossible mission.

Ayansola, that crazed spirit of Africa, symbolized the difficulty for me. Home with his family now, he used to visit us in his traditional African robes while carrying a plastic Snoopy bag inscribed with the word: 'SMILE'.

Every afternoon we set off to discover Ife, at staggered times, like the Monte Carlo Rally. There was a surprising sense of competition about it, each trying to out-do the other with his great discoveries. Also, everyone had become amazingly furtive all of a sudden. Sometimes I'd catch sight of an actor slumped wearily in a bar, busy avoiding the rest of the group slumped wearily in other bars. Or of Brook hurrying urgently through the chaotic streets as if to a secret rendezvous. . . .

You could take a taxi into town, crowding in with several locals going in the same direction.

'Hey, white man!' called a great fat laughing lady crammed between two passengers in the taxi I took one time. 'Hey, white man! Marry me!'

Shrieks of laughter from the rest.

'Do I have time to think it over?' I asked, amid more laughter.

'Yes,' replied the laughing lady. 'You have exactly one second.'

'Then I accept.'

The taxi practically rocked off the road.

'In which case,' said the laughing lady. 'I must return home immediately and inform my husband.'

'What will you *tell* him?'

'I will tell him that I have met a better man in a taxi and he can go take a powder.'

Hysteria!

Africans laugh, and want to laugh, more than anyone alive.

Ife! Though the spiritual home of all Yorubas, it has no fine architecture or exquisite temples. The outsider, perhaps accustomed to such splendours as the Holy See of Rome, won't find the outward symbols of a religious centre. It's more a shanty town. Noise, dirt, chaos, cars driving on their horns, motorbikes whizzing through the crowded streets, goats and chickens strolling about ramshackle markets, people gossiping in tiny tin bars, washing hung from wall to wall, smell of meat cooked on open fires, rat and elephant meat, street salesmen selling everything under the sun, modern dresses for sale, plantain and palm wine, kola nut and Coca Cola, snake necklaces, herbs, red peppers, bundles of wood, silver bangles, potions used for worship, colour and sweat and flies in the simmering shanty town. A fight threatens, and explodes. People dash in all directions, take to the hills. A child carries a huge tray on her head and I note what's on the tray, balanced miraculously: tin of Cadbury's Bournvita, packets of Omo and Soccer Chewing Gum, box of matches, six bars of Goody Goody Toffee, twelve tubes of Trebor Extra Strong Peppermints, St. Louis Sugar, Lux Toilet Soap, tin of Bird's Eye Custard, Bic Biros, a matchet, a dozen eggs and a small plastic bucket, and that's not a bad collection to have on your head.

Perhaps because Ife didn't look like a spiritual centre, I couldn't find it. Perhaps that was its secret. But the world of gods and cults didn't seem accessible to me. How could I, who find it a struggle to believe in one God, now accept the possibility of hundreds? And how could I find them?

An erect phallic monument, said to be a thousand years old, stands on a small hillside by the goat market. It was the shrine of Ogun, God of Iron. But people hurry by, without noticing their god.

A modern building, huge and ugly, built to overshadow the Christian church nearby, is the temple. Inside, an altar and ceremonial drums. But the temple is deserted, like the Christian church nearby.

I would drift back to camp before work began again, more confused and weary than when I left.

I didn't always search for the spiritual world of Ife in the town. I searched for it in the swimming pool. No stone was unturned. The university had a private pool where the bored, white wives of academics sunned themselves, wishing they were some place else. 'Oh, look!' I'd say to myself, feeling a little guilty whenever I went for a swim. 'There are the bored, white wives of academics. And there's the *group*.'

'Can't stop now!' yelled Katsulas, plunging in at the deep end. 'Got to search for spirits. . . .'

But perhaps something of this bewildering African town was begining to influence them. Actors are carriers: however strange and new life is, at some point its influence will crystallize and emerge, carried into their work. Even without being aware of it, actors absorb new impressions, steal them, like magpies. And unusual events had begun to happen.

A young African, a professional actor and singer, took five members of the group back to his home: Mirren, Zeldis, Goldschmidt, Myers and Odim Bossouku, the Gabonese observer who'd joined us in Niger. He took them back for a drink. They sat on the floor of a small room in the back streets of the city, drinking palm wine and talking. The African actor showed them his press-cuttings. The African was vain. Until he disappeared from the room without warning.

271

Then suddenly, he returned wearing a mask. And danced. The others burst out laughing, unable to control themselves at such a dramatic entry. But the African didn't join in the laughter. He continued to dance in his mask. And disappeared again. The others were still laughing to themselves, it seemed so unlikely.

When the African returned this time, he was wearing a shimmering blue costume, robes wrapped round him like a priest. And danced again, differently from before. Sometimes he stopped and explained that he was representing the different gods of the cult for them. 'This is the God of Thunder. This is the God of Disease. Have some more palm wine. . . .' The African seemed amused, mischievous man dancing for them. His audience were too sceptical to involve themselves. One actor performing for other actors: they felt suspicious. But as the African actor continued his strange display, Odim Bossouku, the only other African there, began to stare into space as if suddenly possessed. He sang as his fellow African danced as a god. The others began to feel nervous. Odim Bossouku had completely freaked out.

'Don't fight it,' said the host to his stunned guests. 'It's life.'

And he began to dance marvellously now, gradually involving the sceptics watching him. And laughed at their excitement and fear, goading and hexing. And played with their feelings, one moment good-naturedly, the next with such power and violence that all scepticism vanished. The African had his audience exactly where he wanted them. And his audience knew it. Some mysterious force from within that man had got to them. The dance of the gods had taken over. Those sophisticated European actors were mesmerised and shaken, frightened out of their skins.

We had a shadow in Ife: shadow of the Black American actress and former dancer Barbara Ann Teer, founder of the National Black Theatre in Harlem.

This striking woman, perhaps in her mid-thirties, proud, sharp, sour, would stir things up a little. Unlike Brook who'd gone to Yorubaland not to imitate the cult but to learn from its secrets, she saw herself as returning to her natural home, and would virtually transport the cult back to Harlem. Her theatre there is more of a temple where revivalist rituals are performed with stunning effect for the Afro-American community. 'We are an African people,' she told me of herself and the people she plays for. 'Ours is a temple of liberation. Black people are spirit people! The spirit is within us, housed in our bodies and souls. Africa is the source of the spirit.'

I felt uneasy with her, fearful of an explosion. But when I risked saying the Black American might not have much more in common with Africa than the White American, she took it quite well. For Barbara Ann Teer a historical link with Africa was being renewed, form of destiny which the Black spirit cries out for. As for her theatre in Harlem, she was liberating it from White European values and styles in search of the true spiritual roots of her people. She calls it a process of 'de-crudding'.

An irony! There was someone in theatre who'd travelled to exactly the same destination as Brook for totally different reasons. The founder of Harlem's National Black Theatre was in Africa to begin again by going back to an old culture. Brook was there to begin again in the hope of going forward into a new one. In the past is the future. But which future? Brook searches for the power of the spirit too. But from the suspicious tones of Barbara Ann Teer it was clear she saw him as The White Man searching in a country where he didn't belong.

Hence the highly provocative theory of Brook's, which is called 'The Rainbow Theory'.

According to the gospel of 'The Rainbow Theory', Black or White Man doesn't really exist. To see people as exclusively Black or exclusively White is a unifying limitation on them both. To say that all Black people are African is in itself a form of condescension on all Black people. For part of all mankind is an African and part of an African is all mankind. Man is like a rainbow with the whole range of the prism to be found within him. Man is the microcosm, and Fully Developed Man the world. So the continents of the world and the peoples of the world are all less than the Fully Developed Man. So an African is limited to being an African until he fulfils the vast range within him. So too the Black American and the White European. All are less than Fully Developed Man. For each man carries within him the seeds of all mankind, which is his Africa and his Asia, his America and his Europe. So that if we, the group, were responding to the spirit of Africa we were responding to that part of us which might never have been brought to life, but is our Africa. So the White European has an African somewhere within him. But if 'The Rainbow Theory' is right, the Black American must also have a white European in him.

Or her.

'You know,' Barbara Ann Teer said to me after talking to Brook for a while, 'your group's got problems.'

The work continued, with a vengeance. Brook was working up to a big performance of *The Conference of the Birds* at the end of the week. In the absence of Ted Hughes I awaited the call, feeling I might have some useful material to offer. But the call never came. Only on the final day of the journey when we were back in Algiers did Brook ask me to write my own version.

Familiar disciplines were returned to: shared reference in a new and formless world. The T'ai Chi exercises, the Feldenkrais movements, the musical workshops, relentless research into sound and rhythm, experiments with birds, always the constant squawks and babble of the birds.

Late one night, Brook suddenly called for every cardboard box that was left. For hours and hours, box improvisations: building of a box city, inaccessible to all but those who know its secret. Local students watched, most respectfully.

But in the midst of the box city, Mary Evans, Brook's personal assistant, unexpectedly emerged. She was whispering urgently in his ear. Could only have been evil tidings about the shambles of a camp. 'This should be *perfectly* simple!' snapped Brook, steeling himself once again. He looked so angry that even the traditional silence hushed itself.

Apparently, the lights were falling down more than usual. Nothing personal, right, John? Camp-beds were all over the place. Equipment was lost. No one was doing the washing-up. No one was helping out. People weren't even turning up for the delicious pilchards. As a matter of fact, not even the flies were turning up. Uncertain of the new world we had come to, the camp was going to pieces. The camp was in chaos.

'Is someone translating for Malik?' demanded Brook, looking even more exasperated than usual. 'You see, once again Malik is *not* involved in a vital discussion. For two years he has been with the group yet not one of you can spare the time and energy to translate for him. It's something that should be *sensed*.'

'Wait a minute!' replied Sylvain Corthay, determined for once to speak his mind as the rest of us slumped. 'I am the one who usually translates for Malik and I find it *very* difficult to translate. I do not think Malik even *listens* to me when I translate.'

'I wash my plate every morning,' announced Malik, as if awakening from a dream.

'But do you realize the washing-up bowls have to be filled with water *first*?' asked Katsulas, who had begun to look like the Boston Strangler. 'And what I also wish to say is that if the washing-up bowls *aren't* filled with water, someone has got to go and *get* the water and that someone is always *me*.'

Corthay was now translating at top speed as Malik Bagayogo nodded his head with special emphasis.

'I am very sorry,' François Marthouret confessed in the midst of all this. 'I was under the impression the washing-up rota had been *abandoned*. I wish to say that if there has been a misunderstanding, I am very sorry.'

'You see,' groaned Brook, 'there's a *perfect* example of *one* set of rules being established and someone believing there's *another* set of rules. . . .'

The local students who had watched the work with such fascination now looked stunned.

It was almost two o'clock in the morning.

Brook, drawing on his own reserves of energy, let the conference drift on for its ritual hour or so. And called a halt—

'Are we unable to understand that life in camp goes to the heart of our work? Can't we understand it's about coming face to face with one's own lifeless habits and routines? It's about inter-relating, responding, caring, sensing out the different needs and moods of other people. It's about trying to build a real group. It's about *awareness*. If only you could see the fantastic possibility of changing one's life. Yet I feel I'm talking to the wind. I look at you now. After all this time you still remind me of closed little boxes stamped with the words, "Made In Paris".'

It was the last of such conferences.

Work on *The Conference of the Birds* was abandoned the next morning. A school in the countryside outside Ife had invited the group to perform for the children. A show! A special show would be prepared. But to my exasperation, Brook pointed to Katsulas' shoes. Not the shoes! I groaned inwardly, opposed to the revival. I couldn't see the point of going back to *The Shoe Show* in the world we had come to. I thought the show had run its noble course. Also, I had come to hate the sight of it.

The decision was made, however. Brook often returns to the past when you least expect it. It's a way of measuring progress.

The group retired into the palm trees to find again the mystery of Andreas Katsulas' shoes, really battered now. The actors blinked through sun and sweat, cursing the cruel mosquitoes and maybe Brook and maybe the rotten shoes. If it was progress I saw, it looked suspicious. The show I remembered as light comedy was now emerging before my eyes as a cross between *Madame Butterfly* and *Murder in the Cathedral*. Perhaps it was the strain of the day. And all comedy is a serious business, as those manic depressives called comedians will testify. But as the experiments slogged on, I hated *The Shoe Show* no longer. Blood's thicker than water. I cherished it, suffering privately for its memory. Most inconsiderate of all, François Marthouret, who played a crucial role, keeled over with suspected malaria.

After a decent pause, Brook pressed on with a new experiment more dumbfounding than anything I'd witnessed so far. The group sat in silence among the trees of a bamboo grove, examin-ing and stroking their navels. I didn't know the reason then, and I don't know the reason now. The navel experiment was performed with due solemnity. It was fascinating in its way. I have actually seen people contemplate their navels.

So it is that anyone who watches an experimental theatre group at work eventually feels himself losing his mind.

I thought of an old friend, a famous playwright in Russia called Bulgakov who worked for the great experimental director, Stanislavsky. The result is a renowned book—*Black Snow,* one of the funniest satires ever written about theatre. Yet Bulgakov loved the theatre and couldn't believe his luck when Stanislavsky asked him to write a play. The Moscow Arts Theatre! Fame! Medals! However, Bulgakov was also a man who by temperament felt unable to regard the mighty Stanislavsky with the same uncritical devotion as his disciples. During his version of events he writes and rewrites his play but can't help noticing, for example, that what happens during rehearsals doesn't actually have anything to do with his script. Sinister doubts about Stanislavsky's 'Method' begin to creep into Bulgakov's mind. . . . And reach breaking point when Stanislavsky, accompanied everywhere by a reverential hush, orders the hero of his play to perform a love scene while riding a bicycle.

Passionate love, the great director explains, is expressed by the hero being prepared to do anything for his beloved. Bring on the bicycle! Thus, the hero dutifully wobbles around his beloved until he's too exhausted to cycle any further. 'Empty!' calls Stanislavsky as Bulgakov watches his tender love scene in horror. 'You were riding emptily instead of being filled with your beloved. . . .'

Surfeited with what Bulgakov calls 'new and strange impressions', he returns home from the rehearsal, saying to himself: 'It's all quite extraordinary, but only because I'm a layman. Every art has its rules, its methods and its secrets. A savage might think it most odd for people to clean their teeth with a brush loaded with chalky paste. It must seem just as strange to the uninitiated that before operating a surgeon does a number of incomprehensible things to the patient, such as taking blood tests and so on. . . .'

As I watched Brook and the group contemplating their navels

among the palm trees, I thought fondly of my friend Bulgakov. Perhaps my friendship with him was a little presumptuous, particularly as he died before I was born. Yet I felt a common bond between us and that there were times when I must have understood him better than any man alive.

The following afternoon, we drove through the cocoa plantations outside Ife to perform *The Shoe Show*. Several shrines could be glimpsed on the way, spattered with blood.

The village was called Itagunmodi, twenty miles away. The show was to be for the children.

Our shadow, Miss Barbara Ann Teer, followed.

With her, Professor Beier and his family. He looked intrigued to see what Brook had to offer.

The village was familiar territory to us. Crowds of children: excited and open faces. It wouldn't be difficult to play in this village. The conditions were right for the simplest of shows. Often with Brook, a rehearsal might not go well but a performance can turn out differently. Adrenalin is high. Things come unexpectedly together in the urgency of performing.

With a proviso: never rely on it.

The carpet was laid out in the dust of an open field: a mistake. The group was without shade, at the mercy of the sun.

Handshakes, smiles, only form of contact possible with the children until the show began. We couldn't speak the same language. Yet had our greetings become routine now? The sun was beating down. It had become an effort to say hello.

A bench had been set apart from the audience for those not performing. The rest of us sat there.

Barbara Ann Teer ignored the bench, sitting on the ground among the villagers.

Perhaps I was over-reacting. But the only white people watching the show were sitting on a bench separated from everyone else.

'SHOOOOOOOOOOOOOOOOOOOOOOES!!' screamed Bagayogo, anxious for attention as he held up the shoes for the children. It looked hopeful. The performance no longer resembled the re-

278

hearsal. On the other hand, it no longer resembled the script. 'I buy,' announced Bagayogo. 'You sell.' The actors laughed to themselves. Perhaps mindful of his difficulties during the washing-up conference, Bagayogo had decided to practise his English. 'This is pair of shoe. This is show about shoe. I buy shoe, you sell shoe. It is very cold in Africa. . . .' The children looked blank, unable to understand. Bagayogo was now taking theatrical sniffs at the shoes. 'I buy, you sell.' The in-joke had gone too far. 'Smelly, smelly, smelly shoe.' The children were silent. Brook watched what was happening in stunned disbelief.

Actors ambled listlessly onto the carpet. Others didn't even trouble to perform, watching from the fringes as if they were part of the audience. Astonishingly, scenes were lost or abandoned without much concern, inept and lethargic, crude form of play. A few half-hearted songs: embarrassing and feeble. A dance, token dance performed by actors who looked as if they had given up, no longer seeming to care.

Nothing remotely like this had ever happened on the journey. Even when the group were at their most uninspired, even when nothing would go right, they struggled to find a way out. They tried to create *something*. Respect for the audience had always been paramount, absolute and golden rule even in the midst of the craziest experiments. Yet now the performance was so uncaring it was as if the audience was of little consequence. The hopes and excitement of those children were being treated with a form of indifference. 'I buy, you sell', Bagayogo began again. I watched Professor Beier turn away in disgust. The children stayed bewildered and silent: crucifying, unnatural silence. At the height of the journey, the group looked as if it had gone to pieces.

Perhaps they had their excuses. Two of the actors had been too ill to perform. The rest looked over-tired or near exhaustion. The show had run its course. . . . Yet no actor made an excuse. They looked ashamed.

'What do you feel now?' said Barbara Ann Teer angrily to me. 'Have you got to know anyone here? Have you entertained *one* child? Who have you touched? *Touch* those people! You hear me? *Touch them!* What are you *using* them for? What do you know of Africa? What do any of you know?'

Professor Beier, our contact in Yorubaland, the man who had welcomed us, looked humiliated. His relationship with Brook would never be the same.

'I think you've insulted the people of this village,' he told me. 'Brook's actors can't sing, they can't dance and it doesn't seem they can act. What does it mean? Why have you come here?'

It was little use saying other shows had been different. I felt defeated, along with the others. There was nothing to say. It was as if a finger had been pointed at the Emperor's imaginary suit of clothes.

Brook was badly shaken. He could only mime his apologies and regrets to the village elders, who seemed to understand. Surprisingly, the villagers minded less than anyone. The children didn't seem to mind very much either. Perhaps you can take guilt too far. At least, the crestfallen faces of the actors told the village how sorry they were. Now if the children had grabbed the sticks lying on the edge of the carpet and beaten the actors into a decent performance, that would have been something. It happened to Brook's group once.

It was the first public performance the group ever gave. And it was also for children. It's not just that children don't set up defences and barriers. The child asks the question 'Why?' The child forces the sophisticated actor to relearn the steps. Faced with the natural openness and spontaneity and perhaps the cruelty of children, actors have much to learn. The actor, like any adult, can't fake it for a child. But when Brook's group gave their first children's show, they thought it wouldn't take much effort. They thought it a low-level form of work. Hadn't they joined the centre to find the key of life?

Unfortunately for the actors, the children ran riot. They were so dissatisfied with their show that they set on the group, chasing and beating them with the bamboo sticks. No matter what the actors tried, it wasn't good enough. The kids had been patronised and taken for granted, dished up second best. The kids charged at the terrified actors again and again, lashing them with the sticks. It was a historic show. The actors actually fled, traumatised.

It was thought at the time they would never again take performing for children lightly. Yet now in Africa, the group had fallen into the same trap. The sense of shock was just as traumatic. That the African kids were too polite or timid to beat them into a pulp made no difference. In effect, the group had given the same terrible show they'd performed years ago. And perhaps the shock went deeper. For just at the moment in the journey when the group was struggling to break through to the spiritual world, they'd been given the most timely lesson of all.

For the first time in the journey Daniel Charlot, the young French observer, spoke in a conference. He said just this:

'Watching you perform reminded me of the white Europeans who visited Mali when I lived there. You went to perform like snobbish colonials sightseeing among African villages. You forgot that a simple show for children is as valuable to you as the most mysterious show for adults. You felt that you had seen it all. But the more you see, the less you understand.'

There was no need for Brook or anyone else to add anything.

Far from the longed-for breakthrough in the work, I sensed only that the journey was falling apart now. The hard psychological blow had sapped the actors of confidence, as all defeat does. But there seemed only strain and turmoil in its place. The group returned to work with little heart for the challenge ahead.

There was less then a day to throw together a big performance of *The Conference of the Birds*. Brook's reputation had preceded him into Ife. People were expected from all over the place for this performance. The university had printed leaflets, advertising it.

Brook drove on with the work, looking drained now himself. When in doubt: work. The group struggled on with the new material sent over by Ted Hughes, as if defying what was left of their energy to give out completely. The material was adapted into special bird chants and songs, crazed sounds shrieked out

through the forest—useful form of psychic release, if nothing else.
AAAAAAAAAAAAAAIIIA! O!O!O! TSOOOOOOOR! OKAKAKAKAKA-
KAKAKAKAKAK!

YAKYAK! HUNWEEEE! ZIYAWOSSSS! and SHOPATIKETPAHO-
HOPATITSE. . . .

Hughes had given the rough translation for that last word as
'set your feet dancing'. SHOPATIKETPAHOHOPATITSE was a
word-sound for set your feet dancing. For Godsake.

It was the end for me. I couldn't take any more. It's just that
in my opinion the word SHOPATIKETPAHOHOPATITSE, whether
spoken or shrieked by the finest actor in the world, sung by the
finest singer in the world, produced by the most miraculous
means from whatever mysterious source in the world, will
never in a million years convey the meaning of the words 'set
your feet dancing'. I could be wrong. I believed it might be
possible to find the sounds able to convey the source of emotion,
and every emotion. For what is music? But when I'd listened
for hour after hour to the sounds of the mad-house, I wanted to
throw in the towel. I couldn't even laugh any more. If an actor
wants to set your feet dancing, I don't think he should trouble
with SHOPATIKETPAHOHOPATITSE. I think he should shut up
and dance.

Swados looked half-dead in that session. She seemed in despair
now, painfully thin, virtually living off chocolate and cigarettes,
coughing badly, unable even to hear well. I'd begun to fear for her.
The worst of all imaginable things had happened to Swados. This
incredible composer was being drained of music. I didn't think
she had anything left.

Somehow she was still composing feverishly, as if her life
depended on it. Often she worked right through the night,
unable to stop—impossible strain in the heat of the day. I used
to see her kicking ant hills, pounding termites. Each day more and
more work, tear round town, work with local musicians, hunt for
chocolate, kick a few shrines, back to the group, work on technique, rhythm, pitch, pauses, breaths, kick a few actors, conference
with Brook, kick Brook, more songs, more ideas, sleep maybe,
wake to birds, more birds, more work, on and on. . . . The

strings of her guitar were popping one by one in the stifling heat. Swados was like that now. She was almost finished.

'Well here we all are,' she said to me during a break from the bird session. 'Going bananas. Seen any spirits yet? Seen anyone *possessed*?'

'Nope.'

'Jesus, you're bleeding. Your arm is sort of. . . . You don't want me to go into it, huh? Well how do I know you're telling the *truth* about the possession stuff? How do I know it isn't a sacred-secret with you?'

'I've had an offer of marriage. That's about it, really.'

'Is she Jewish? What the hell. Listen! Do you want to hear the most *miraculous* song ever composed? You want to hear my latest song or not? I'll teach you to sing it. You can sing it at the wedding ceremony.'

'Sing!'

So she sang her song. And she was right. Miraculous! I couldn't believe it! The song had a *lyric, words, language*! Real, live English *language*! Not bird language, not bird sound, not even the sound that encompasses all sound. *Rock 'n Roll!!* Spirit of Chuck Berry! Sweet, *sweet* music! Swados The Genius grinned from ear to ear happier than for centuries, rocking on in the forest until, cruel fate, she fell in a ditch. Slap in the middle of the most miraculous song ever composed, a battered guitar flew one way and a rocking deaf American composer flew another. She'd rocked headlong into the shit. She couldn't even move. She just lay there. She just sank into the ditch, laughing till it hurt.

The bird session perked up—

AAAAAAAAAAAAAAAAAAAAAAAIIIIIIIIIIIIIAAAA!!
O!O!O!O!O!O!O!O!O!O!KAKAKAKAKAKAKAKAKAKAKAKAAA!!
TSOOOOOOOOOOOOOOORR!!.
UMUM!! YAKYAK!! HUNWEEEEE!! HOHOKYUN!! HYA!! HYA!!
TOTOTOTOTOTOTOTOTOTOTOTOTO!!

It grows on you after a while, maybe. But I left the group to it. My head was spinning. I felt in need of help, and there was one man in Ife who might be able to give it to me. I skipped work and

283

went to see the man known as 'the father of secrets', the *babalowo*, who is the Oracle of Ife.

Sometimes dismissed in the West as a 'witchdoctor' or 'medicine man', the Oracle holds a vital position in the community, perhaps second only to the King. He's a man of many mysterious parts, a healer, a clairvoyant, perhaps a prophet, a philosopher, a man with extraordinary powers and gifts, a religious man, a priest. The oracle of Ife isn't just the most important in the area, he's the spiritual head of every priest in Yorubaland. People come from far and wide to visit him. They go for help and guidance.

A young actor called Yomi Fawole, a student at the university, went with me. He spoke perfect English and agreed kindly to translate the words of the Oracle. Yomi was part of the growing middle-class intelligentsia of Ife, worldly and quite sophisticated, the son of a doctor. Yet he still worshipped the god of his ancestors and believed absolutely in the power of the Oracle.

We walked up a hillside full of mud and rubble in the centre of the city, past old and decaying buildings as far as a derelict house which seemed no more than a shell. It was the house of the Oracle.

The doorway was low so that you were forced to bow inside.

Yomi led the way and immediately knelt before the Oracle, as a Catholic might do before his priest. The Oracle was introduced, shaking my hand. I felt awkward, for his eyes never left mine.

He must have been about sixty years old, though very alert and fit: a presence. His skin seemed to have been wrapped tightly round him. He was bare chested, wearing only baggy black shorts, more like a skirt. His head was shaven. On his wrist, a silver watch.

For the moment, he did not seem approachable. There was a sense of formality about him. He was a man whom you met on his own terms. He was seated in a chair, quite high, like a throne.

Yomi pointed to a low stool where I was to sit facing the Oracle.

Two other old men were in the room, assistant priests, toothless in string vests. They looked roguish and suspicious of me: unwelcoming, or so it seemed.

The room where we sat was amazing—in a state of squalor and mess which at once seemed entirely natural to it. Hens clucked about the small room and pigeons flew among the cobwebs of its rafters. A stone altar decorated with palm fronds was tucked into a recess of a wall. The hens crapped on the altar and most places. In every corner and on every shelf were different-sized bottles filled with potions and herbs. They were covered in dust, as was the room.

The Oracle offered me a small glass of palm wine, smiling when I nodded my thanks. And announced that he would try to answer whatever I asked.

'Your potions are said to have magical power,' I began, feeling it best to be bold. 'It is said that you can prevent anything happening and that you can make things happen.'

'Yes,' replied the Oracle, still fixing his eyes on mine.

'Well I would like you to stop every mosquito in Africa from biting people, and me in particular. I would be most interested to see you do this.'

The Oracle and his toothless assistants roared with laughter when the translation came through. Instantly, more palm wine was offered.

'There's nothing I can do!' replied the Oracle, laughing. 'It's *natural* for mosquitoes to bite people. They don't even have to make an effort! You see, God has given them the power to bite. And they use it!'

'But what of your magic potions?' I asked.

'I have certain medicines,' the Oracle replied now. 'And perhaps I can help you after all.'

His tone had become serious.

'There is a place in the market where I believe you can find what you need.'

'Where in the market?' I asked urgently.

'Where the goats are kept,' replied the Oracle.

'But who do I *ask* for?'

'You ask for the chemist and he will give you anti-mosquito ointment.'

Howls of laughter, from all of us now.

'Now you laugh!' said the Oracle. 'Now you are my friend! Now I *sleep* with you!'

'Take it easy,' I thought. But the atmosphere was no longer forbidding and I put a few shillings on the ground as Yomi had warned me to. Only a token amount was necessary and perhaps I gave more than I had to, for luck.

Then the Oracle of Ife came down from his chair, touched the ground with his forehead and threw a chain of cowrie shells to the ground. The chain was the symbolic link with the gods: system of divination. According to the pattern made by the chain, the Oracle will choose certain poems from hundreds in his collection. Among his duties, he's the custodian of ritual poetry in Yorubaland and his knowledge of it will be unique. The formation of the shells guides him to the appropriate poems. It's a complex and mathematical system, not entirely a matter of showmanship or luck. The poems tell of stories and legends which help him foresee events and advise his visitor.

He blew into the cowrie shells, muttering strange incantations. And handed the chain to me. As he did so, he pointed to his eyes.

'You must whisper into the shells,' advised Yomi. 'The Oracle says you must do this. You must whisper into them what you want to happen in your life.'

I whispered, taking it seriously. I'm superstitious.

'Please make everything okay,' I whispered into the shells. 'Please give me some energy. Please see all my family and friends are happy and well. Please help me understand what's going on. That's all for now. . . .'

When I finished, I had to blow into the shells.

Then the Oracle took them, throwing them down several times into different formations. As he did this, no one moved or made a sound.

Eventually he spoke. I heard a sigh of relief from his assistants, as if the news awaiting me had hung in the balance.

'What's he say?' I asked Yomi excitedly.

'The news is *good!*' came the reply.

'Everything is good for you!' said the Oracle, who was smiling now. I felt relieved myself.

286

'You are going to be placed above others. You will be loved and honoured!'

I thought to myself: 'This man takes me for a fool.' Yet I couldn't help feeling pleased at what he said. I mean, if there was just the slightest chance. . . .

'Anything else?' I asked.

'You are going to be fantastically *rich*! The money will be so much you won't know what to do with it!'

'Have you any idea how much?'

'A fantastic amount. A million pounds—at least.'

This was too good to be true. I began to laugh, not knowing what to say. But the Oracle suddenly looked stern, talking urgently to Yomi who translated back to me.

'The Oracle says you must not despise what he says or think it untrue. He says only what he sees. It might not happen to-morrow or the next day, *but it will happen*. The Oracle says to you, "It is today one sees. The eyes do not see tomorrow." But what he sees will happen.'

I apologised immediately, aware my laughter had given offence.

But now the Oracle asked a question.

He pointed to a large rock in the room. The rock looked old, a symbol perhaps.

'If you wish to break the rock,' he asked, taking me by surprise, 'how would you do it?'

I replied that it was too heavy to lift. I would try to break the rock with an axe.

Immediately, everyone laughed and shook their heads.

'But how can you break something which has lasted for centuries?' asked the Oracle.

The Oracle smiled when I did not reply, and pointed to his eyes.

The rock was a symbol of faith.

Then he took the chain of divination again, throwing it to the ground as I watched carefully. Each time he threw the shells, he spoke. Then he turned to me, saying:

'There is something in the home where you were born, some-

287

thing in the room where you lived. It belonged to your grandfather. It's an object of some sort. There is iron in the object. The object is connected with iron. Do not neglect the object. You must try to keep contact with it and worship it. It will help you in your life.'

I went cold. I had the object. It's always been kept in my room at home. And it belonged to my grandfather.

The Oracle could never have known of its existence.

I can't even be sure why I've kept the object for so many years. I suppose it's a sentimental memory of my grandfather. He was a deeply religious man and though I didn't share his views I felt close to him and loved him. As a child I used to go to the synagogue just to be with him, rather proud to be sitting next to a man so respected. He didn't seem to mind me sneaking off to the football match afterwards. He was kind and good, a handsome little man from Poland with a white goatee beard and gravy stains down his tie. He always wore a pin-stripe suit, looking most correct. I remember him sitting in his musty flat surrounded by strange-looking men arguing the finer points of the Talmud. When I asked him once about Christ, he went 'Pah!' and refused to discuss the matter. He would sometimes stand quietly in a corner of a room and pray. I was fourteen when he died. I remember my mother screaming. People loved him. He was the first of my family to die.

When the family gathered I asked if I could keep the object which the Oracle of Ife now referred to. It was a plaque the congregation had given to my grandfather in honour of him. It was found buried away in a cupboard. The Oracle had said the object was connected in some way to iron. It seems so unlikely, yet it's true. The plaque is attached to a chain of iron.

'You must keep in touch with the object,' said the Oracle. 'You must worship its spirit.'

He pointed to his eyes again.

And asked why I had come to Ife.

I explained a little of the journey and the work, saying we had come to Ife to try to learn something of the spiritual world.

And the Oracle replied by way of a story, the story of the

creation of the world within his city. He told me how the father of all the gods created human beings out of clay, how life was breathed into the clay and the gods descended to earth.

'You have come to the place where all life began,' said the Oracle. 'All life came from this city and all people are our children. You and your ancestors migrated from Ife and now you have returned to it. Take care of the object within your home, for there and in Ife the spirits are working together. It is the same everywhere. You have travelled to Ife only to find something which is already with you.'

The assistants of the Oracle smiled now. And the Oracle smiled too, and pointed to his eyes for the last time. It was the moment to leave. He had given me his advice. Perhaps I had sensed the simple truth he was trying to tell me before even we left for Africa. That the spiritual life we wanted so much to experience cannot be found in a special place, a church, a strange city, a country of secret traditions or in anything or anyone except ourselves. Yet without my visit to the Oracle of Ife I do not think I would have truly known it. The Oracle was smiling because he knew that in one sense our long journey had been in vain. What we searched for was already with us, within and everywhere.

'I will make a sacrifice for you!' called the Oracle as I left. 'You will be blessed! You will have plenty of money! You will have plenty of wives! Your journey will come to a happy end. You will have good fortune. What I see will happen. The gods be with you.'

The Oracle of Ife blew air at me, as though the air were life.

I left feeling very, very good. I'd forgotten about the performance.

The *show*! I dashed to the small open-air amphitheatre on the other side of the city, just in time.

The place was packed. The artistic community of Ife was out in force, the dons and intellectuals, an audience which for the first time in the journey seemed almost exclusively middle class. Quite a few Europeans were there. Barbara Ann Teer and the Beiers, and other faces I knew now. Many students had travelled specially from Ibadan, anxious like the rest to see something of Brook's work. But the excited audience was unusually formal, like an audience in Europe. After so much time in the rough and tumble of the villages it seemed an unnatural atmosphere: uncomfortable. I can't remember seeing any children: too quiet. . . .

I slipped backstage to wish the actors luck, in itself a tradition that belonged to another life.

The actors looked tense in their white costumes, waiting for the firing squad.

Without quite knowing what they were going to perform, the group was about to face an audience which more than any other on the journey expected something worthwhile from them and perhaps great events. In many ways, the audience had come to see Brook: 'A Brook Production'. Yet neither Brook nor the group had one. They didn't have a production. I had to remind myself sometimes. They didn't even have a script. Even at this stage of the game they had only the rough outline of that impossible mystery tour called *The Conference of the Birds*.

Just to get through an occasion as demanding as this struck me as near miraculous. Sometimes they didn't, of course. But the day was saved this time and with it, the journey. If the performance had fallen to pieces like the children's show I don't think the group would have recovered. They were too exhausted now. Another disaster would have been the knock-out blow. Yet somehow the actors dredged up what reserves of energy were left and the performance held together. Nothing too dangerous was risked. A number of scenes were from the group's own repertoire: the safety-net. But they worked. God bless the Oracle of Ife! He had brought us luck.

The group survived.

Perhaps the audience were a little too respectful of Brook's reputation. The applause at the end seemed too self-conscious. It was the applause which verges on something which often happens in 'serious' drama. The audience ends up applauding itself.

Not everyone, though.

'Worst thing I've ever seen in my life,' snapped Professor Beier afterwards.

Miss Barbara Ann Teer looked thoughtful.

'I see,' she said. 'I see what Brook's getting at now. But it's still *rotten*.'

The actors were very relieved when it was over, like Brook.

He hadn't watched the show too much. He'd watched the audience. It's something he does. If you want to see a show, watch the audience.

Brook could see what was happening on the stage written on the faces of the audience. People were intrigued and interested in the world of the birds, but no one was fully engaged in the action. Silence can be deceptive and the audience which keeps quiet should be watched. Also, it might turn out more entertaining than the show. Those pained expressions, the stifled yawns, the lady choking on a hacking cough, the man dying for a pee, the critic so busily scribbling notes he misses the vital scene, those sly shuffles when people seize their chance to get comfortable. Maybe that's the answer to Brook's search for a new theatre! The audience should be the show, and the actors should be the audience. . . .

But what Brook saw this time was a reflection in the audience of something absolutely central to his work and still missing from it.

For we'd seen another performance in this theatre two nights before. And another audience. We saw a Yoruba adaptation of *Oedipus* performed by African actors. And that was a marvellous occasion, a real event, so alive and unpredictable that the audience ebbed and flowed with every second of the action, one moment stunned into silence, the next convulsed with laughter, but always this wonderful sense of movement and lightning response. For Brook, the exciting atmosphere touched his ideal: richness of the Elizabethan experience.

It didn't happen with us. In search of the mystery of the spiritual world, the actors imposed mere style. Style can carry with it invaluable moments of intensity, but I was also learning that it can turn into a false purity and a false god. 'Not by awe alone,' said Brook afterwards. The moment theatre imposes a style, it limits itself. The style becomes formalized at the expense of the full diversity of human response. It creates a barrier.

At the time when the future of the journey balanced on a knife-edge, the group held together in nerve-racking circumstances. They lived to fight another day (which would be tomorrow). But just as the show for children had taken them back in time into an old trap, so they fell into another with the big performance. The actors assumed too much. They took it for granted they could skip the steps. The performance of *The Conference of the Birds* had begun and ended too 'high', just as the production of *Orghast* had done more than a year before.

It's a danger with Brook. For all his natural instincts he forgets that spirits laugh too. The high seriousness which goes with myths and spirits, with grandiose themes and mystical journeys, creates its own barriers. In the higher realms of mysticism there's a temptation to treat the rest of life as mundane. And it's why the audience couldn't involve themselves in the performance beyond the level of mere curiosity. It was too remote. The group had created the distance of 'style' and 'artiness'. The spiritual world Brook wants so much to reach can't be rarefied or set apart from the rest of life. Nor can it be found on a different plain called 'Mystery' or 'Art'. The actor who fails to link the high with the low will not gain access into the invisible world, and nor will his audience. It was clearer than ever now. Theatre can't rely on the abstract alone. It cuts off all contact with emotional involvement, ending up like the 'stripes school' of modern art. It might look clever and mysterious, beautifully constructed no doubt. But in the end, it just isn't that meaningful.

The answer could only be found in that basic and most difficult search of Brook's: the quality of openness. The form must be open to the fullest range. Laughter isn't always essential or even appropriate. But the performance confirmed the necessity that the outer language must always be naïve. Brecht was right when he told Brook that his term for the theatre of the future would be 'Theatre of Naïvety'. Within true simplicity might be found the whole of life. The book of *The Conference of the Birds*, the very thing the group was struggling to recreate, showed them the key. For there, the most meaningful of stories always begins from an outer simplicity. It's as if you're lulled into the deeper aspects. Each story, however serious at its centre, is expressed in the simplest of forms. And it's in this way that the door opens on the mysterious. A man prays: 'O Lord, open a door that I may come to you.' And the book gives the reply: 'O idiot! Is the door closed?'

In search of the miraculous, the group had lost touch with the naïvety which went to the root and heart of its work. For the vital slot still missing from the spectrum were all those rough and popular elements of the best village shows. Without them, the group was stranded in mid air. It was as if they believed the concrete world somehow downgrades the mysterious. But the reverse is true. And it was the most valuable lesson of all. The popular form of theatre might be called 'the lower level' and the élite form 'the higher level'. But the lower levels are the foundation on which even the most mysterious of phenomena are built. They build a ladder to it.

So the actor who skips the step falls. Maybe it was a long way to come in search of such a conclusion. But if the group could grasp a real understanding of it now, the work would be transformed. The spiritual world can be approached step by step. For the universe is well ordered and the spirits themselves are practical.

Even Jacob used a ladder. Also, the gods of Ife.

'The spirits came down to earth on a chain,' the Oracle said and laughed, to see such fun.

The next day we took the yellow brick road to Oshogbo and its sacred forest.

25

By way of preface to our last days in Yorubaland, I asked Brook why we had come to the sacred forest of Oshogbo. He remained in lengthy silence at first: Brook silence, which signals an unusual reply.

Then he told me this:

Suppose a child is perfectly normal until he's five years old. Suddenly he goes deaf. And with his deafness, his power of speech becomes difficult. The child isn't the same as someone born deaf. He's had impressions of hearing. But his hearing and speaking are warped—with all the psychological barriers and confusions that involves. He functions in a diminished capacity for almost all his childhood and early youth. Whereupon a new treatment comes into existence.

With it, his hearing begins to come back a fraction. Other treatments are tried, but the hearing is still slight. And then by some miraculous freak, a totally different form of treatment is discovered. This involves transplanting electrodes into the brain which enable the patient to recover his hearing totally. But only for one hour.

The doctors are concerned. Will it be psychologically kind or unkind to return someone's hearing for so short a time? The patient might blow his mind. The sense of loss could be too great to bear when the deafness returns again. So the doctors put their dilemma to the patient. Is he prepared to take this treatment knowing he's going to experience something quite real, like a vision, which might take him twenty years or more of further experiments to re-acquire? Even then, there can be no guarantee. But the patient says he wants it.

He takes the treatment. And for an hour he can hear perfectly. Suddenly, he's aware why he's been struggling almost all his life to decipher half-sounds. He understands why he's been trying to hear and speak the way he can now. Miraculously, everything is in its place. Misunderstanding and confusion are swept away. The treatment confirms all his deepest hunches and memories. The patient is in a totally changed state. Then his hearing goes again.

He is back where he was. And yet at the same time, all isn't lost. The direction of his life has been clarified. However uncertain and crude the treatment in the future, he'll take it with a new awareness. And he'll bring to it renewed hope and confidence. For a short while, he lived in a more complete sense of reality. He awoke to a vision of life. And that is the characteristic and virtue of a sacred place.

But Oshogbo is a town of startling contrasts and the sacred mingles happily with the profane.

It's an amazing, eccentric town, perhaps the only place in the world which has a petrol station of real artistic interest. The Esso petrol station has been transformed by a local sculptor. The local sculptor didn't like the hideous Esso petrol station. So he built cement sculptures round it. The one I liked best was of cars being filled with petrol.

Like Ife, it's a town of some 120,000 people, modernized in the sense of having electricity, running water, more or less compulsory education. But it's a town in a terrific state of flux, hybrid mixture of traditional African life and Western influence, bizarre city that's bursting with vitality and amazing rituals. Each year the people of Oshogbo dance into the streets insulting any high-ranking official with impunity. A king, a chief, a judge: two fingers.

People enjoy life, welcoming strangers, excited by the new and unexpected. People kept throwing parties for us and handing Brook the bill. Drinks on you! Welcome! Listen, someone's got to pay for the band. . . .

It's a town where the ancient meets the new and maybe they compete. But they don't collide. On the one hand, the exuberant 'highlife', the music and gaiety which exploded in the '60s, losing a bit of its sparkle now. On the other, the secret societies and cults of the forest where the river Goddess Oshun is worshipped, watching over the fortunes of the people. Every year thousands of cult worshippers, including Muslims and Christians, follow the King to pay homage to Oshun. In return, she protects them.

And it's the town of an exotic personality known as Twins Seven-Seven, who was our host.

We camped in the back yard of his small home, which eventually led to Brook's arrest by the local police.

By fantastic coincidence, Miss Barbara Ann Teer had that very day moved in with the family of Mr. Twins Seven-Seven. Our shadow was still with us.

Twins Seven-Seven, who is no relation to Hawaii Five O, might have invented his name. It's possible. The story goes that his mother lost six pairs of twins and he's the survivor of the seventh pair. Swore it was true to me.

He's the best-known artist in Oshogbo, a former dancer who was discovered by Ulli Beier and encouraged to take an interest in art. His weird etchings and gouaches are exhibited successfully in America. He's lectured there. Before the journey began I'd seen his work in a chic London art gallery. And now here he was, in the flesh.

Young, late twenties, hip clothes, bangles and beads, a celebrity, a showman, leader of the pack. 'Hi, Twins! What's shakin' baby?' Camp followers. Twins Seven-Seven is low, *everyone* is low. Twins Seven-Seven is high, *everyone* is high. Everyone gotta be high. I liked Twins Seven-Seven. He was soft and generous. He made a speech when we arrived in his back yard, wondering what had hit us:

'Peace, love, brotherhood to all men! Welcome to Oshogbo! Relax here! Feel at home here! You want to shit we got a toilet! You want to shit *African-style* we got a tree. . . .' Then he struck up an amazingly tuneless band, which he conducted. 'Peace and love to all nations on earth! A one, a two, a one, two, three, *four* . . .'

Thus, expecting a sacred forest we were thrown into the

highlife: welcoming party from Twins Seven-Seven with love and squalor.

Brook looked pained, as if he'd suddenly gone deaf.

Still, he joined in the unexpected party, dancing with the rest of us by the camp-beds in the rubble of a crowded field.

We were outside the centre of Oshogbo, virtually in the bush. Good to dance and get drunk again. I'd forgotten.

After a while, I lurched off following howls and chants coming from a hut in the distance. I peeped inside and saw several old women dancing together. They were wild, form of possession, stoned on drugs.

When I asked Twins about it he said I must have been seeing things. 'Peace and love, Twins. But what *gives* here?' He smiled and replied, 'A Yoruba doesn't put all the clothes he washes in the sun.'

I could hear drums from the bush, talking. They never stopped in the night.

Ayansola suddenly turned up at the party, looking gorgeous. He talked to Helen Mirren for a while in Yoruba. And talked, and talked. He'd talked to her every night this way, from the Sahara Desert to Ife, constant talk never understood. She was the only one who would listen to him. But for once there was a chance for someone to translate. Ayansola quickly fetched one of the guests.

To Mirren's astonishment, it turned out he hadn't been speaking to her in everyday language, but poetry. The talk that had bored and irritated her so much in the past was heard now as nothing more wonderful than the fine traditional poetry of his country. She listened to him differently now.

But the translator stopped, and wouldn't continue. He was laughing too much. Outraged, Ayansola kept going—determined his words be translated. He talked on, weaving his tender poetry. But again the translator laughed and laughed. 'Listen to me!' Ayansola was saying, forgetting his poetic turn of phrase occasionally. 'I'm a drummer. I'm a poet. But I'm also a *king*! Who are *you*? Who do you think you are? You're an actress. I'm a *king*! I command you! I *command* you to do what I say! And

what I say is the moon and the stars are all very well but SCREW
ME!! SCREW ME!!' And Ayansola and Mirren were both laughing
now. But the translator wasn't. Because no one need listen to a
drummer and no one need listen to a poet, but who would dare
disobey the command of a king?

Masquerade! Local masqueraders had arrived to perform.
The party was stopped immediately. Cabaret! A circle was
formed for the masqueraders.

They were like rag dolls: ancient costumes, worn and frayed,
mongrel combination of African prints and modern material,
lurex and tinsel, handwoven cloths and Victorian flower prints,
knitted wools and bright dyes, carved masks and plastic masks,
costumes that seemed moulded to their bodies. According to
superstition, to show any part of their skin means death to the
onlooker.

There were six performers, medieval circus troupe out-doing
each other with tricks and acrobatics, tumbling round the field.
A black tongue snaked out of the mouthpiece of a pink mask.
'Howdoyoudo,' mimicked a voice from behind the mask. 'Howdoyoudo.'

Europeans are always satirized.

Europeans are stiff and clumsy.

A marionette sex dance follows, mating human puppets,
horny display in the carnival atmosphere.

Grotesque policeman, traditional caricature.

Pantomime cow with a great pair of balls.

'Howdoyoudo. Howdoyoudo.'

Money! You hand over your thanks.

One masquerader walked forward shrouded completely in rush
matting. You couldn't even see his head. He lunged at you in the
semi-darkness, a spirit. Then amazingly, he turned the matting
inside out without showing any sign of his body. It seemed impossible. It was as if he disappeared.

The surprise party went on, though we were out on our feet.
Great offence was given to Twins Seven-Seven when we had to
decline his offer of another party the next night. We just didn't
have the energy. Also, Brook didn't have the money.

Brook was arrested the next day.

The charge was breaking and entering private property, trespass and theft. Just when things were going so well. . . .

Brook had left the camp first thing in the morning when the police swooped. He was driving into town to fix a visit to the sacred forest. The police stopped the Land-Rover, confiscated Sylvain Corthay's driving licence and placed Brook under a form of house arrest.

He returned to camp, blazing with anger.

'It's *absurd*!' he shouted, storming round the camp under police escort. 'They say we've stolen a mattress.'

A mattress?

'Well of course,' announced the Leader. 'This is just what I've been afraid of.'

'Should we organize a search party?' I asked.

'That's right! *Laugh!*' replied the Leader. 'But you won't be laughing when we're all in jail.'

The crew were back after their rest in Lagos.

But Deirdre, the official cook, senior in rank even to Marva Katsulas, was about to take a plane home. The strain of the long journey had been too much. Unfortunately, while buying fresh supplies of food for the return desert crossing she had concentrated on building up a collection of extremely large tins of chocolate pudding.

'It's a *farce*!' groaned Brook, unable to believe what was happening.

The tribe who couldn't get it together drifted over in ones and twos, some half-dressed, others clutching their heads. 'Anyone know what's happening?' 'Oh, Peter's been arrested. . . .'

'Who's your superior?' snapped Brook at the police.

'The magistrate!' came the reply.

'Well why aren't we in *town* with the magistrate?'

'No need,' one of the policemen answered cheerfully. 'He's here.'

'He's *here*?' said Brook, taken aback. 'Well, good. That's *excellent!* That's just what I wanted to know. Let's *meet* the magistrate!'

299

He strode purposefully across the field towards a squat little man dressed in a formal black suit, like an undertaker. Despite the heat, he wore a stiff white collar and tie.

'Good morning,' said Brook to the magistrate, 'I believe we have stolen a mattress.'

And the magistrate replied that he believed it was so.

'And may I enquire to whom the mattress belongs?' asked Brook.

'Yes,' replied the magistrate. 'It belongs to me.'

There was chaos after that.

'But this is Peter Brook!' yelled a large man who'd turned up from nowhere.

Peter *who*?

The large man had come to welcome Brook to Oshogbo. Daru Lapidu: best-known actor in Nigeria. Huge and lovable, he's a man who sort of makes things wonderfully worse in a crisis.

'I'll deal with the magistrate, Peter!' he announced. 'The magistrate is stupid in the head!'

At which the police were now helpless with laughter.

Brook was stranded in the confusion as a virtual lynch mob gathered round the tiny magistrate and the great Daru Lapidu took over the case for the defence.

But the case for the prosecution was interesting.

We had spread out beyond Twins Seven-Seven's property, camping in a neighbouring field. It turned out the field belonged to the magistrate. Also, a small house in the corner of the field, furnished accommodation which the magistrate rented from the Ministry of Works. The mattress had disappeared from the house.

Technically, we were therefore guilty of trespass. We'd camped on the magistrate's land.

'It's a frame-up,' said Twins Seven-Seven. 'I asked for permission to use the land. I asked the police. Love all,' he added 'Trust few.'

He meant the police. Perhaps the magistrate too.

'Look at him in his stiff white collar!' mocked Twins. 'He's been to Europe. He thinks he's *clever*. . . .'

'It all looks fishy to me,' the Leader was saying warily. 'It all looks extremely *fishy* to me.'

'But this is my grandfather!' exploded Daru Lapidu, suddenly breaking off from his row with the magistrate.

Most unexpected twist of all! If the magistrate was his grandfather, all was saved.

'Your *grandfather*?' asked Brook, looking stunned.

'What grandfather?' replied Daru Lapidu. 'This is my palaver. *Palaver!* Do not concern yourselves! I'll fix everything!'

'Aren't you the actor, by the way?' asked the magistrate unexpectedly.

'It is *I*,' replied the great Lapidu, taking a regal bow.

'I saw you in a play. You wore a fine costume.'

'And now,' replied Daru Lapidu, holding out the jacket of his baggy suit, 'I am *respectable*.'

'Very good,' added the magistrate, smiling. 'Now come this way to the police station.'

'*Stupid!*' yelled Lapidu. 'This man's stupid in the head!'

The police were convulsed with laughter again. Brook looked dazed. Apparently, we were confined to camp.

'Leave this to me, Peter my friend!' called Lapidu as he swept off to find his car. 'We will settle the affair of the mattress and prove the magistrate is stupid in the head!'

He struggled with the door of his battered car, which wouldn't open, though kicked many times.

'He is as stupid as the door of my car!' he cried.

His four wives were waiting patiently inside: one to sing, one to dance, one to act, and one to look after the children.

I jumped in the back, excited to see how events would turn out.

When Daru Lapidu finally managed to get into the driver's seat, and the car finally managed to start, he roared off to the police station singing happily.

I wasn't allowed into the meeting with the police. But after only a few minutes, he breezed out again.

'It's all settled!' he announced, beaming.

'Terrific!'

'We pay for the mattress.'

'We *pay*?'

'Yes, it's all settled! An amicable solution!'

'But nobody stole a mattress.'

'True,' replied the great Daru Lapidu, smiling happier than ever. 'That's true!'

So it was that I was able to return to the group, explaining how all was settled and the journey could continue.

Brook was now to spend every available moment in the sacred forest.

The group worked there, preparing *The Conference of the Birds* for performance in Daru Lapidu's open-air theatre.

They worked by the river, before the shrine of the river Goddess.

All other areas of the forest were closed to us.

A gate, sometimes locked, guards the entrance to the forest. The gate represents a gigantic tortoise: symbol of the earth.

Outside the gates to the shrine of the river Goddess, a vestal virgin stands under a tree. She is eleven years old.

A priest watches permanently over the shrine, praying before it and singing. He sings tiny, gentle songs to the gods. He dances fish dances, bird dances, smooth simple easy lifts and pulls, stories. He laughs sometimes.

The statue of the river Goddess stands twelve feet high, arms outstretched, guarding the moss-green river, still river, alive with frogs and fish. The feet of the Goddess are planted in the open mouth of a giant fish. She stands in a mangle of roots spreading down to the river among the rocks and everywhere.

The wall surrounding the shrine is sculptured with strange figures and signs, as are the trees and the earth. The wall warns off strangers and, it's said, sinister people who misuse the power of the Goddess to give strength to various medicines and spells.

The gods reside in the forest undisturbed. The holy grove of Ogun where a sacred spot of earth carries magic powers for the cult worshippers, earth fed through the blood sacrifice of hunters performing death rituals when one among them dies. Further on through the forest many other groves, forbidden ground to outsiders and even Yorubas. The oldest cult: temple of Ontoto inhabited by flying red earth and river spirits. The spirits are hot tempered here. Trees, poisonous snakes, monkeys, birds, everything in this grove receives the power of the hot and wild spirits. By order of the Oracle the shrine itself is of Obatala, god of creation. Obatala controls the dangerous emotions of Ontoto. Obatala is cool.

A white priestess restores the shrines and the walls of the forest.

Yoruba builders and carpenters help her.

I met her, sceptical of her role, white priestess in an African cult.

She is called Suzanne Wenger, an artist who was born in Austria and came to live in Africa twenty-five years ago.

She lives in the centre of Oshogbo and agreed to see me in her home, though reluctantly. Her house was set apart from others with their tin roofs and open doors. It looked grand and intimidating, built on three storeys, like the set of a horror film inside. The hallway is dark. The narrow twisting staircase creaks. The rooms branching off the staircase are in disarray, as if a storm has blown through them. Monkeys claw at a cage. Dogs yelp. On beams like totem poles, on every shutter and every wall, everything in the house has been carved and sculptured. The rocking chair I sat in was carved as a snake.

She brought in tea in tiny china cups.

Strange woman with darting eyes. Pale blue eyes, gentle sometimes. Her lips are painted bright red. She looks like Bette Davis. Some of her teeth are missing. She wears a white dress, child's dress. Nervy, strange lady, said by some to be a witch.

So I asked her if it was true.

She rocked with laughter so much, great cackle of laughter so piercing I was convinced she must be.

But she denied it, speaking in a thick Austrian accent:

'No, young man! I haven't paid my dues to the Society of Witches. Witchcraft is a *perversion* of ritual. It might be used by a priest to bring people into the correct state of psychic force. It's part of a priest's equipment. But the difference is that the witch uses her power for personal aims. I'm no pudding. But I'm no witch.'

She cackled with laughter again. But when I asked her to say more about the priest's power of 'witchcraft', she changed the subject.

Children were scampering about the house: reassuring. Six African children have been adopted by her.

One of her husbands was Professor Beier, now married to an English artist. Another turned out to be King Ayansola, no less.

The strange Austrian priestess talked about the cult for a little while, expressing what she wanted to say very simply. For her, all religions are connected in the fundamental truths. The mythology of the Yoruba cult speaks in a different language from the mythology of the Catholic mass. Both talk of the same mystery.

Could it be so? In the sacred forest, the Yoruba sees the spirit in every flower, in every stone, every tree, every blade of grass, every bird, everything. 'Split the tree and you will find me, raise the stone and I am there,' Christ said.

I began to ask lots of questions now—but she cut me short. 'Talk! Talk! Talk!' she snapped suddenly. 'Give the secret of life! Tell me this, tell me that. Questions, always questions! How they pour out of your pretty mouth! But if you want me to answer your questions about spirits I would have to persuade my drummers and dancers to be with you for a few hours. Then you would be less worried and more satisfied, and might begin to understand.'

In time she was to arrange that meeting for all the group. And the journey was transformed by it.

I was more or less shown the door now. But before I left, she told me this about herself:

When she was a child in Austria she rarely went to school, though her father was a school-teacher. She used to go to a forest. Often she lived in the forest alone for months at a time. She was quite renowned for it. She became a child of the forest.

304

In her room in Oshogbo is a painting of the forest she had done as a child. And she showed it to me. It was exactly like the sacred forest of Oshogbo.

The group entered the sacred forest, eager for the fray.

'But it's just like Disneyland!' cried Yoshi Oida, looking pleased.

Mr. Zeldis was serenading the shrines with a flute, as he'd done sand-dunes.

'We shouldn't be tampering with any of this,' said Myers, genuinely fearful. 'We don't belong here.'

Others were tearing round as if it were the rush hour in Piccadilly Circus.

Others kept silent, like Brook.

Suddenly—

'I hope you're all grabbing your MYSTICAL EXPERIENCE in there!!'

The voice of Andreas Katsulas.

When we weren't working in the forest, he never went there as the others liked to. He stayed in camp, washing Land-Rovers. 'There you go, honey,' Marva would say to him. 'Here's a nice cup of tea. Watch you don't slop it over the car now.' Rather than go to the forest he washed the Land-Rovers till they gleamed.

'Anyway, I'm fulfilled washing cars,' he explained to me. 'I wash dishes. I wash cars. I'm a *washer*. Well you know what they say?'

'What do they say, Andreas?'

'Why should I tell *you*? It takes people a lifetime to discover what they say.'

'If you tell me what they say I promise I'll never let the lights fall down again.'

'They say Mecca is where you are.'

So he carried on washing the cars.

Kasulas studied Drama at university. But the subject he chose to study with it was Divinity. . . .

Extreme rejection of the place we had come to, extreme acceptance. But soon people began to take things more quietly,

305

gathering what they could. The counterfeit searches faded.

The cynics, including myself, would be blown to pieces sooner or later. It took time to get used to this alien, sacred place.

One morning Swados went to the forest before dawn. She was sleeping in a field miles away from the crowded camp when two bewildered herdsmen woke her, prodding her with a stick as if she were a scorpion. They were surprised to find a naked white girl stretched out in the middle of their field.

She decided to visit the forest, since she was awake. It would be a chance to see it on her own. Perhaps it would tell her something.

She walked to the forest, quite a way. It was almost dawn when she arrived. But as she opened the gates to the forest, something pulled her away. She swung round and saw the eleven-year-old vestal virgin.

The virgin carries the calabash during rituals. But she guarded the entrance that night. She barred the way, refusing to let Swados enter.

'*Money!*' the child demanded suddenly. '*Money! Money!*' So Swados gave her some and the child opened the gates to the forest, and disappeared in the half-light.

Swados took the path towards the shrine of the river Goddess, forgetting about her. 'Hey, white girl!' The child was back, circling her. 'Money, white girl! I want money, money white girl!' Swados kept walking, trying to shrug her off. But the child went for her, slapping her arms. 'Money, white girl! I want money, white girl!' She was half-singing the words now, the same words over and over again, kicking and taunting her. 'Give money! Want money, white girl! Give money! Want money . . .!' Swados screamed at the child to leave her alone. The child's eyes were insane. But the child only haunted the intruder more and more, circling the gates which led to the shrine of the river Goddess. Swados seized a stick impulsively. The child of the forest wasn't letting her into the shrine.

'MONEY!'

Swados held the stick ready to swing.

The child went for her.

306

'YOU GIVE!' screamed Swados suddenly. 'You give *me* money! Give *me* money!'

'*Money!*' screamed back the child. 'You give *me* money. Give *me* money!'

The child went for her again.

For a split second Swados had a vision of blood. And started to run.

But the child stuck to her, mocking and kicking her, spitting contempt at her presence there. And both were wild now, insane children fighting the money battle through the sacred forest. 'YOU GIVE!' Swados screamed. 'Give, black girl! Want your money, black girl!' On and on. Until they were driven back to the entrance of the forest. 'Want money, white girl! Give *me* money, want money! MONEY!' The child wasn't letting her out. 'GIVE!' shrieked Swados. 'Give, black girl! Money, black girl! Give me! Give me!! GIVE!!' Until the child gave at last. And opened the gates of the forest to let her out. The child-protector of the forest had won the insane battle.

It had taken Swados almost three hours to get past her and out of the forest she had gone to discover. The child laughed now, evil brat.

Work on *The Conference of the Birds* drove on for many hours each day, though the sun and humidity were more killing than ever.

For the only time in the journey, no stranger ever watched. We were completely alone in the sacred forest.

But the work was strained and hopeless.

Brook had said that the virtue of a sacred place is the vision of life to be found within it. Yet in the first days in the forest, the work lost all direction and form. Nothing was clarified, except the state of our own confusion.

I wasn't even sure why we were there or even if we had any right to be. I felt it from the day Professor Beier first took me to the forest, the day he kicked the American tourists out. We had stood together in silence before Oshun, Goddess of the river, guardian spirit of Oshogbo. The two white men stood before the African god. But my eyes strayed from the statue and watched the Professor. I knew he loved the forest and had come to understand many of its secrets. Yet could a white man really sense the mystery of this forest, Africa's heritage? Oh, I knew it must be an extraordinary place, for few such places exist. But I felt that I didn't belong there. I felt no awe or mystery as I knew I should. And wanted to, longed to in a way.

What I saw then seemed only a bizarre sanctuary from the outside world, no more. What could the African gods ever mean to me, the white European who lives in Kensington, London? Was it surprising the gods didn't speak? Except to say in a weary way, 'Call us names.' What ammunition the sculptors of the forest gave such worldly eyes! The white priestess and her Yoruba disciples had restored the crumbling groves with their own art. But there at second and third glance spirits were made absurd. Look at the God of Iron! Patron of the strong, their figure of him looked no more powerful than a garden gnome. Look at the Goddess of the river with her outstretched arms and ridiculous pointed head! What phoney shamans these? Spiritual Disneyland, said the Japanese actor who lives in Paris, France. And knowing it was an insult to the gods and the people who worshipped them, I agreed.

Later, Professor Beier told me how the sculptures came there.

The African priestesses hired two bricklayers to rebuild the ancient walls of the forest which white ants and time had destroyed. So the bricklayers set to work. But as they worked, they started to make little reliefs in cement which depicted the spirits of the forest. Amazingly, the reliefs grew. And soon the wall they built was covered in them.

'They restored the past?' I asked the Professor.

'They continued it,' he replied.

I began going back to look more carefully at the wall people:

Man-woman figure points a gun. Three heads dance. Cow sleeps. Bird flies. Spirits play a game of draughts. . . . The more I looked, the more mysterious they seemed. It was as if they had been created in a fever.

When the builders first worked on the wall they went to the ceremonies of Alijare, a god who inspires people to create. And the builders created their wall people. But Alijare inspires art in different ways, preferring life to be rich and varied.

For instance, the priest who protects the shrines likes to sing. But it slowly dawned on me that that tender man could do everything Swados loves most in music. And in another sense, he could do everything Brook longs for in theatre.

It's a kind of talk and a kind of prayer he sings so gently. And he talks and sings to the gods, saying, 'Well here I am again, gods. And I'll tell you what I've done today. And I'll tell you what I did a hundred years ago.' And out comes this incredible music. It's so informal and so natural and so full of love. You know the skills behind it come from long traditions. You know the music has that kind of naïve, expert musicianship which always deceives in its simplicity. But what he does is far beyond technique, far beyond performing or culture. It's that rarest of all things, something Brook would give anything for: a completely natural happening. There's no sense of deep ritual or mysticism or art. The priest's music is miraculous. He is what he is, singing a completely natural song.

Gradually I felt that I was at last beginning to sense something of the mystery of this forest, as the others must have been.

For work on *The Conference of the Birds*, that perfect reflection of the state of the group, was slowly coming together again. In the midst of all the confusion and strain, powerful qualities were beginning to emerge. And one spectacular breakthrough.

Brook was still working hard on a scene begun months before. It was as if he had a fixation about it—the scene when the birds decide to commit themselves to the long journey ahead of them.

It's the crucial point of the Sufi fable, for only then do the birds of the allegory glimpse an understanding of immortality. Even so, their leader warns them:

'All that you have heard or seen or known is not even the beginning of what you must know, and since the ruined habitation of this world is not your place you must renounce it. Seek the trunk of the tree, and do not worry about whether the branches do or do not exist.'

So Brook's actors set off in the sacred forest, to seek the trunk of the tree, as it were. They gathered as birds and in sound and movement set off for about the tenth time that day. But the heat was so stifling the actors could scarcely move. Some bird-actors didn't even make the first valley of the imaginary journey: too exhausted. The real birds of the forest watched from the trees, scoffing. It wasn't going too well that day.

Suddenly, Lou Zeldis the flute player began to walk round the forest in a circle: the famous *Walking Show*. He just walked round, expanding the circle little by little.

And very slowly began to change into a bird.

As he walked, he transformed. And quickened in pace. And was a bird, absolutely. And flew. He *flew*! I saw him do it. He became a bird and flew over the trees and up to the sky. Applause from the real birds watching from the trees! They knew they had seen a supreme moment of theatre. An actor, human they say, flew.

Ah, but did his feet really leave the ground?

It was the hugest discovery for me! It doesn't matter! It doesn't matter a damn, provided you fly.

The next morning, the actors began work in the forest without Brook. He was busy seeing people in Oshogbo, which meant something important was brewing.

The group exercised conscientiously, feeling the Brook spirit present. Until after an hour or so, it came to life. Brook came hurrying across the forest towards us. He looked in a terrific state of excitement, unable to hide his feelings. The forbidden territory of the forest was about to be opened to us.

It was the breakthrough we had longed for. Suzanne Wenger had persuaded her cult dancers and drummers to show us something of their secrets. Such people do not usually open themselves to outsiders. We would see the finest form of possession the world knows.

The meeting wasn't to take place in the forest. Instead, we went that afternoon to Suzanne Wenger's strange house in the centre of Oshogbo.

We were tense and quiet, wondering what to expect. We'd come so far in search of this moment there was a danger it might not live up to it. We were nervous. Talk of secret rituals and cults, world of spirits: what awaited us? I expected to be frightened, and perhaps the others felt the same.

We were shown into a narrow room, perhaps twenty-five feet long. Like the rest of the house, every part of it had been sculptured with animals and half-human creatures. Suzanne Wenger came in: nervous too. Her eyes kept darting at the ceiling.

We waited quite a while. Until at last, several women entered the room. They were old and beautiful. Their grey hair was plaited. They wore beads, dressed very simply. They were the reverse of intimidating. They were gentle and calm, smiling at us with shy eyes. I couldn't take my eyes off them. When they shook our hands they drew the hands close to them, kissed them and gently wiped their eyes with the kiss.

Two drummers sat at one end of the room.

They were younger than the women, very relaxed. They waved hello.

We hushed in anticipation of a start. But there seemed to be a delay. We talked among ourselves for a while, uncertain what was happening. We couldn't speak the same language as the women. They talked quietly in their own group.

Without warning, one of the drummers began.

The room was shot through with a thunderclap. The room shook. The women danced.

In that split second the atmosphere in the room was totally transformed. My eyes were opened and astonished. The old women danced and were young.

They danced alone within their group, flowing and amazing. Without effort or apparent will, their bodies vanished and burned. The old and beautiful women of the forest were spirits, dancing for joy. They were so proud and so gentle. The whole of life was held in their movements and gestures, rhythms of gods, changing and mesmerising. When the drums switched rhythm, the women changed and turned even before the signal had finished. Worlds turned on them. The spirits of the forest had shown themselves to us. Human bodies became a vehicle for the spirit. And the spirit spoke. Life of reason. Life of so much hope and love. Never had I seen even a dream like this. Yet I can neither describe nor explain it. That in a room I received a vision of sheer existence. And that God passed before our eyes.

Epilogue

The group went on to give its performance of *The Conference of the Birds* in Oshogbo.

It took place in Daru Lapidu's open-air theatre, a rough concrete stage at the back of a crumbling colonial residence. The theatre was in the busy centre of the town, yet behind the stage was another forest.

The night before we had seen Lapidu's troupe perform a Yoruba legend there, and as many as a thousand excited locals crammed into the courtyard to see him. How they cheered! At the end of the show, the great Daru Lapidu stepped forward, ignored the rest of the cast, and took one wondrous bow after another. Then he made a curtain speech: 'Thank you, thank you. Most kind. More applause? Thank you, thank you so much. By the way, come and see my good friend Peter Brook tomorrow night. . . .'

The place was bursting when we arrived for the show. Swados had teamed up with several local musicians, drummers mostly. We had a band! The crowd jostled for a better view, scrambling for the best seats, yelling and laughing. 'How do I get to join the group?' asked one Yoruba. 'I hear you travel, have a good time. And so I ask myself, "Why not me?" '

And the show began.

On top of the walls which surrounded the courtyard and from the forest behind the concrete stage, the actors appeared as half-human birds, and called to each other, gathering for a journey.

The crowd erupted as if they were at a bullfight! And there, the stretched catapult was released at last. Actors, Stanislavsky's kings and rulers of the stage, sprang to life sweeping the excited audience along with them. So exhausted during rehearsals that they could hardly move in the stifling heat, the group hit back in the urgency of performing and gave the show every last ounce of energy they had left. Incredibly it was as if the shape and form of Brook's longed-for theatre of the future were at last bursting open. And something wonderful, something more that Brook had waited years to see. For there was the unique and individual colour of a real group, sensing each other out, playing with danger and care, care for each other, but performing as one, absolutely as one true group of people who have come together to share what they have to offer. For myself, whenever glimpsed, such moments in theatre are always touching. It isn't a matter of fine acting performances or of those talents which always impress through expertise and technique, however special. It's more a question of heart. That in an empty space, a group of performers simply and openly show themselves for what they are, and hope to be.

And in sound and movement, very transparent, a new range and depth began to emerge. For the first time in the long journey, a true sense of this mysterious search of the birds was captured in the twilight. But just as quickly as it had been caught, it was gone again. They lost it! Like the high-wire act that begins to wobble, up there, the actors seemed to lose their nerve. On the verge of breaking through, it was as if they were suddenly afraid of going any further. The old routines and familiar images were returning as their energy evaporated in the pressure and heat. Invisible barriers and safety-nets came up, protecting. The birds who gathered for the long journey ahead of them had at last set out in search of their vision understanding what knowledge and commitment it involved, yet they lost their way.

Was the lack of energy to blame? No, it couldn't be so. The spirits of the sacred forest had found the miraculous only after a lifetime, and many others have failed.

The generous crowd in Oshogbo carried the tired actors along with them until the performance ended. But for all that, something priceless had sprung from it.

It was a seed, and a beginning.

The following morning we left Yorubaland, crossed the border

314

into Dahomy and camped on the empty beaches facing the Atlantic Ocean. We rested there for three days, and swam, and slept.

Cripples and beggars and blind men surrounded us.

On exactly the spot where we camped on the beach, by a shrine to the dead and the husk of a canoe, the locals told us an important ceremony would take place within our stay. Every twenty-five years, the High Priest of Ouida leads the entire town down to the sea-shore. He leads a white bull, and sings. Then the High Priest sings to the sea, and the sea parts. And so he leads the white bull into the path between the waves, further and further, until they both disappear. The townsfolk who watch the ceremony remain silent. Eventually, they hear singing from beneath the sea. Then the High Priest appears again, riding a white horse.

The locals swore it had happened in the past, and since the twenty-fifth anniversary of the ceremony was now due we would be able to see for ourselves. Alas, when the moment came the High Priest was suddenly taken ill. Also, we were told, he'd never done this particular thing before.

We turned north now, for home.

'Let's go!' called Katsulas, revving up his Land-Rover. 'Let's get the hell out of here before the bugs drive me crazy!'

The humidity count in the area was at breaking point. It was as if the sky longed to burst open, and rain. Our energy hadn't recovered during the three-day rest. Bodies were lean and fit, yet the faces of everyone in the group remained lined and tense. It was more than fatigue. In different ways we had all been deeply shaken by the Ife-Oshogbo experience. Only Malik Bagayogo, the African, troubled to play the game of outward appearances. He was still learning English diligently. 'Today the weather is most cold. It is a good morning! How are *you*, my friend?'

For the others, even a minor revolt against the group's own disciplines was necessary. Perhaps it was an attempt to relieve the pressure and confusion, but to my surprise the group confronted Brook—questioning the very reason for their work.

'It makes me feel guilty,' said Miriam Goldschmidt. 'It makes me feel as if I'm in church.'

'There's an empty space,' was all Brook would reply. 'There are several people and an empty space. Some approach it timidly. Others scream. Still more turn away. Who will face the empty space?'

'Are we meant to take this personally?' said Katsulas.

Now the convoy sped north through Dahomey towards a village of fetishists and madness, where the women of the village were preparing a special ceremony. They ran from the forest surrounding the village, transformed into human birds! They were *birds*! In return, the group performed our own bird story. And more carpet shows followed in the villages we passed through. And more and more memories—

A dance before a king, said to be a hundred and thirty years old, certainly ancient, waxed like an exhibit in Madame Tussauds. The actors danced for the King, each taking his turn. And when all had finished, the waxwork King danced, twirling his walking stick above his head like a Samurai.

A purple haystack appears walking along a dusty road. Inside, a fetish on his way to a ceremony. Muffled sounds come from inside the purple haystack: 'If you take photos, you have to pay. . . .'

A man plays a flute. Child sings. Another begs. Africans smiling. . . .

We drove fast through Dahomey and into Niger again. We were behind schedule and the Land-Rovers were long since due back in Algiers. The Leader resumed command of the convoy, wearing his black *cheche*. Gradually, everyone changed back into the army surplus and heavy overcoats, the boots and clothes we had left in: protection against the freezing nights of the return journey through the desert.

One hundred days after we left the Sahara Desert, we re-entered its void. Yet that limitless horizon no longer seemed as strange or mysterious.

Brook and the group returned to Paris, though not to the studio of their research centre. For the first time in his life, Brook eventually opened his own theatre, rebuilding a derelict music hall on the north side of Paris.

There, the nucleus of the original group took the fruits of their research directly to the public. Some went their separate ways—

Lou Zeldis was last believed to be living in the hills of Peru.

Sylvain Corthay formed his own acting group.

Helen Mirren returned to the London stage.

Swados returned to work in New York.

The last I heard of Brook he was in Egypt, setting up a film he wanted to make about Gurdjieff's *Meetings With Remarkable Men*.

His new theatre in Paris opened with two successful productions: *Timon of Athens* with François Marthouret as Timon. And a new play called *The Ik*, which was based on Colin Turnbull's true story of an African tribe who chose to starve to death rather than adapt to a modern way of life.

Both plays, something of a breakthrough in Brook's non-verbal world, were performed in French.

But perhaps at midnight in his theatre, perhaps with only a few hours' notice, the group would return to *The Conference of the Birds* and play it for anyone who cared to watch. Almost six years after it first began, no final version of *The Conference of the Birds* has been reached.